Weight Lifting Pro Tips For Strength and Conditioning Weight Training & Muscle Building Tactics

SHAKRUDDIN KHAN

Published by SHAKRUDDIN KHAN, 2024.

Also by SHAKRUDDIN KHAN

The Smart Way To Personal Finance Success
Goal Setting 101 Achieve More Goals Than Ever! Faster!
Blockchain Masterclass for Businesses and Corporations
Master Your Mindset & Brain Framestorm Your Way To
Success
Manipulation Techniques: How Can We Influence People's
Thoughts And Behaviors
Leadership How To Influence, Inspire And Impact As A
Leader
Learn How To Create A Safe Working Environment For
Your Team
Productivity Hacks For Easily Distractible Entrepreneurs
IT / Non-IT Recruiter Training To Become A Recruiter
(Junior)
Weight Lifting Pro Tips For Strength and Conditioning
Weight Training & Muscle Building Tactics

Table of Contents

Copyright 1

About 2

Introduction 3

Mindset Of A Champion 4

Workouts For Increasing Muscle Mass 9

Power Building Lifestyle 14

Diet For Increasing Muscle Mass 19

Muscle Boosting Supplements 24

Cardio For Muscle Building 29

Tracking Your Progress 34

Best Fitness Apps To Measure Progress 39

Recap 44

Mindful Meditation 45

Understanding Mindful Meditation 49

How To Practice Mindful Meditation 52

Still More Mindful Meditation Techniques 56

Mindful Meditation & Your Brain 59

Why Is Awareness So Important 61

Mindful Meditation & Work...66

Mindful Meditation & Relationships 69

Mindful Meditation & Happiness............................72

Famous & Successful People Who Meditate 75

Great Mindful Meditation Apps............................77

The Many Benefits Of Mindful Meditation 80

How To Create A Mindful Life................................86

Thoughts & Tips..89

Beginning Concepts..90

What Is Eczema..92

Beating The Eczema Itch 96

Eczema & Your Emotions 100

Eczema & The Magic Of Meditation 105

Eczema & Skin Hydration 108

Great Home Remedies For Eczema 112

Coping With Eczema 116

Allergy-Proof Your Home.. 120

Eczema & Children.. 123

Final Ideas & Tips.. 127

Insomnia 131

The Science Behind Insomnia 132

The Brain Of An Insomniac 138

Sleep Starvation 144

The Insomnia Cure 150

Lifestyle Modifications For 156

Switching Off 159

Thoughts & Tips 163

Keto Diet 164

What Is The Ketogenic Diet 165

Benefits Of The Keto Diet 167

Keto Diet & Cancer 172

Keto Diet & Epilepsy 175

Keto Diet & Blood Pressure 177

What To Eat On Keto Diet 179

How Keto Diet Works For Weight Loss 184

Getting Started On The Keto Diet 189

Great Keto Recipes 194

Final Thoughts & Tips 203

Beginners Guide To Juicing 206

The Science Of Juicing 209

Juice Cleanse 215

Juicing & Anti-Aging 219

Juicing & Energy 221

Store Bought Or Homemade - Pros & Cons 224

The Many Benefits Of Juicing 230

Great Recipes For Juicing 235

Going Beyond Juicing 238

Why Your Healthy Lifestyle Is Important 243

Intermittent Fasting 247

What Is Intermittent Fasting 249

The Many Benefits Of Intermittent Fasting 253

How Intermittent Fasting Really Helps Weight Loss 256

Is Intermittent Fasting Safe? 259

A Protocol For Intermittent Fasting 264

Intermittent Fasting 24 Hour Protocol 267

Other Types Of Intermittent Fasting 269

Maximize Your Intermittent Fasting Results 272

How To Get Started With Intermittent Fasting.............. 275

Common Questions About Intermittent Fasting............ 278

Thoughts & Ideas.. 284

Yoga Is Something Different 286

Science Of Yoga & Health Benefits 288

Yoga History 292

Emotions & Mind-Body Connection 296

Yoga Strength & Flexibility 299

Yoga Cardio & Weight Loss 302

Types Of Yoga.. 305

Yoga Poses & Better Immunity................................. 309

How To Get Started Doing Yoga 314

Yoga & Meditation... 321

Conclusion 326

Copyright

WeightLifting Pro Tips For Strength and Conditioning Weight Training & Muscle Building Tactics

Book Design by **SHAKRUDDIN KHAN**

About

Welcome to a concise yet profound journey into the world of bodybuilding and weight training! In this Book, you will gain years' worth of in-depth knowledge, empowering you to elevate your weightlifting game to a whole new level.

Our expert-led training draws from professional lifters who have achieved remarkable muscle-building results. You will learn how to tailor and enhance your workouts to maximize muscle growth stimulus, while gaining the ability to design personalized routines aligned with your evolving goals.

In the realm of bodybuilding and muscle growth, there is an overwhelming pool of information – some effective, some not. To save you from wasting time and effort on futile strategies, we present a practical approach with noticeable results. This Book delivers high-quality, applicable information that you can immediately implement in your next gym session, bypassing fruitless experimentation.

Enroll in this Book to unlock your true muscle-building potential. This Book condenses extensive knowledge into practical techniques that deliver results you can witness and feel. As you apply the strategies, you'll gain confidence in designing effective workouts for yourself and others, making a lasting impact on your fitness journey. Take this opportunity to invest in yourself and embrace the transformative power of expert-guided muscle building. Get ready to achieve your fitness goals like never before!

Introduction

Bulking up, as in bodybuilding, is often seen as synonymous with lifting weights, and for most people, that's where the equation ends. As long as they lift weights, they believe they'll get jacked. However, there's much more than just weight lifting when it comes to bodybuilding essentials. In fact, it's an entire series of components, including nutrition, supplementation and training. Then comes rest and recovery, along with lifestyle changes that will help you gain muscle and keep it that way. You will need to incorporate these and other essentials to get results. And while weights are integral to becoming ripped, you won't get anywhere alone. So here we will look at what you need to do and what routines to follow to reach your goals.

Mindset Of A Champion

In this chapter, we'll talk about the mindset of a champion, mental toughness is a trait required for success in any field. It's what gives your goals. Resilience gets you over adversity and lets you follow through on what you set out to do in the first place. When it comes to bodybuilding, you don't just need your body, but also your mind to collaborate together. You have to put your mind to the game to win it. For many people, bodybuilding doesn't work out because they don't have their mind in the game. What separates the successful from others is not only their dedication or motivation, but also their mindset. So it's not only your physical competency that will set you apart, but also your mental attitude towards getting to your goals.

Here's what you need to look for in the mindset of a champion unwavering dedication. If you want to build quality muscle mass, you'll need to be very dedicated to your goals. It's a strong set of beliefs you'll need to follow where your goals are defined. Clearly, your dedication may at times be dictated by your physical strength, stamina and endurance. On other occasions, you may be driven on by your eagerness to learn. But whatever the case, you need to believe wholeheartedly that you are cut out to achieve your goals. There will be times when your dedication and determination may waver, but you need to stay on Book.

You'll need constant reminders of why you started this journey in the first place, and that thought should keep you on track. Dedication can also be reinforced if you're always willing to learn. This willingness becomes the driving force for continuing and improving your craft by constant practice. This way, your mindset becomes one of continuous growth. For added motivation. You could have posters of professionals on your walls or on your phone. This is another way to stay focused. When you look at these pictures, you'll be reminded of why you started in the first place. Fight, distraction. Distractions can make you derail from your priorities and goals. When you lose focus, you lose the game.

That's why it's absolutely imperative that you keep distractions away. Even when you're faced with distractions, you need to muster up the determination to ignore them completely. For instance, if you already chalked out a workout routine, you need to stick to it no matter what. Champion athletes and bodybuilders know that they have the potential to improve and don't let distractions get in the way. Missing out one day of training can quickly evolve into a pattern of laziness, but champions never let it get to that point. One thing that works quite well is planning your day beforehand. When you've already planned your day, you're more likely to follow through.

Being spontaneous is great, but doesn't always deliver when you have an agenda to follow. Having said that, you can't completely get rid of distractions because they're an integral part of productivity. However, you can train your mind to ignore any distraction that comes your way. Look at the bigger picture and keep yourself focused on that. Finish what you started. Many people start their muscle building routine with a lot of excitement and passion, but they don't finish because they either get distracted or become lazy on the way. You need to keep the same level of motivation going on as you had the first day of your training. Something that works well for this is to keep track of your progress.

If you can see how you're progressing, you'll be tempted to finish what you've started to make things easier. You could make a checklist for yourself, right? The different exercises that you have to do on every day of the week, just ticking off the task from your list will give you a sense of satisfaction. This is necessary. If you want to reach the finish line without tiring or losing focus, keep telling yourself how close you are to your goals and how much you've achieved so far, set both short and long term goals to keep going. The short term goals can act as catalysts for the long term ones to build positive mental habits.

It's very important to build positive mental habits. You'd be surprised how much influence your brain has on your body to start off, stop comparing yourself to others. This is one of those mental habits that will always leave you unsatisfied and ungrateful. Stop comparing yourself to other bodybuilders or your buddies in the gym. You have your own goals and they have theirs. Another mental habit that often brings you down is thinking that you're a failure. So you weren't able to finish your reps because you had a long day at work. It doesn't make you a failure. It's just one day to pick yourself up and work harder the next day.

If you have a champion mindset, you won't let any limiting benefits or destructive self-taught get in the way. Instead, you'll have mastered your mind in such a way that only the positive makes an impression and the negative doesn't become a deterrent. At the same time, being a perfectionist is also a mental habit that can limit you. If you want everything to be perfect, you end up not even meeting yours. Own standards, instead, you always criticize yourself. This attitude can easily overwhelm you, and that is never good for anything. If you want to be good at something that's awesome, you must always remember that everything can't and won't ever be perfect.

Don't give yourself a hard time just because you ate one unhealthy snack in a week. That snack might not affect your muscle gains, but that's self demotivating will definitely affect your mind. You have to be your biggest influencer because no one else is going to do it for you. Push yourself beyond normal limits. Always push yourself forward. If you think you've learned how to do one thing perfectly, it's time to move on to a harder level. The trick is to get out of your comfort zone and you'd be surprised at the potential your body has put this potential to the test and train your body to do harder and better things. It's a step by step procedure where your body will learn one thing first and then advance to another level.

Don't limit yourself to the same exercises that you've been doing for months now. Try new things and test your potential to keep your motivation going. Get your inspiration from people around you. If you think there's no one to inspire you, go online, talk to Bodybuilder's from around the world, read about people who started with thin schoolboy bodies and are now ripped. You'll feel the urge to push harder once you realize that it can be done and others have done it. If you've got your mind under control, your body will definitely follow.

Workouts For Increasing Muscle Mass

In this chapter, we'll discuss the mindset of a champion. The way you work out to gain muscle will, Of course, determine the outcome of your efforts. And that's why it's so important to find a routine that caters to your body the best. And for that, you need to consider a few things. First, while the general idea is to lift heavy weights or build muscles, you need to start off by strengthening muscle first. If you're new to this, you may want to engage in some strength and endurance moves before you tackle the weights. For instance, you could start off with some body weight exercises to strengthen muscles and then move on to lifting weights.

And Of course, as you make progress, you can then add in more weight, along with expanding the number of reps as well. Some important considerations when doing so include the following choice of exercises for building mass. Low volume training is highly recommended. In broad terms, this training technique prescribes one to eight sets for each muscle group. The session can last anywhere from 20 to 45 minutes. The basics of low volume training dictate that the workout routine should have the right stimulation restoration ratio. What this means is that you need to put a stimulus on the body significant enough to increase muscle without exceeding the body's capacity to tolerate the stress.

So basically balance is key. You can, Of course, increase the magnitude of training by adding more volume training more often or taking rest for a shorter duration between sets. You can also lift heavier weights and train harder on each set. But since it's a low volume session, you can only increase the volume by so much. So you focus on how to do the few sets that you do. The sets should be stressful enough so that you can only do a few at a time. At best you should be able to do three to six work sets for most muscle groups and up to eight for the back. Being a more complex structure, the exercises for beginners, intermediates and experts are different.

You can always start with easier workout routines and then progress to the tougher ones. Number of sets, low volume workout. One way to engage in a low volume program is to follow the five three one approach. Before you take this approach, know that you're one rep. Max is about the amount of weight you can lift for one rep without compromising form. So you need to know you're one rep Max or one R.M. for squats, deadlifts, bench presses and military presses. Once you have the numbers, you can move along. You can get to train three to four times a week and do one of the four workouts on your training days.

One squat and assistants work to bench press and assistants work. Three deadlifts and assistants work for overhead and assistants work. You perform each workout once every day with rest days in between. Follow the cycle for four to six weeks, then start over again by increasing your stress load. Now you're at the stage where you don't just pick a heavier weight five or three or one times more per set. Instead you use ninety percent of your one rep max. This program is best suited for those who are new to weight training and will see the most results. With this system, you can realistically accomplish a goal with every one of your workouts, high volume workout to take your training to the next level, you can engage in high volume training.

This technique allows you to get the most effective pumps with heavier weights. Three ways to do so include lifting weights more in the same set or reps scheme, lifting the same weight for more reps, preset performing more sets per workout. When you increase volume, you may be doing so for gaining size or for strength. At the same time, you're also flaunting higher levels of muscle with lower levels of body fat. The technique brings together a combination of compound and isolation exercises. You can prioritize the compound exercises that use multiple joints and lots of muscle mass so that you have the physical and mental capacity to get more plates on the bar.

When you combine compound and isolation exercises, vary your repetitions to focus on multi joint lifts, you can use higher repetition ranges for isolation exercises. Resistance resistance exercises are extremely helpful in building muscle mass. These are specific moves in which you push against a weight. Using a resistance band is a popular way to create tension through your range of motion. It produces something called progressive tension, giving you more tension at the end of every repetition. There are a few resistance exercises that you can add to your workout routine bicep curls for this exercise. Keep your legs in a parallel position, using a resistance band for this exercise, stand in the center, keep the other end around your wrists.

Your arms must be close to your body. Now you need to lift and move the band up and down slowly when the arm is curling up, squeeze your bicep. Do 20 or 30 reps of this exercise. Oblique twists for this exercise. You also have to stand with your legs in a parallel position, but they must be more than hip distance apart. Keep your arms straight at your chest level and hold the resistance band twist from one side to the other. The trick is to begin this movement from your waist and then twist as you do so. Squeeze your stomach, do 20 to 30 reps of this exercise, triceps, kickbacks. For this exercise, you have to keep the same stature as the bicep curl, stand in the center of your resistance band and keep the other ends around your wrists.

This is quite similar to a dumbbell kickback as you have to squeeze your arms and shoulder blades using the resistance and start squeezing from the top. You need to do 20 to 30 reps of this exercise to the point of doing so many reps is to fatigue the muscles. That's how resistance works. Once a certain muscle group is fatigued, you move on to the next one. If you want the exercise to be most effective, you have to do one after another. In this way, all muscle groups work to their full potential. At the same time, this helps make muscles stronger and induce division in the musculature between sets. When you do sets, you need to rest for some time between successive sets. And while this is true for most types of workouts, things tend to be a little different when you're trying to gain muscle.

When you rest in between sets, when training you can flex and pose. This helps blood flow to your muscles, keeping them pumped and warm. Not only does flexing impose you better control over your muscles, it also lowers the risk of injury. Also, when you flex and pose, you improve the ability to hold the pose for an extended time. This prevents your muscles from cramping as well. You can also stretch in between sets for serious muscle gain. Stretching increases flexibility, which can bring about greater muscle recruitment. Flexibility also improves form and gives you a greater range of motion. The same also reduces the risk of injury, prevents soreness and promotes faster recovery.

Power Building Lifestyle

In this chapter, we'll talk about power building, lifestyle, body building or building muscle mass doesn't mean that you have to lead a life of deprivation. You need to keep a balance in your life so that all your efforts at building strength or muscle mass are not lost. If your lifestyle is in accordance with the muscle building regime you are following, then you're golden. While the general idea is to lift heavy weights for building muscles, you need to start off by strengthening muscles first. If you're new to all this, then you may want to engage in some strength and endurance moves before you tackle the weights.

Once you attain your muscle building goals, you also have to maintain them or get better. If you thought getting to the goals was hard. You'd be surprised to know that maintaining your gains is even harder. You need to alter your lifestyle according to your muscle building routine so that you can create a balance and keep your gains, making your workouts good muscle. Building lifestyle needs timely changes in workouts. You should add variety to your workout plan so that your exercises don't end up being ineffective. For instance, if you've been doing five sets of a particular exercise every day for the past three months, a time will come when your body reaches a plateau. At this point, you may still be gaining muscle and the exercise may be effective, but your body can do better.

You need to increase the resistance level of your body and expose it to newer and harder challenges. There's a difference between your endurance levels at month one and month six. So as your endurance levels change, your workouts should change to also bring some change in your workouts so that your body doesn't end up being injured. Do you ever get bored of things just because you're doing them so much? Well, the same happens with workouts. When you keep doing the same exercise every single day, you'll surely get bored of it and you won't even try to enjoy it. Mix up your workouts and bring some change in your routine so that you can also feel excited to try out new exercises.

Adequate sleep for eight to 10 hours daily is very important for your muscle building routine. During slumber, the body breaks down the proteins present in it to yield amino acids and then use them for energy. But when you eat before going to bed, this process is reversed. Your body starts to make proteins using the food that you've eaten. Some experts also encourage nocturnal sleeping, which is waking up in the middle of the night to eat. Also during slumber, growth takes place as someone looking to gain quality muscle mass. This is very important for men. More than 50 percent of the human growth hormone is secreted when the body's in a sleep cycle. This means that if you don't get adequate sleep, the levels of this hormone reduce significantly.

As a result of this, your muscle gain also suffers. And you don't want all your efforts in the gym to go to waste, do you? When you sleep, your body repairs damaged muscle cells and replenishes immune cells. This is also important for bodybuilders because the human body needs substantial recovery time if it's to perform in the gym daily. Sleeping also recharges your brain because the levels of adenosine are reduced during slumber. This keeps you alert during your workouts. Without proper sleep, you won't have the motivation that comes with alertness if you struggle with your sleep patterns, cut down on alcohol and caffeine levels. Also, don't take sleeping pills as they only work initially and later cause disturbed sleep patterns.

Train your body to sleep at certain times every night, and eventually your body will adapt to this routine schedule. Regular recovery time recovery is very important. Some people completely overlook this essential factor and train without any planning. You need to give your body time to repair. Otherwise there can be problems. You won't have the same strength level to work every day. If you don't give your body time to rest. Your endurance will also decrease if you train the same muscles without giving them a break. If you overdo overdoing exercise, your body can get injured and you may have to face muscle sprains or tears. So if you don't give your muscles time to rebuild, you'll probably end up doing more harm than good to yourself.

Your body will only start repairing once it gets adequate rest. As such, it's essential to plan your workout accordingly. Ideally, you should take a break of two to three days before you train the same muscles again. For example, if you do an intense forearm workout one day, then you must wait for 48 to 72 hours before you train your forearms again. Studies regarding this issue show evidence of this to be true. One such study involved working with three different groups. All the groups did the same volume of workout, but the. Pattern was different bodybuilder's from one group that the assigned volume in one day, the others two days, while the third group did the same volume of workouts in three days with breaks, it was seen that the group, which worked out three days a week with breaks, had more gains, even though the volume of workout was the same as the other two groups.

Hydration water is the most important nutrient for the human body, as it's the medium for transport and numerous bodily reactions. Not only does water hydrate, it also keeps your joints healthy. Your joints contain synovial fluids, which is mostly water, and a lack of water weakens your joints by reducing synovial fluid. This fluid reduces friction between joints to prevent inflammation and increases flexibility. When the levels of this fluid reduce, you find it hard to exercise and there's a greater likelihood of you getting injured. When you workout, you lose a lot of water through sweat and need to replenish this water loss by drinking lots of water.

Lack of water also increases fatigue. If you don't drink enough water, you'll face problems with low endurance levels and fatigue. While water doesn't give energy directly to the body, it's the medium in which major reactions occur. It also keeps your brain healthy. In the absence of sufficient amounts of water, your brain will be tired and that will decrease your levels of alertness and concentration. What is also important for making your muscles State-Owned? If you don't drink enough water, your skin becomes saggy. And on the contrary, sufficient levels of water help make your muscles more resilient and toned.

For most individuals, eight to 13 glasses of water a day are recommended. But if you're trying to increase muscle mass, you need to drink more water. This is because you lose more water through physical activity in the form of sweat. Always keep a water bottle with you in the gym and outside. It's evident that your lifestyle has a huge impact on the overall results of your bodybuilding endeavors. So make sure your lifestyle complements your routine in the gym.

Diet For Increasing Muscle Mass

In this chapter, we'll talk about a diet for increasing muscle mass. Diet is perhaps that component of your muscle building program, which will make achieving your goals so much easier when planned correctly. So you know that you can work out all that you want, but if you eat the wrong foods, you won't get the results. Here are some tips on how to eat right when you want to increase your muscle mass, eat at home. Eating out frequently doesn't only affect your health, but can also slow down the process of increasing lean muscle mass. Most of the food that you eat outside is processed. This food is low in nutrients, so doesn't really benefit the muscles much. It also has a very low fiber and protein count, which further contributes to the problem.

Processed food is also rich in refined carbohydrates and sugar ingredients. These ingredients don't help in muscle building at all and are harmful if over consumed. Cooking at home means that you have complete control over what you eat and what you avoid. You can try out different recipes that aim at building muscle mass. Plenty of protein. Broadly speaking, building muscle mass is divided into two main phases. In the first phase, breakdown of components takes place. This happens when you workout or do resistance training. The second phase is the synthesis phase in which synthesis of muscle cells takes place. This is the phase for which you need to take a lot of proteins.

Protein is the essential nutrient for muscle building. Proteins are involved in the repair of damaged muscle cells and building up new muscle fibers. The muscle fibers are made up of two main proteins called actin and myosin. To synthesize these proteins, you need to take in different amino acids. Some of the amino acids are present in the body and are called non-essential, while the ones you take in from food are called essential amino acids. You can get these proteins from foods like eggs, meat, cheese and fish. You can either get your proteins from food or use protein supplements. These formulas are present in powder and soft gel forms.

Health experts suggest that you must have at least 20 grams of protein in every meal or snack you eat if you want to build muscle mass. It's also important to snack often if you want to increase muscle mass, the trick is to build up on your intake of nutrients, especially proteins. With many hardy options available. It's easy enough to sneak proteins into the mix. Protein snacks will keep you energized and also provide your body with nutrients needed to make new muscle cells and for muscle proteins. Contrary to popular snacking trends, you shouldn't eat sugary foods as these can slow you down. Instead, you need to eat healthy snacks or build muscle mass. Some snack ideas for building muscle mass are given below.

Have a tin of tuna. You can also eat it with brown rice to increase the carb and protein intake. Smoothies are great muscle building snacks as they have milk which is rich in casein protein. Cheese is a protein rich snack. Greek yogurt helps build muscle mass. You can make a snack out of it by adding berries or almonds to it. If you're on the go, you can make power bites to keep you boosted. You can make these without making them and keep them in the refrigerator for later use. To make these bites. You blend together a quarter cup of raw oats, two scoops of a protein powder, chocolate or vanilla, two tablespoons of honey and a spoon of natural peanut butter.

Roll the mixture into small balls to really boost up the calorie count. You can also add dried fruits or nuts to this mixture. If you develop a taste for these, you might never need to buy a protein bar again. Best foods to bulk up. There are a lot of foods that are high in nutrients best suited for building muscle mass. Just consuming a few grams of these foods will give you a lot of calories. Some of these foods are mentioned below: nuts. Nuts are rich and energy rich because they have monounsaturated fats that are healthy for you. Making nuts. A good choice for bulking up is the fact that even a small serving of nuts can give you a lot of calories. Only 50 grams of nuts contains 300 calories to make things even better.

Nuts are a dense source of magnesium, selenium and phosphorus. All of these minerals are essential for building muscle mass. Nut butters are also rich in calories. So you can snack on anything that has peanut butter in it for bulking up one sandwich. Using peanut butter contains four hundred and twenty calories and fifteen grams of proteins. It's also rich in copper, magnesium, potassium and different vitamins. This is a low cost, bulky and tasteful snack option for people looking to increase muscle mass egg whites. Not only are eggs a rich source of protein, they're also great for bulking up. Each egg contains about 90 calories with a protein to fat ratio of 60 to one, plus the protein content in egg whites is readily utilized for protein synthesis.

An omelet for breakfast is a great way to start your day with a filling meal. Smoothies are an effective way to bulk up, especially if you're too busy to prepare elaborate meals. A smoothie made with whey protein, milk and bananas contains about 400 calories. Along with that, it also contains 31 grams of proteins and 10 grams of fat due to the presence of healthy ingredients. Smoothies are also rich in vitamins and minerals, coupled with the high calorie count. This factor further assists in increasing lean muscle mass beans and legumes. Not only are beans and legumes an excellent source of protein, they are also chock full of fiber.

While the benefits of protein from muscle building are obvious, fiber does its part by maintaining proper insulin response. This is critical for muscle growth as it enhances glycogen levels in muscle cells and creates a favorable environment for growth. Salmon eating fatty fish is recommended even for the general population. And if you're doing extensive workouts, you should eat at least three servings of salmon or other fatty fish in a week. Salmon is rich in healthy fats and proteins. The healthy omega three monounsaturated fat present in fatty fish are very good for lean bulking. Fish is not only rich in calories but also helps to improve joint care.

This factors in significantly as you need to have healthy joints. If you want to continue your intense training sessions. Beefsteak each steak of beef contains about 320 calories. It is the most protein rich food on this list containing thirty six grams. Also two grams of carbohydrates and 15 grams of fat are present in a single beefsteak. Beef is a rich source of creatine, which is an amino acid needed for muscle growth. Eating only a pound of beef gives you five grams of creatine. This assists in increasing muscle strength and accelerates the process of muscle growth.

Beef provides three more grams of creatine as compared to red meat or lamb meat. Avocado avocado on toast is a great snack option for people who want to bulk up eating two slices of toast with half an avocado spread on it gives you four hundred and eighty five calories. Although the snack is a bit low in protein, it contains about thirty eight grams of fats. The high concentration of minerals, vitamin A and healthy fats make up for the lack of protein in this snack. So if you couple your resistance training with the right kind of foods, you'll get your results faster.

Muscle Boosting Supplements

In this chapter, we'll talk about supplements for muscle mass. If you're aiming to build muscle mass, you're probably familiar with a number of supplements to enhance results. However, you have to remember that supplements are exactly just that, supplements that are meant to supplement your diet and not replace it. Well, they can add to achieving results. They can by no means act as substitutes for a well-balanced diet and a solid training program. Importance of supplements for bodybuilding. The right supplements can be extremely important for bodybuilding. These are compounds that aren't naturally present in your body and aren't present in sufficient amounts, which makes it essential to take them from the outside.

If you have a routine where you consume more calories than you burn and have more protein than you break down, you are well on your way. Plus, when you pair this up with a challenging exercise program, you set yourself up for success. Adding in certain supplements that cater to muscle gain needs specifically can help you go a long way. The following may help you gain more muscle with the right diet and exercise program. Creatine creatine is an organic acid which is nitrogenous in nature. It contains amino acids like glycine, methionine and arginine. These amino acids play a role in increasing muscle mass by repairing any damaged muscle tissue and forming new muscle cells. Our body already has creatine in skeletal muscles and the brain creatine assists in muscle building.

By allowing your body to work harder and for a longer time, it lets you do more sets and reps. Supplements containing creatine help to increase the phosphor creatine reserves present in the body when needed for energy. These reserves are broken down and the energy can be used in intense workout sessions. Health experts believe creatine is the most effective supplement for increasing lean muscle mass and making muscles strong. It enhances performance in anaerobic exercises and increases the fiber size in the muscles. Muscles are made up of actin and myosin fibers. When the fiber size is increased, muscles grow and that increases muscle mass as a whole.

Creatine also improves endurance in the muscles, which means that muscles are able to perform a longer time without tiring for increasing muscle mass. You should take about three to six grams of creatine every day. There's a process called creatine loading in which the user takes 10 to 20 grams of the supplement for about two weeks. This reduces the time you need for seeing the results of the supplement. After this time, you can go back to using three grams each day. There are two different forms of creatine, but the best one for muscle building is creatine monohydrate. This form is cheaper than others and has a better bioavailability when using supplements for muscle building. Users are also concerned about the possible side effects.

Creatine, being the most studied supplement for muscle building, hasn't shown any side effects so far. It doesn't tear out the muscle cells or harm the kidneys, as some people speculate, along with men. Women who want to build muscle mass can also use creatine as it's safe for both genders. Beta alanine. Beta alanine is an amino acid that's naturally found in the body in skeletal muscles. This amino acid isn't directly involved in forming muscle cells or even proteins. Instead, it actually forms carnitine in the body by joining with al histo dine. The amount of carnitine your body can make doesn't depend on the amount of histo time present, but on the amount of beta alanine. Although the body has processes for forming beta alanine, the best way to get this amino acid is from supplements. It helps form carnitine and then plays a role in increasing muscle performance for intense workouts.

During high intensity workouts, the lactic acid concentration in the muscles increases. This increases acidity in the muscles and causes fatigue. Carnitine assists in reducing this acidity so that you don't tire quickly. Carnitine has buffering capabilities and it levels out hydrogen ions that accumulate in the muscles during workouts. Most supplement plans include taking beta alanine for twenty eight days so that the current assigned levels in the body are maximized. Beta alanine also increases endurance during intense anaerobic exercises such as sprinting and weight lifting. Your body has a veto to Max, which is the percentage of oxygen that the body can make use of in the presence of beta alanine.

Your body's volume, max, increases from 90 to 115 percent. With such high oxygen consumption, muscles get a sufficient amount of oxygen that they need. For better performance, beta alanine does have a side effect that it causes paresthesia. This is a condition in which the user feels a prickly sensation on the hands and face that's going to last for more than an hour if high doses of beta alanine are taken. Despite that, beta alanine helps boost muscle building by forming carnitine, which increases fatigue, threshold and Buffer's muscle acidity.

A study published by International Journal of Sports, Nutrition and Exercise Metabolism showed the beta alanine actually helped enhance the effect of creatine when taken in conjunction, Becka's amino acids are the monomers that form proteins. Since muscles are made up of proteins, any supplement that contains amino acids is good for muscle building. Branched chain amino acids are those amino acids that have branched side chains. The three major Bekas are Lucene Vallen and ISO Lucene BKK aides are involved in the synthesis of glutamine, which is important for muscle building.

It helps in protein synthesis and balance of the nitrogen levels. Both these factors contribute to muscle building on their own. Becka's reduce fatigue in the muscle cells. When the body needs extra energy during workouts, it breaks down these amino acids for energy so you can work out for a longer time. Also, these amino acids accelerate recovery time. Your muscles need to recover for the next workout. So Bekas play a role in recovering and rejuvenating your muscles. Bekas are also involved in enhancing protein absorption in the body so that these nutrients are not lost and can be put to good use in the muscles.

During exercise, the body produces a hormone called serotonin, which also increases fatigue. Branched chain amino acids lower the levels of this hormone to reduce fatigue. These amino acids are present in legumes, meat and dairy products. If your diet is rich in these foods, you may not need to take synthetic supplements for getting these amino acids. All three branched chain amino acids are equally important. A ratio of three to one to one for Lucene, to Aissa, Lucene and Vallentine is good for building muscle mass. HMV, HMV or Beta Hydroxy Beta Methylbutyrate is produced in the body during Lucene processing. It's helpful in preventing muscle breakdown during higher intensity workout muscles.

HMV prevents this from happening so that minimum muscle loss takes place. It also increases the levels of protein synthesis, which is a great way for increasing muscle mass. Studies have shown that people who take three to six grams of HMV daily have more gains than people who don't. HMV also improves recovery during exercise. Your muscles undergo Microtel and get sore. Due to a buildup of hydrogen ions. HMV reduces the time needed for recovery by elevating the protein synthesis to repair the muscles that have been damaged. Being able to exercise harder and longer. You will experience an increase in muscle mass before you take any supplementation for building muscle mass. Read up on the side effects of the synthetic supplements and only take the recommended dosage.

Cardio For Muscle Building

In this chapter, we'll discuss cardio for muscle building. Many bodybuilders flinch at the mention of the word cardio as they know that cardio burns fats. If the whole point of your tough exercise and diet regime is to gain muscle, why would you want to do something that burns fats? It just defeats the whole purpose, doesn't it? There is scientific evidence to back up this fact. A study was published in the Journal of Applied Physiology, which touched on this subject. The study included a group performing 10 weeks of intense training along with cardio. It was found that cardio burns more fat as compared to only weightlifting. The downside was that the cardio also reduced the strength gains.

There are also other studies to prove that cardio does cut down the muscle gain when integrated with resistance training importance of cardio muscle building. So cardio becomes a controversial topic when trying to bulk up. The question remains, does cardio counter muscle gain? Well, it certainly can if you do it wrong, but it's not all that bad if you know how to do it properly. When you workout to gain muscle, think of cardio as conditioning. It's the means through which you can improve your heart health. A healthy heart means better blood flow to the muscles, which further means a sufficient supply of oxygen and nutrients to the musculature. But it's important that you do cardio without losing any muscle.

According to Jobholder, a Nike coach, you need to train both your aerobic and anaerobic systems if you want your cardio to complement your muscle building routine. Your anaerobic system provides energy for a short span of time, ranging from a few seconds to a minute. At this time, no oxygen is involved. The anaerobic phase is further divided into the lactic and lactic phase. Lactic acid is produced in the lactic phase while it's absent in the electric phase. On the other hand, the aerobics system involves oxygen and provides energy for long term use by breaking down essential nutrients to the body.

Duse of cardio. If you plan on integrating cardio into your existing exercise routine, you need to do it properly and with extreme thought. First of all, you need to consider the number of days you'll be doing cardio for. Experts suggest that you should do cardio only for two days a week if you don't want to lose muscle. The maximum number of days could be three. But if you exceed that, you'll end up losing muscle. Sprint exercises are the best kind of cardio that you can do to preserve your muscle mass. You may have seen professional runners being so buff despite running all the time. Well, it's because sprints work your anaerobic system, which means the energy comes from short spurts rather than burning off any major nutrient to the body.

Also, sprints help improve recovery. They give your body time to build itself and repair any torn muscle. It will also help you in the gym because sprinting exercises increase your work capacity and give you massive energy. Do ten rounds of sprints on a treadmill at a speed of ten miles per hour, make each round ten seconds and take a ten second rest between each round to skip the part where the treadmill is accelerating. It's good to jump on the treadmill when your desired speed has been achieved. It might seem very easy when you read it here, but this routine really pumps you up. Try to take shorter breaks, limit your cardio to less than twenty minutes. It's been seen in different studies that cardio done longer than that actually burns muscle mass.

Low intensity cardio is much better if you want to preserve muscle mass during low intensity cardio, your body burns less fat as compared to high intensity cardio. Also, it builds endurance, so you have a better performance during your gym routine. At the same time, low intensity cardio is easier on the joints. This is also a considering factor for bodybuilders as they don't want to get injured doing cardio. This can easily render them unfit for their actual muscle building exercises. Another smart way to incorporate cardio into your routine is to use it as a warm up for your strength training.

Limit the cardio time to ten minutes so that it doesn't interfere with your workouts. Later, performing a longer, low intensity cardio session before intense training not only burns more fat, but also interferes with increasing gains. Don'ts of cardio high intensity cardio is good for a lot of things, but not necessarily for bulking up. In fact, it's one of the don'ts. When you want to build or maintain muscle mass. It's been seen in studies that high intensity cardio is better at burning fat than low intensity. It gives your body the ability to burn fat even after the workout is done. Also, it increases the aerobics capacity of the body.

This means the body goes in an aerobics phase where it burns nutrients for energy in the presence of oxygen. The same also increases oxygen consumption after workouts, which only. Added to the Arabic capacity, high intensity cardio is suitable for utilizing muscle mass, which is something you need to avoid when your strength training another don't have cardio is long sessions don't do cardio for too long. Even when you do low intensity cardio, make sure the sessions are not longer than 20 minutes. Also, don't do longer cardio sessions right before resistance training. It'll only leave you exhausted and in bad shape for training when you want to bulk up.

There's definitely no need to do cardio every day. As mentioned earlier, you can do cardio in two or three days. If you do high intensity cardio, mix it up and maybe do low intensity for two days and high intensity for one. And most importantly, don't make your cardio exercises a chore that you get sick of. Enjoy your cardio and make it a fun routine for yourself. Sprints or cycling or even swimming can be a boring task for some people if they're not made for it. For some people, bodybuilding and weightlifting is the only fun thing. But you have to make your cardio fun so that you are tempted to do it. Cardio is supposed to condition your heart, so make your routine full of variety.

Don't stick to one pattern, change your cardio pattern, just like you change your intense workout routine for the first week of the month. Try to do low intensity than moderate intensity for the next week, for the first week of the month, try to do low intensity and then moderate intensity for the next week and high intensity every once in a while. Don't let your leg day and cardio fall on the same day. It'll leave you exhausted and you won't be able to do either of them with concentration or motivation. At least let there be a one day break between your leg day and your high intensity cardio day. So you can say that cardio is a good way for you to keep on track and to condition your body and heart. Just remember not to overdo anything because your body needs a break from time to time.

Tracking Your Progress

In this chapter, we'll talk about tracking progress when you start an intense training program and you've got the supplements and diet plan ready, you need to work towards keeping track of your progress, too. It's something that most people tend to ignore if they don't realize the importance of this practice. You need to keep a track of your progress so that you can monitor how soon and how many gains you're making. Based on this info, you can then make changes to your diet or exercise plan if you don't track your progress. How do you know if your struggle has given any results? Similarly, you wouldn't know if you need to increase the amount of sets or reps you do.

Some people have set a time frame for themselves in which they have to reach a certain goal to reach this goal. In the time span, you need to track your progress. Here are a few ways in which you could track your progress and make changes in your muscle gain routine. Along the way, keep a journal. Journals can be tedious and boring, but are probably the most effective method of tracking your progress for muscle gain. You need to have a workout routine with varying reps and sets for each exercise. Also, your diet should contain snacks and meals specific for muscle gain.

Since it's not possible to keep all this information in your head without getting confused or mixing it all up, it's best to record it all. To keep a track of all this, get a journal and pen down your daily eating plan and exercise habits. If you use supplements, you can also record results you've seen from that supplement in your journal. Experts suggest that you should change your plan after every two months. When you do that, either get a new journal or change the format of your existing one. This will make it easier for you to track your progress with different plans.

For instance, if you change a supplement after two months, you can write all the pros and cons in your journal. This will give you a clear idea of which formula works best for you or which workout plan is the most effective. You can also write your short term goals in your journal that you need to reach in two or three months time. If your goal is to reach ten sets of any particular exercise, your journal will help you monitor how quickly you reach your goal and how close you are to it. You can write the following things in your journal, write about the amount of time you spend in the gym every day. Also, you can write if you felt energized or fatigued during your visit to the gym any day, write about how a particular supplement changed the way you feel or how long you were able to work out.

Weighing scale. It's very convenient to track your progress using a weighing scale because it's something that is easily accessible. You might not be able to observe any changes on a daily basis, but you'll be able to see any noticeable changes if you check your weight after each week of your plan. If your plan includes bulking up on high calorie foods to build muscle, then you'll be able to see the results on a weighing scale. One important thing to remember is that the weight gain you see on a weighing scale may not necessarily be muscle. The weight could be water, weight or fat. If you're clean bulking, then there's likelihood that the weight gain you see on your scale is muscle. You should still measure your body muscle composition to see if the weight you are gaining is actually muscle or not body fat composition. You can measure your body fat composition using body calipers.

These are special devices that measure fats from several regions of the body where fat deposition is maximum. These regions are different for men and women, but mainly involve the abdomen, hips, arms, thighs and chest. When measuring muscle mass, you have to assume that the mass you've put on is fat. To track your progress, you must first know your body weight before you start your muscle building plan of that weight, you must measure the fat mass. This can be done by various methods and you can get it determined by an expert for accurate measurements. You have to measure the fat composition by subtracting the amount of fat in kilograms from the total body fat.

If you weigh fifty kilograms and five kilograms of that is fat mass, then you have to measure your further fat composition from that information. Say, after you start your muscle building routine, your weight increases to 70 kilograms. If five kilograms of fifty was fat, then it means that of the 20 kilograms you put on, the same percentage would be fat. From that amount to that percentage would be 10 percent and the 10 percent of 20 kilograms is two kilograms. This means now your overall body weight is 70 kilograms, of which seven kilograms is fat mass and the rest is your body, organs, blood and water. In this way, you can keep track of how much fat you've put on.

It's just an assumption that this is muscle mass, which it could be. Since you're bulking up measurements, another way to track your progress is to make. This is probably the simplest way to track your progress and to visibly monitor how much muscle you've gained for this, you need to take a measuring tape and measure your biceps, chest, calves and legs. You can also measure your stomach and forearms to see how much muscle gain you've achieved. You can actually measure a lot of different parts of the body. But these are the main areas that you should measure to track your progress. For example, if you started with your biceps at eight inches and after a few months of training, the size increases to 10 or 12 inches, it'll give you a clear idea that your routine is working well and you've actually gained muscle.

Take pictures, this is one of the more fun ways to keep track of your progress when you start your routine for building muscle mass, take a picture of yourself in the mirror, then track your progress by taking a picture every week or two times a month. When you put all these pictures together, you'll be able to see how much change has occurred in your body over time if you want. You can also print out the pictures and paste them in your journal to keep your log updated. This is a great way to keep yourself motivated. Sometimes the results may be a bit subtle and you won't really see them yourself.

But when you put all the pictures together and compare them, it becomes easier to see the difference in your gains. If you feel that the pictures aren't showing any difference, then you may need to make some changes in your diet, workout or even your supplements. Tracking your progress is a great way of ensuring that you don't end up wasting your time and not getting any results. You should check your progress every week so that you can reach your short term and long term goals on time.

Best Fitness Apps To Measure Progress

In this chapter, we'll discuss the best fitness apps to measure progress. You can even use technology to measure the progress that you make. There are so many apps that you use for a number of things every day. But did you know that there are apps for tracking your progress, too? There are apps set up by different developers that you can use for tracking your progress and measuring your gains. Nike Training Club. This is an app developed by the leading producer of athletic products in the world. Their app gives you access to more than 180 personalized workouts and all for free.

Just think of this app as your own personal trainer for gaining muscle mass. These workouts are aimed at increasing endurance and muscle gain if you want to track your progress. You can do it with this app as it adapts the workout plans to your needs. The notable feature of this app is that it is suited for everyone, whether you're a beginner or an intermediate level exerciser. This app caters to your needs. It has a pick for you feature which tells you about workouts that are suitable for you. You can choose the kind of workouts you want to do, such as the ones that increase muscle mass and the app will recommend them for you on a daily basis.

The app also gives you expert advice, which comes from leading Nike trainers with tips included on increasing muscle mass and getting toned muscles with time based and rep based options. You can choose the one that is suitable for you. In this way. You can track the amount of time you spend in the gym every day, or the number of reps you're able to pull off if you do any other activities than just training in the gym, such as playing basketball or running, that can also be tracked by this app. Your runs will be stored by the app and the progress of other activities will also be monitored by the app. Garmin Fit. Garmin Fit is another app that can be used to track progress. You compare it with a compatible Garmin device and track your physical activity.

The app has a my day page on which you can see your health data weighing scale. Just turn on your GPS and you can measure your distance if you're running or your elevation. If you're training for building muscle on the app, you can create your own workouts personalized to your needs. This app can also sync with other apps such as Strava or My Fitness Pal, allowing you to track your progress from different apps on one platform. One distinguishing feature of this app is that it lets you connect with other users so you can track your progress against other users. The app also tracks the amount of calories you take in or you need based on your age, height and weight. With the app open, you can also listen to your favorite music while you plan Jefford Workout Tracker.

The Gethard app is a fitness tracker app that you can use for tracking your progress in the gym. It's a gym trainer app which is filled with free fitness programs that are aimed at keeping the user fit. There are thirteen hundred different exercises in the app and the developers have also added animations for the user to see how these exercises are done.

The fitness tracker gives you a progress report so that you can see how well you're doing or which changes you need to make. There's a resting time or two so that you can rest for an optimum time between successive workouts. The app also gives you an option for goal setting that it will then track for you. One of the most noteworthy features of this app is that it gives different kinds of workout plans.

You can customize the plans for yourself to three day, four day or five day splints, or you can sink your data on cloud. If you don't have Wi-Fi, the apostille works offline. The interface is quite user friendly and overall the app is free. Fitness Pal Fitness Pal is an app that many people are aware of. It has a calorie counter for the user to track their calories. If you do muscle building exercises, you can use the calorie counter to see if you have gained weight. Also, there's a BMI and body fat calculator. This is very important for keeping track of your progress in muscle building routines. Body fat mass is used to determine the amount of muscle gained. There are different gym exercises on the app with instructions and animations.

If you're not happy with the results you get from your existing routine, you can learn new muscle building exercises from the app. There are also meal plans on the app for people working for muscle building so you can track your progress in the gym and monitor the calorie intake at the same time. Create your workout log in the app and you can track your intense workouts as well as the results. You can also track your calories with the building calorie tracker and use the pedometer to track the steps you're taking if you've taken up walking as an extra activity. My fitness pal also has a heart tracker to track your heart rate.

The good news is that it's free, works offline and can also sync with other apps such as Garmin Fit. I muscle, i muscle is a tracking app for people who want to gain muscle in a specific part of the body, there's an anatomical figure on the app from where you can choose which part of the body you won't workout plans for. There's also detailed animation of different muscles on the app so that you can see how you need to train along with primary exercises. The app also tracks your secondary muscle gains. You can track the statistics for individual exercises you do or for the whole workout. There's also an option to track your body measurements. This is suitable for people who want to gain muscle mass.

They can monitor the different parts of the body and how they have increased in size. The app tracks workouts with weight and the number of reps and sets you do. There's a digital trainer to give you tips and advice on how to make your workouts more fruitful. Workout Trainer. This is another fitness app that you can use for tracking your progress. The app lets you choose any stage, whether you are a beginner, intermediate or expert. Set a goal for yourself and the Apple Track how close you are to your goal.

You can also connect this app to your smartwatch for better tracking. If you subscribe to the app, you can also get a one on one fitness trainer for yourself online. This trainer will customize the workouts for you and you will also be accountable to this trainer. If you don't want to pay, you can still enjoy different workout plans that are devised by expert coaches. As you can see, it's quite easy to track your performance with an app since your smartphone is almost always with you. Also, different apps are equipped with training, ticker, customized workouts and calorie trackers.

Recap

So now that you know a bit more about the essentials of muscle gain and strength, you can put together a more comprehensive plan to execute beginners. It may still be the lucky ones in the bunch. As no matter what they do, they're bound to put on some muscle. But when you work on a more advanced level, knowing how to optimize results is the only way to enhance your bodybuilding results.

Mindful Meditation

Ten million people in America practice mindful meditation. That's quite a lot, mindful meditation has become popular as more and more people enjoy living a better, less stressful, more productive life. Why are these people turning to meditation to improve their daily lives? The easy answer is meditation works. The more complex answer is that today we're suffering from information overload and stress more than previous generations. Some meditators want to reduce stress and enjoy greater peace. Others seek more awareness to create a more purposeful life. Still others want to gain greater awareness and align their thoughts with their actions.

Mindful meditation is useful for all these purposes. What is true for everyone, however, is that the more you know about your thinking, the more you are in control of your life. Whatever the reason, mindful meditation can be a powerful force like music. Life has many layers and mindful meditation can help you become aware of all the nuances. Mindful meditation isn't magic. It allows you to concentrate your awareness on the here and now. All too frequently, our attention can scatter into the past or the future. We become distracted and unable to focus on what is important in the present. Mindful meditation gives us power to focus on the here and now.

It increases our mental energy, allowing us to perform better and achieve more. Quite simply, mindful meditation makes us more efficient in many areas of our lives. More importantly, it puts us in control. The mind is an extremely complex labyrinth where the subconscious can rule and throw roadblocks in our path. There are times we behave in certain ways without being consciously aware of why mindful meditation increases our awareness and opens our minds to more answers. Our senses are heightened as we enjoy the present more fully. Everyday activities from what we eat, how we enjoy art and listen to music and how we respond to friends and family become more vivid as mental walls crumble.

Mindful meditation relaxes us with awareness, stress and unpleasant thoughts become less threatening and easier to handle. We become more relaxed and are able to let more joy and peace into our lives. Today, we live in a state of impermanence more than ever before in history. More than a hundred years ago, most people spent their lives in the town in which they were born. They knew all their neighbors, their station in life determined their job. It may not sound ideal to us, but it certainly wasn't stressful. These days, we live very fragmented lives. We may move regularly and barely know our neighbors. We switched jobs and friends on a regular basis.

Constant change has become the one permanence on which we can rely. There's no denying that modern knowledge and conveniences have brought us untold advantages. However, at the same time, we've lost our connection to others and to our surroundings. Mindful meditation brings back that important lost connection to what is happening inside of us and around us. It's not an antidote to the problem of living in the 21st century, but it can provide the skills to help us cope with many of its problems. Did you know that you don't have to be a yogi to reap the benefits of mindful meditation? The more you practice, the better you'll become.

It's like exercise for the mind. You know what daily exercise does for your body. It strengthens and firms those muscles in much the same way. Daily mindful meditation strengthens your mind and honors your thinking process. It's both simple and complex and at all times it's a choice. Hopefully this chapter, Of course, will help you make the right one for you. Consistency is the key to successful practice. Even a short meditation period every day is more effective than sporadic longer meditations like physical exercise. Mindful meditation is a process. Success doesn't happen overnight, but it will happen when you begin your meditation journey. You may find it difficult to sit quietly for fifteen or twenty minutes at a time.

You may start making excuses why it's OK to skip meditation for just one day. This will make it harder to resume meditating the following day and you'll easily find an excuse why you shouldn't. You're too tired to. Busy, too frustrated, any excuse will do. That's why I'm making a commitment to regular meditation. Ask yourself what motivated you in the first place? Make a pact with yourself that you will get up half an hour earlier in the morning to meditate with a firm commitment, you will gain momentum and see the results. Mindful meditation is unrivaled in its ability to open your mind. If you are new at mindful meditation, it is helpful that you ask yourself what has motivated you to start meditating at this time? There is, however, no right or wrong reason.

Understanding Mindful Meditation

In this chapter, we'll learn about what mindful meditation is, mindful meditation is actually very simple, yet it comes with great benefits. It's a Western practice with roots in thousands of years of Buddhism, where it's referred to as insight meditation. As that name suggests, it's meant to develop our mental skills and become more aware. However, mindful meditation is not associated with any specific ideology. Mindfulness is a skill we all possess, but not all of us develop and cultivate fully. The unique thing about mindful meditation is that it allows us to take an active part in our thinking process instead of remaining passive. It's more than being aware of the world around us. It specifically refers to that exciting and sometimes mysterious world inside of us.

Mindfulness increases our awareness of ourselves and how we think it's an effective way of knowing ourselves better. Mindful meditation is always purposeful and nonjudgmental. We calmly accept and acknowledge what it is. Instead of moving through the day on autopilot, mindful meditation allows us to be more present and gain more control over our thoughts and activities. This invariably enriches our lives beyond measure. When we practice mindful meditation consistently, we gain an inner calm that will help us deal with life's many challenges. How often have we become so stressed that we have consciously avoided thinking about our problems, which then only worsen as we become more stressed? Sometimes it may feel easier not to think at all, but in the long run, reality will take over.

Nonjudgmental awareness allows us to remove ourselves mentally from the mental tsunami and remain calm in times of adversity. We become more connected to our experiences in a healthy, non-threatening way. On a basic human level, it's natural for us to push aside unpleasant thoughts by distracting ourselves from what is really important. Addictions to alcohol, drugs and social media are just some of the ways we avoid dealing with the present. This obviously is not helpful and merely generates greater anxiety and stress daily. Mindful meditation keeps us focused on the present and helps us deal with problems rather than avoiding them.

Fortunately, becoming more aware is a skill that can be learned, like playing a musical instrument or a sport. The more we practice, the better we become at it. Mindful meditation has moved from the mystical to mainstream. Many studies have confirmed the benefits of regular mindful meditation, less stress related illnesses, better sleeping habits, lower blood pressure, better immune system, more energy, better pain management, better decision making ability, greater resilience when faced with adversity. The reason mindful meditation has proven so powerful is that the body and mind are intricately connected. When our emotional state suffers, so does our body.

This is especially relevant to stress, which can cause many physical problems. As a result, mindful meditation not only improves our mental health, but our physical health as well.

In the past, doctors have concentrated on prescribing medication for anxiety and stress related symptoms. However, following a myriad of studies in recent years, doctors are now recognizing the value of mindfulness and recommending mindful meditation as an adjustment to or instead of medications. A study at Johns Hopkins University showed that 20 percent of 3500 patients using mindful meditation showed improvement in symptoms of depression as opposed to the placebo group. These numbers are the same for patients using antidepressants. That means meditation has the same effect on our brain as medication.

Interestingly, these patients only meditated two and a half hours each week. That's how powerful, mindful meditation can be. The study concluded that if patients were to spend even more time meditating, they would see even better results. Neuroscience has revealed that people who meditate regularly show an increase in gray matter in brain regions that regulate emotions and learning. Similar studies have found that areas of the brain that process fear decrease in size. Science is providing a connection between meditating and brain waves, and studies are continuing. Another study showed. Three months of regular meditation affect enzyme activity that controls how we age. This important finding could link meditation to a slowing of the aging process.

How To Practice Mindful Meditation

In this chapter, we'll learn how to practice mindful meditation with all of its benefits, practicing mindful meditation is extremely easy. Let's go through the steps where comfortable clothing, you don't want to have your focus interrupted by a tight pair of pants or skirt, find a comfortable seat. Ideally, it will be in a peaceful spot without clutter and noise. You can meditate indoors or outdoors. Start your meditation with short sessions of around 10 minutes. This will make it easy to develop the habit of meditating and working your way up to half an hour or even a full hour. Mornings or evenings are the best times.

But any time you spend meditating, you can also split your meditation sessions and do half when you get up and the second half before going to bed. Either sit in the traditional lotus position or simply relax in a comfortable chair with your feet resting on the floor. Keep your spine straight but not stiff. Let your head hang naturally with a downward gaze. Your hands should be resting comfortably on your thighs. You can keep your eyes open, but most people seem to prefer closing them. Do whatever works best for you. The goal is to get completely comfortable and not to worry about whether you're doing it right or wrong. Just do it and you will enjoy the results.

Start focusing on your breathing. All your attention should be on how the air feels as you inhale deeply through your nose, down to your stomach, then exhale. Notice the physical sensations of the air moving down your body, then being expelled through the nose. Become aware of the rise and fall in your chest as you inhale and exhale. Don't worry if your attention wanders, this is perfectly normal. What is important is that you don't try to stop those intruding thoughts. Just let them flow through your mind, nonjudgmentally, and return your focus to your breathing. If you find your thoughts wandering too often, don't worry. Simply observe whatever's happening.

Don't judge or blame yourself. Just observe what your mind is doing when you're done meditating. Sit quietly for a moment before opening your eyes. Take a minute and observe what you are feeling again. It's important not to judge yourself when you are ready. Go about your day. Mindful meditation may sound simple, but it isn't. The act of focusing on your breath helps you become aware of your thoughts and emotions. The more you meditate, the more aware you become. And as we'll discuss in the next chapter, meditation is all about increasing your awareness daily. Mindful meditation will help you cope with stress, but even normal days can make it challenging to remain in focus and mindful. Your boss wants to see you in his office now. Your spouse has been argumentative all week.

Your child, who has just received his or her driver's license yesterday, has disappeared with your car and five best friends. It's stressful and it's called life. Mindfulness can help you cope with these adversities before seeing the boss arguing with your spouse or writing your air out of the will. Take a deep breath literally, even if it's at your desk. Sit quietly and spend two minutes inhaling and exhaling. However, you can do this exercise anywhere, such as in an elevator or while waiting for a streetlight to change. There's remarkable power in breathing. Just a few minutes will help calm you for whatever you need to face.

These short breathing moments can be your own mini health spa. You'll also find that taking a mindful walk and greatly elevating your mood, all it takes is 10 or 15 minutes. You can do this outdoors or in the hallway of your office. A walking meditation helps focus your scattered thoughts. It's a chance to work through the mental tsunami that can invariably ruin your day. You can do it anywhere while walking to the store to work or through a park. Take care while crossing the street. So when we walk in a normal fashion, we do so automatically without awareness. We simply move forward from point A to point B. Not so with a walking meditation during walking meditation.

Keep your hands wherever they're the most comfortable at your side or in front of you. You may find it useful to mentally count out ten steps at a time as you walk. Instead of focusing on the rising and falling of your breath, you will focus on your feet as they rise and fall with each step. Be aware of your body as it shifts its weight. As you walk, as in a sitting meditation, thoughts will intrude. You will notice sights and sounds as you move. That's fine.

Be aware of the intruding thoughts and gently shift your attention back to your feet. Another form of walking meditation is to focus on your environment instead of your body as you walk, become aware of the sounds and smells around you, notice colors and shapes and don't judge or react, simply remain aware. If your mind wanders, pull it back into focus. Whether you do a regular half hour meditation session at home or a mindful walking meditation on the way to the store, incorporating mindfulness into your day should become a natural part of your lifestyle. You deserve it.

Still More Mindful Meditation Techniques

In this chapter, we'll learn about more mindful meditation techniques. In addition to breathing meditation, there are additional techniques that will help you enhance your awareness and become more mindful. So much is going on around us at all times, yet most of the time we move through the day on autopilot. These exercises are designed to strengthen your mind in the same way pushups are meant to strengthen your body. They are also fun and will make your day more enjoyable and alive. Focus on a specific object of meditation. You'll be keeping your eyes open for this meditation. The exercise is enormously helpful in preventing your focus from wandering. Start by choosing an object.

It can be anything: a flower, a picture, an interesting design, a candle, anything that touches your fancy. It should be the right size for you to observe it easily in its entirety. The purpose of the object is to be your focal point. When your attention strays, start by closing your eyes and focusing on your breathing for five minutes to become relaxed. When you feel ready, open your eyes and observe the chosen object. Notice any lights and shadows falling on the object. Notice the texture. Is it smooth, bumpy, silky? Imagine what it would feel to the touch. Notice the different shades of color. Keep breathing slowly, make no judgments about the object, you're simply an observer, continue as long as you wish.

Ten minutes is a good time. If your mind wanders, let your awareness return to the object. Since modern life can assault our senses on a daily basis, we can remain oblivious to the beauty around us. How often do we really notice our surroundings? This quiet exercise is helpful in keeping your focus sharp body scan meditation. This mindful meditation is useful in releasing tension at the end of a day and in helping you fall asleep easily. Tension can frequently settle in specific areas of the body, such as shoulders bringing on aches and fatigue. This will draw attention to trouble spots and help you relax, sit or lay anywhere you're comfortable.

Close your eyes and breathe in and out for five minutes to enhance relaxation. Shift your focus to your body as you breathe. Become aware of various body parts. Start with the toes and feet. Move to the ankles and up the legs. As you notice any tension, breathe into it, then exhale. Keep breathing. As your awareness moves past your hips to your torso, breathe into any tension that you may notice. Keep breathing and notice your arms. Hands and fingers continue to breathe into spots that feel tense as you continue to breathe. Move your awareness to your shoulders, neck, face and skull. Breathe slowly into any tension spots. Spend as much time on any ten spots as necessary. This is a wonderful exercise to relieve tension, calm your mind and hone the way we deal with stress.

Counting, mindful meditation, as with all other meditations, sit comfortably and practice the basic breathing meditation for five minutes to relax, take a deep breath and inhale. Wait a second and exhale while counting out the number one in your mind. Take another deep breath and inhale weight and count out the number to continue doing this until you've counted to number ten. Repeat this counting process by starting with the number nine and going backward to one. If at any time during this exercise you lose track of a number, start over from the beginning. As you get better, you can increase the base number to twenty or even thirty, find your happy place of meditation, sit comfortably and enjoy five minutes of mindful breathing meditation.

Now imagine you're in a peaceful, beautiful place. It could be a place you've been to or a place you imagine, whichever is very relaxing and soothing and there's no place you'd rather be. Look around and experience the sights, sounds and colors around you. Notice how your body feels. Allow yourself to become lost in the beauty of your special place. Take all the time you want. Notice the sense of peace and calm flooding through your body. When you're ready to leave, take a deep breath and open your eyes. You're now ready to face the challenges of your day.

Mindful Meditation & Your Brain

In this chapter, we'll talk about mindful meditation and the brain. Until recently, scientists regarded the brain as mass inside our head, nothing more and nothing less. It was believed that as adults, we are stuck with the neurology cards we were handed at birth for life. That theory has been proven to be false. With the use of MRI, neuroscientists have discovered that we have far more control over our brain than previously thought. Changes in the brain can be quantified and seen. We can change our thinking to improve our lives. The fact is, our brain keeps changing throughout our life. The remarkable truth about mindful meditation is that it allows us to control those changes. For centuries, we have enjoyed the truth that Renea discards words.

I think therefore I am. Modern science now allows us to amend that bit of wisdom to I think therefore I control who I am. The realization that we have the power to influence the workings of our brain has many far reaching potentials. We are seeing that a mere 30 minutes of mindful meditation each day can have a measurable effect on various areas of the brain. Let's take a look at what is being discovered. A study conducted at UCLA shows that people who have practiced mindful meditation for 20 years or more had a greater amount of gray matter within the entire brain.

The results of this study can have life changing effects on aging diseases such as dementia and Alzheimer's and how we age in general. A study at Yale University has found that mindful meditation decreases brain chattering or monkey mind. Buddhists call it monkey brain because our brain can resemble the chattering noise in clamoring of monkeys, especially when driven by fear. The Yale study and others have shown that mindful meditation serves the function of a volume control. Toning down the noise and allowing for some mental peace and quiet.

Studies at Johns Hopkins University have found mindful meditation has a similar effect as medication on the brain and its ability to ease depression and anxiety, while mindful meditation may appear to be just sitting there. In reality, it has a powerful healing effect on the brain. A Harvard study has shown that mindful meditation increases brain areas responsible for learning and emotions at the same time decreases the brain area that deals with stress and fear. In that same study, it was shown that the perception of fear in the participants also changes. In other words, mindful meditation can control the amount and intensity of fear that we experience.

A study at the University of Massachusetts confirms that mindful meditation reduced the level of anxiety in participants. At the same time, as the level of fear decreases, the level of awareness increases, in effect, taking up the new available space in the brain. Studies about the effect of mindful meditation on the brain are ongoing. But the fact that we can tone our brain muscles in the same way we tone our thighs and abs is encouraging wider interest in the scientific community.

Why Is Awareness So Important

In this chapter, we'll discover why awareness is so important, greater self awareness is at the root of mindful meditation. Prior to the 1970s, self-awareness was a somewhat vague concept. At the time, psychologist Shelley Duvall and Robert Wickland defined and advanced the link between behavior and thoughts. If we could understand our thoughts, we could increase our awareness as to why we behave in a certain way. This led to further studies and the conclusion that we can monitor thoughts and feelings as they happen. Much of the inner life lies below the surface in the vast region of the subconscious.

Our lives are governed by patterns set long ago, sometimes at birth. Perhaps the first words out of your parents mouth when you were born was Here's my future doctor. Growing up, much was expected of you and your career path was clear. Good schools, perfect grades, best college, then medical school. After an appropriate period, there would be a suitable spouse, a desirable house followed by two adorable and well-behaved children. If this is our internal blueprint, we might never question it. We may never be totally aware that this has been our path from birth. It's as if we moved on a kind of automatic pilot with us just along for the ride.

If at age 30, we drift into a state of depression, we become utterly confused. We have achieved our dream. What could possibly be wrong? Our mind can be conditioned in many ways. With the help of mindful meditation, we can recognize a pattern of behavior. It's this awareness that allows us to take that first proactive step toward change. We are now in the driver's seat. There are countless ways when our conditioning simply bypasses our inner self, we are someone else's creation, not a person in our own right. Our thoughts and feelings are so deeply buried, we're no longer aware of them, except on some level we are aware. But our only clue may be anger, sadness or simply a deadening numbness.

We lose interest in things that used to excite us. We deliberately sabotage relationships because then at least we have a logical reason for feeling miserable. Maybe we turn to drink and drugs. Self-awareness isn't a magic pill, but when we practice mindful meditation and examine new thoughts and feelings, it serves as a roadmap to different choices and opportunities. If you want a clue as to how awareness or the lack of it affects behavior, look around you. Do you have a friend who is in constant financial difficulties but spends every weekend at the mall buying more shoes and makeup? Do you have a coworker who constantly argues with him, belittles people, yet wonders why he has no friends? The link between thoughts and behavior couldn't be clearer. People sleepwalk through life and act on sheer impulse.

They are unable to control their behavior because they are not in control of their mind and feelings. Their feelings are controlling them. There's another reason awareness is so important. If we wish to move forward, many of us ruminate about past wrongs. Some of us even obsess about them. Anger and bitterness can take over our minds and leave little room for anything else. At the same time, studies show that our memories can be very difficult from reality. Maybe we were bullied a few times in school. What we remember is not the bullying, but the emotions that were a part of the experience. Shame, anger, helplessness. When we recall the bullying, what we really remember are those negative feelings.

This can significantly affect how we see ourselves and how we behave towards others. Maybe we are overwhelmed by shame and feel worthless, or we thrive on anger and start bullying others before they have a chance to bully us. These behaviors become ingrained habits, and we react automatically without understanding why. Sadly, many people go through their lives chained to a script. The dialogue for these scripts can be written in childhood, and we spend our days reacting to established clues growing up where you called stupid, unattractive or clumsy, it may be twenty or thirty years later. Maybe the people who labeled you are no longer here, but their voices still resound in your brain whether you are consciously aware of them or not. Every time you tell yourself I can't do this, why bother? No one worthwhile will ever love me.

Your mind plays a script that determines your actions. The path you're walking now was set long ago. The band has stopped playing, but you're still dancing to the music as you'd be. I'm aware of your life's script, it may seem like a case of mistaken identity, every fiber of your being is arguing, but this isn't me. Whatever your pattern, it moves you further and further from your true essence. This can be a painful realization. At the same time, it could be the key to the release from a lifetime of mental bondage. The more you engage in mindful meditation, the more you will understand the reasons for your past actions and will be able to develop a new alternative life script. It is never too late to change.

As a matter of fact, mindful meditation makes it easier to open our mind and accept a different, perhaps unexplored path. With mindful meditation, you become aware of the negative dialogue that guides your behavior, the opportunity to change the life script you've been living and open doors to better, more life affirming choices is both exciting and challenging. But it's always worth it. There's a possibility that some of the new awareness will make you uncomfortable. We're all human. We've all behaved badly or made mistakes we would rather not think about. And here comes mindful meditation to make us confront behavior we'd rather forget. It can seem scary at first. To quote Dr. Phil, you can't change what you don't acknowledge.

The unwanted behavior will continue until you face it. Denial is a luxury you can't afford if you want to move forward. It's a matter of fact. The problem will only worsen. Know that it is never too late to change. Sometimes it does take some courage. The point is so critical, it bears repeating. You can't change what you don't acknowledge. Change isn't always easy, but it may be necessary to become a better version of you. There are other forms of meditation that urge us to brush away bad thoughts as if they were unwelcome and unpleasant intruders. What they are in effect saying is that you are your thoughts. You probably felt the effect of bad thoughts. I'm a bad person. You identify yourself with your thoughts.

That gives one particular thought an extraordinary power. The fault with that logic is that you're not your thoughts. Perhaps you are a person who has done a bad thing, but you are not a bad person. The difference is crucial when we attempt to change. Bad thoughts aren't the real problem. Thoughts in themselves are neutral. When we strive for greater awareness, the issue becomes our inclination to resist accepting negative thoughts. That just makes them more powerful and prevents us from exploring them in a nonjudgmental, mindful way. When we start to label ourselves as bad or lazy, we accept that our entire essence can be defined with one word. When that happens, we act in ways to ensure that the label fits the deed labels become prophetic. We act badly and lazily mindful.

Meditation brings awareness to this destructive type of self labeling. It lets us view our thoughts, nonjudgmental apart from ourselves, and begin to challenge the truth of any label. Behavior is never set in stone. When you challenge labels, your behavior will change accordingly, using mindfulness. The next time you think of yourself as a bad person, you can stop the thought as it happens. Tell yourself, here's that silly label again. This is not who I am. Mindful meditation allows us to recognize the labels we have accepted with nonjudgmental awareness. We can act in ways that diminish the power of labels.

Mindful Meditation & Work

In this chapter, we'll talk about mindful meditation and work. Mindful meditation is proven to help reduce stress and deal more effectively with change. And the office is a place where you'll find an abundance of both. Work is where you spend most of your time. If you're stressed out at work, this will affect you psychologically, physically and impact other areas of your life. Work related anxiety is known to cause headaches and insomnia. If it persists, it can cause high blood pressure, depression and weaken your immune system. To add to the problem, many people suffering from work related stress resort to unhealthy means of coping, such as smoking, binge eating, alcohol and even abuse of those closest to them. The ability to control our responses to others is critical at the office.

It's a bad idea to tell the boss off and annoying your co-workers will only add more stress. When we're aware and in control of our emotions, we are more able to suppress improper, aggressive responses and reactions. When we're in a Problem-Solving environment such as work, it is crucial that our brain remains in an open, resilient mode instead of getting bogged down by negative thoughts and feelings. Dealing with daily change and pressures is a necessary skill for high level performance and consistent inner calm and mindful meditation can make work a challenge instead of an emotional hazard zone. The good news is that many companies are starting to embrace mindfulness and are organizing on site meditation programs.

If your company doesn't have a program, you can still engage in mindful meditation. Short breathing meditation can be done at a desk and can quickly shift your mind to Problem-Solving stance instead of panic mode. When work pressures become overwhelming, use mindful meditation to keep yourself in a calm zone. All kinds of ideas may be flowing through your mind. My report isn't good enough. The boss will fire me. Your mind is scattering into all kinds of areas except focusing on the report. As you take control and change those intruding thoughts, it will be easier to approach the problem in a more productive way. Tell yourself the reasons why the situation won't be as bad as it appears.

Then give yourself two ways of dealing with a worst case scenario. If the boss really does hate the report, what actions can you take to resolve the problem? Instead of merely reacting, you are proactively seeking solutions. A quick, mindful meditation at your desk or away from your desk, when necessary, will have immediate, soothing consequences if possible. Practice at a happy place. Meditation described in this chapter Book as its excellent preparation for facing adversity. Instead of remaining overwhelmed by what the boss may do, you'll be more prepared to listen mindfully to what is being said and form a more reasoned response.

Many of us don't listen carefully when we're upset. We're too busy preparing our reply to really listen to and hear what is being said. Look into the speaker's eyes. Keep your mind focused on what is being said. Instead of thinking about how you will answer. It's all too common to talk without thinking and say things that we wish we could take back. Mindful listening improves how we communicate with others. You hear the words and the intent behind the words. When people notice that you are genuinely paying attention, they're far more likely to listen to what you have to say. More mindful actions you can take at work before leaving for work in the morning.

Tell yourself that you will remain calm and mindful. This will set the tone for the day before you leave the house. Become aware of how your thoughts add to your stress. Expecting things to go wrong will also set the tone for the day, although in a very negative way. Have lunch with a friend or eat alone instead of lunching with coworkers, getting away from the office, whether physically or mentally can relieve work related anxiety. Take regular mindful breathing breaks.

Mindful Meditation & Relationships

In this chapter, we'll talk about mindful meditation and relationships. Relationships are confusing and can bring out the worst behavior in anyone, whether it's your family, a date friend or co-workers. Even good relationships prevent constant challenges. One of the reasons relationships turn problematic is that many of us remain unaware of the other person's needs. We tend to be more focused on what we want. We have discussed the importance of self-awareness. However, when there are other people in our lives, we need to extend awareness to them as well. If we don't, we will find ourselves engaging in a constant struggle for power. The standard advice for relationship problems is to work on the relationship, usually with a counselor.

While this can certainly be beneficial, it's also crucial that we overcome our own insecurities and become more loving and understanding toward our partner. We need to work on ourselves when we are in conflict with another person, especially a loved one. We're more likely to be talking and expressing our grievances instead of listening. We've already discussed the importance of mindful listening. It's the basis of any important relationship. When we just hear words, we quickly label and follow them away without being aware of really what's being said. We're too busy framing a reply to really get it. This leaves the other person frustrated and unheard.

Imagine your spouse telling you you forgot to pick up the dry cleaning like you promised. What you hear is you're too stupid to be trusted with a simple task. Instead of mindfully listening to what is being said, you react to the unspoken words. All you do is nag. We're wired for a fight or flight response. For cavemen, it was a matter of survival for us. Thankfully, there are other options to quote Tibetan Lama Jom Yang. We think that we have successful communication with others. In fact, we only have successful miscommunication without being aware of it. Instead of blindly responding. Take a deep breath. Think about what you're going to say.

Instead of reacting with the first thought that enters your mind, consider how your words will affect the other person. Make a conscious choice to use a normal tone of voice instead of attacking. When you engage in a more mindful conversation, you eliminate many misunderstandings that can damage a relationship. Mindfulness is always nonjudgmental. Most of us yearn to improve our relationships. Mindful meditation helps us clear our mind so that we're able to listen without judging and embrace kindness to avoid confrontations. The next time you're tempted to engage in a confrontation with somebody, simply stop. Become aware of any tension developing in your body, is your breathing becoming shallow? Is your heart pounding? Are your muscles tensing? Simply notice without the need to judge or condemn.

Now breathe into the tension. Focus on your right hand as you make a fist. Imagine the tension flowing into your hand. Now open your fist and release the tension. Do this regardless of what the other person is saying or doing. Forget about proving that you're right. Simply focus on your body. It only takes seconds. But in those moments you have shifted your awareness to your anxiety and have chosen not to react, but to remain in focused control. Instead, becoming more mindful can have a tremendously positive effect on your relationships.

Mindful Meditation & Happiness

In this chapter, we'll talk about mindful meditation and happiness. We all want to be happy, it's our natural condition. It used to be believed that our capacity for happiness is innate. We're born with a certain happiness threshold, and that was the baseline. There is evidence that circumstances may raise or lower that baseline, but that it will eventually return to the original level. For example, when someone experiences something exciting, such as receiving a much wanted gift or a dream vacation, the happiness meter rises immensely for a while, then naturally levels off. These bursts of occasional positivity really don't affect the overall quality of our life.

In the case of severe grief, our natural happiness level may plummet, but eventually it will return to the normal level. Neither extreme joy or extreme grief has a permanent effect on our happiness. Does that mean that we cannot enhance our happiness? Before we discuss meditation, it's important to point out that our basic level of happiness consists not of some single circumstance. Instead, it's the small daily joys that elevate our mood. A beautiful sunset lunch with a friend, a good book all have the power to raise our spirits. We need to become aware of these mood elevators and consciously pursue them.

It's important to savor these moments and give gratitude for the experience. Happy people make a deliberate decision to pursue these moments when it comes to moods, researchers have long focused on the negatives, such as depression and anxiety. It's as if happiness isn't worth studying, but that is changing. Dr Richard Davidson of the University of Wisconsin has spent considerable time studying Tibetan monks. More recently, he followed employees taking part in an eight week mindful meditation program. The results of Dr.

Davidson's findings show that in all cases, a program of mindful meditation can elevate a person's mood. You need to be a monk to reap the benefits. Following the meditation program, participants reported enhanced positive moods and decreased negative feelings. New research has found that about 50 percent of our baseline mood level is derived from genetics. 10 percent of our mood depends on circumstances, good or bad. That leaves 40 percent of our mood in our control. Happiness is something that we can consciously cultivate and grow. This is very exciting news indeed.

Mindful meditation has proven to be a solid foundation on which to build positive emotions, along with savoring all of life's small pleasures. Shame and anger can be a tremendous barrier to happiness. To let go of those negative feelings, do the following forgiveness, meditation, sit comfortably, close your eyes and practice mindful breathing for five minutes. Allow thoughts, words or images of someone you can't forgive yourself to surface in your mind. It can be someone you've hurt and you have regretted your actions ever since. Let your mind wander to how much you cared for this person and the pain that you caused.

If you're remorseful, feel those emotions, accept what happened in the past. It's done. It is time to forgive yourself in your mind. Think I forgive myself. I have made mistakes and caused pain, either deliberately or not. I am not the same person. I have learned much from life. It is time for me to move on. I forgive myself. I am ready to let joy back into my heart. Feel free to use words appropriate to your situation. This exercise will lift the burden from your heart and allow feelings of happiness in its place. If you feel bitter toward another person who has caused you pain, do the same exercise. But change the word I to you.

Famous & Successful People Who Meditate

In this chapter, we'll talk about successful people who meditate. Many successful people are crediting meditation as part of their regime to grow values, character and improve their overall health. For them, it becomes a winning lifestyle that provides the tools for a higher quality of life. Padmasree Warrior, CTO of Cisco Systems Warrior, meditates regularly. She has stated that meditation helps her manage her large corporation and considers it a reboot for your brain and soul. Rupert Murdoch, chairman of News Corp.. Murdoch, has admitted that he is new to meditation but has expressed an interest in discovering its possibilities. Tony Schwartz, CEO of the Energy Project.

Schwartz is a longtime meditator. He credits successfully dealing with migraine headaches to meditation. He always believes it has improved his on the job performance. Energy requires refueling intermittently. Bill Ford, executive chairman, Ford Motor Company. Ford has stated he uses meditation to develop greater compassion. Oprah Winfrey CEO, Harpo Productions Inc.. Oprah practices meditation twice daily for 20 minutes. She also has encouraged meditation among her employees, states Oprah. I walked away feeling fuller than when I'd come in full of hope, a sense of contentment and deep joy, knowing for sure that even in the daily craziness that bombards us from every direction, there is still the consistency of stillness. Only from that space can you create your best work and your best life. Larry.

Brilliant CEO, Skoll Global Threats Fund. Brilliant learned to meditate in the Himalayas and emphasizes its ability to calm the mind. Ray Dalio, founder of Bridgewater Associates USA Dalio, has stated that meditation has given me centredness and creativity. It's also giving me peace and health. Russell Simmons, founder of Global Grind Dotcom Simmons, has been a long time proponent of meditation. Quote, You don't have to believe in meditation for it to work. You just have to take the time to do it. The old truth is still true today. God helps those who help themselves.

My advice is to meditate. Robert Stihler, CEO, Green Mountain Coffee Roasters, Inc, Stihler has a meditation room in his office and it is a dedicated practitioner, quote, Meditation helps develop your abilities to focus better and to accomplish your tasks. Arianna Huffington, editor in chief, Huffington Post Media Group Huffington practices meditation in the morning. Her company offers weekly meditation classes for its employees, quote, Stress reduction and mindfulness don't just make us happier and healthier. They're approving competition advantages for any business that wants one. Mindful meditation is being seen by more and more people as a crucial tool to enhance performance and create a more fulfilling life.

Great Mindful Meditation Apps

In this chapter, we'll talk about great mindful meditation apps. It's somewhat ironic that while modern technology can cause a lot of stress, there are downloadable, mindful meditation apps that can help guide you through some soothing, mindful meditations. You can choose from a variety of specific topics such as sleep, anxiety, depression, stress, etc., or participate in an entire mindful meditation program. Make them a part of your daily routine. These apps can be downloaded to your Android device from the App Store for free. Some more complex programs offer a paid subscription.

It's certainly a worthwhile investment. There are hundreds of meditation apps. So let's look at some of the most popular ones. Headspace has over eight million users and counting, including entrepreneurs such as Richard Branson. The app teaches correct breathing techniques and guides the listener through various visualization exercises and walking meditations. It is considered the best meditation app for beginners. Headspace offers a more intensive 10 day meditation program for a monthly subscription of Ten Dollars Mindfulness Daily. Mindfulness Daily offers daily 15 minute guided meditations and lessons on how to integrate mindfulness into your daily life. The package is available for thirty seven dollars.

Smiling at this mindful meditation app is free. It's divided into eight specific categories for younger children, teenagers and adults. There are also meditations specifically for sports and the workplace. Each meditation has a number of daily sessions to integrate and expand on a particular topic. Insight Taimur Insight. Taimur offers four thousand guided meditations that can be listened to in any random order. The app attempts to create a community feeling by announcing how many other people are currently meditating. Ora Ora works on a slightly different premise than some of the other apps, it sends you a new meditation every day so you don't have to listen to the same one twice.

The app is personalized for you according to age and specific mindful meditation interests on a certain day, different meditations for different moods. The app allows you to save the meditation, to listen to it again, to personalize the experience and are initially asked about your age and how stressed, optimistic and interested in mindfulness you are. You inform the app of your mood on a specific day and it will send you a complimentary meditation to match. You can save any daily meditation for repeated listening. I'm gonna offer beginners intermediate and advanced 20 minute meditations, there are 75 free meditations from which to choose, but there's no guidance as to which one might be best for you in a particular situation.

Stop, breathe and think. Stop, breathe and think is unique in that it actually explains the process of meditation, how it works and can benefit the meditator before the meditator starts to make use of the thirty free meditations. The ten minute meditations revolve around breathing kindness, staying calm and nature sounds. The app tracks how often you meditate, calm. The cool map has a number of soothing natural sounds, breathing exercises, relaxation meditations and sleep inducing bedtime stories to lure the listener to sleep. There are 16 meditations in all, each lasting from three minutes to half an hour.

The mindful app, the Mindful App, has options for everyone, it's a subscription app that can be downloaded with free features. Five guided meditations, relaxing nature sounds and daily reminders are free. The subscription also includes 20 meditation Books and 200 meditations, specifically for relationships, calmness, body and focus. The annual subscription fee is fifty nine dollars. Why not let a calming meditation app become part of your daily routine?

The Many Benefits Of Mindful Meditation

In this chapter, we'll discover the benefits of mindful meditation as you learn to understand yourself, you will develop a better understanding of why you act in certain ways. Some habits may be helpful, but other automatic behavior may be holding you back. That's what makes mindful meditation so effective. Greater awareness leads to opening doors in many areas of your life. Recent studies on mindfulness have shown that the benefits of regular mindfulness meditation go far from what was originally believed. The mind and body do work together as a team.

The practice has shifted from guru led hippies chanting to scientific studies at institutions such as Johns Hopkins University and physicians recommending the practice to their patients. And the results have been phenomenal. Let's look at some of the proven benefits of mindful meditation. One mindful meditation can reduce pain. Many of us suffer from chronic pain, while mindful meditation is not a cure all. Studies have shown it can greatly alleviate suffering in clinical trials. Mindful meditation has shown that mindful meditators experience over 50 percent less chronic pain, while long term meditators have reduced their chronic pain by 90 percent.

How's that possible? Pain can come in two forms, physical and mental. When the brain reacts negatively to pain, the pain becomes amplified. By controlling how we react to the pain, we can greatly reduce its intensity. Mindful meditation includes actually focusing on the areas of the body that feel pain, observe and release. The struggle, both physically and mentally, to mindful meditation can improve sexual experience. Many people find it difficult to discuss sexual dysfunction, even though it can be a pervasive problem from low libido, poor self-esteem and body image to feelings of anxiety and depression, the brain can wreak havoc with sexual enjoyment. Nonjudgmental mindfulness enables partners to communicate more effectively about sexual needs and concerns.

Three Mindful Meditations can improve mood. We all have moods. The happiest people can feel down for a while, and the blue a person can feel up on occasions. But many people's moods get bogged down with chronic depression and anxiety until there's little else. Research has shown that people with severe mood disorders actually show changes in certain areas of the brain. People suffering from depression and anxiety frequently live in the past or the future. Their mind can ruminate on hurts and injustices that happened years ago, with mental narratives obsessing around should haves, or else they can worry about things that have not yet happened and aren't likely to happen.

Mindful meditation is the perfect tool to bring troubled thoughts back to the present. For mindful meditation enhances empathy, stress, anxiety and depression can keep the brain stuck in negativity and self-absorption, thus reducing opportunities for compassion and empathy towards others. Through mindful meditation, the brain can be retrained to enhance these positive emotions. Five Mindful Meditations can enhance focus. We live in a world of distractions. People proudly boast of multitasking, although multitasking decreases efficiency rather than increasing productivity. When we check email while on the phone and at the same time read an important report, neither task has our full attention.

Our brain, too, can multitask. When we need our attention on a project, it can intrude with worries about unpaid bills, unhappy relationships or an updating event for the weekend. And while our mind is attempting to deal with this mental tsunami, we remember an overdue library book and phone message. We failed to return. For many people, this out of focus state of mind is a normal occurrence. When the brain is overwhelmed with a flood of unrelated thoughts and keeps jumping from one thought to the next, it cannot concentrate on the task at hand. Regular mindful meditation lets us control our wandering mind.

We learn to recognize interruptions and set them aside for a more appropriate time. Mindful meditation allows us to get more done because it keeps our mind focused on the present. Six Mindful meditation reduces stress. We have already discussed that mindful meditation will relieve stress, but it's so critical it bears a closer look. We experience thoughts and emotions every moment of our waking life. It's important to understand that emotions are neither. Good or bad, they simply are, the problem is not the emotions themselves, but how we respond to them. These negative emotions are frequently caused by something that has happened long in the past or hasn't happened at all.

By increasing our awareness, mindful meditation keeps us from dwelling on these negatives that are utterly irrelevant to the present. When our brain becomes jumbled with emotions, mindfulness helps clarify what's important and what is not. As we let go of mental stressors, our body automatically functions on a higher level, enhancing health and alleviating life threatening diseases. Statistics from the Center for Disease Control reveal that one hundred and ten million deaths each year are the result of stress related illnesses. That is a staggering number. Mindful meditation can greatly increase your chances of not becoming a statistic.

Seven mindful meditation and resilience, bad things can happen to good people, to quote Nelson Mandela, do not judge me by my success, judge me by how many times I fell down and got back up again. That is the essence of resilience, not our failures, but how we deal with them. Resilience lets us deal with the ups and downs of life. Change and challenges are seen as just another opportunity for growth. Resilience is the ability to get back up after adversity. Due to the unpredictability of life, there will always be joys and sorrows. Resilient people are able to greet change and difficulty as an opportunity for self reflection, learning and growing. How we react to life's stressors is a choice.

We can turn fearful, bitter and blame the world for being unfair. Or we can use mindfulness to change our thinking. We can't control the world, but we can certainly control how we react to it. A study published in the Journal of Personality and Individual Differences showed that mindfulness helps people cope with hard times and there will always be some hard times. Instead of reacting, mindful meditation allows us to hit a mental pause button and simply accept. Bad feelings or thoughts aren't the enemy, the problem is our reaction to those thoughts when we use mindful meditation to become aware of these thoughts. We have the power to accept and move forward.

Eight mindful meditation boosts creativity. By creativity, we're not just talking about art, music, every day we face situations and questions where some creativity could move us to the head of the line. How do I get the boss to notice my report? How do I approach this popular person and ask for a date? How do I dress for success on my limited budget? The reptilian part of our brain approaches these situations with severe caution. Its sole purpose is to ensure our survival so anything new and different is automatically seen as dangerous. This part of our brain immediately calls for safety. Don't make waves, don't rock the boat, don't do anything crazy.

Anything new and creative has a hard time getting past this reptilian brain. But mindful meditation can calm the reptilian brain and make it less reactive. This allows new creative ideas to flourish. Some of the world's most creative companies, such as Walt Disney, General Mills and Google, encourage innovation and creativity in their employees by making meditation rooms available to their employees. Studies have shown that people who practice mindful meditation are less rigid in their approach to new ideas and Problem-Solving methods. The next time you're stuck while preparing a report, mindful meditation helps you stand out from the crowd that plays it safe and get noticed.

How To Create A Mindful Life

In this chapter, we'll learn how to create a mindful life, mindful meditation can change your life. You learn that the thoughts flowing through your mind are not reality. What you do about those thoughts is reality. In addition to meditation, you can use mindful strategies to enjoy mindfulness throughout the day. Mindfulness doesn't stop at meditation. It's a lifestyle. It puts mindful meditation into daily action. Here are a few easy strategies you can use to inject more mindfulness in everything you do. One use short, one minute breathing meditation throughout your day. It's a great way to stay in focus too. When speaking to another person. Really listen to what he or she is saying instead of preparing your response.

Three chores like laundry can be mindless instead of being bored, focus all your attention on the task, remember how much fun doing simple things was when you were a child. That's because you were totally engaged instead of trying to get it over with when doing the wash, for example, turning your awareness to the texture and colors of the clothes. Notice that just washing smells, make folding laundry again by paying attention to how your hands move. Be in the present for a few of us. Eat mindfully. We can barely remember what we had for breakfast. Not only is gulping down food a waste, it can cause weight gain.

Focus fully on what you are eating instead of watching television or answering your email. Eating is one of our greatest pleasures. Prepare a colorful plate of healthy ingredients. Enjoy the aroma of freshly cooked food. Notice the texture. As you eat, an orange will feel entirely different from an apple. Can you discern the different spices as they hit your palate? Make each meal a gastronomic and mindful adventure. Savor each bite. Pay attention to the types of food you eat. Sugars, simple carbs, prepared foods and unhealthy fats can cause fatigue and lead to serious diseases. You want both your mind and your body to be at peak performance level.

Eat lots of produce nuts, wheat products and lean meats and fish. Five, slow down. What's your hurry anyway? Many of us take pride in being busy regarding it as a badge of productivity, we race through our day without awareness, like robots rushing around without knowing where we are or where we're going. Racing through life mindlessly does not add to our happiness. Quite the opposite. Without living in the present moment, we are far more likely to make careless mistakes. When we physically slow down. We also slow down our brain, take time for a mindful walking meditation, sit in a park, watch the squirrels chase each other, stop for fifteen minutes and listen to your favorite music.

Take a break and reconnect with yourself. Six, like rushing through life, multitasking renders us mindless to the present. We're not focusing on one task, but are scrambling mindlessly to do several tasks at once. We're not accomplishing more. We're just paying less attention and making more mistakes. It's not only healthier, but far more efficient to focus on one task at a time. Life is not a race.

It's a journey to be savored. Mindfulness helps you stay in the moment as you perform one task, then the next. It's also much less stressful. Seven, develop the habit of checking in with your mind mindfully, observe your thoughts and emotions on a regular basis, become aware of how you feel when called to the boss's office or pulling into your driveway.

At the end of the day, the more you do this, the more you will recognize script patterns as they pop up. This will help you control the torrent of negative self talk instead of becoming overwhelmed. Any time you increase awareness, you are practicing mindfulness. Keep in mind, mindfulness isn't about always feeling positive. It means always being aware of what you are feeling closely related to slowing down and equally as important is doing nothing. Almost every day someone asks us, How's it going? We automatically reply, Oh, busy, busy, as if it were a badge of honor.

This dialogue, which seems to happen constantly, is as mindless as multitasking. Our energy level flows and ebbs, and downtime becomes a physical necessity to boost up our optimal performance. Instead of feeling guilty for spending an afternoon relaxing at the beach or enjoying a movie, schedule it into your mindful lifestyle on a regular basis. The benefit of regular downtime is that we can sit back and simply enjoy the present while using all our senses, smell the flowers, hear the birds, watch a puppy frolic and enjoy all that. Life has to offer more and in greater detail.

Thoughts & Tips

Mindful meditation and other mindful practices can dramatically improve how you live each day, all you need to do is get started. Imagine getting to know the real you and reaching your full potential. Imagine enjoying each day to the fullest. It's not magic. It's about reclaiming our authentic self.

There is much in life over which we have no control. Mindful meditation gives us control over ourselves, how we think and how we behave. Our actions are no longer random and self-destructive.

Begin slowly by meditating for just a few minutes each day, then gradually increasing the time. You may not notice the changes immediately, but they will happen. All you need to do is get started on this powerful journey.

Beginning Concepts

Eczema, that horrible, itchy rash on your skin isn't new. Ancient Egyptians suffered from eczema and sought relief with oatmeal baths, and it worked. Hippocrates, the father of modern medicine, discussed the role of skin disease, sweating and itching over 2000 years ago. 30 million Americans suffer from eczema, including children. Doctors have discovered a genetic link for eczema between parent and child. If a parent suffers from eczema, the child may be predisposed to eczema as well. One in five school age children have this rash. One in 12 adults suffer from eczema.

This condition can affect their self-image, self-esteem and their health. It can affect everyday life and cause a lack of sleep. It can also be embarrassing. This chapter will discuss exactly what eczema is and how it can be treated to reduce the symptoms. It's not a disease and there is no cure, but the symptoms of itch and inflammation can be contained. Eczema can't be caught from someone else. It's an immune disorder that can flare up because of environmental and emotional causes. And those are matters we can control.

We will discuss the lifestyle changes necessary to alleviate the worst of the eczema symptoms or get rid of the rash altogether. Although the eczema rash has been around for thousands of years, we still know far too little about it. Research is just beginning and it has shown that changes in lifestyle habits can have a tremendously beneficial effect on eczema. Eczema fixes how to get rid of eczema naturally and permanently places the control of this disorder in your hands. There may not be a cure for eczema, but you no longer need to suffer from its debilitating effects. Eczema is an autoimmune disease where the body refuses to function, as it should be aware that the same auto immune dysfunctions can simultaneously bring about other autoimmune problems, such as Crohn's disease and allergies.

By easing the symptoms of eczema, you may well be helping your body cope with other autoimmune challenges. The standard medical cure for eczema is hydrocortisone. Steroids cream. This works well at alleviating the symptoms, but it does nothing to address the underlying causes of eczema. That is what this chapter does to help you become eczema free for life. Certain changes in your daily life can do much to rid yourself of eczema. Most rashes have very specific triggers, which this chapter will discuss. Once you identify the triggers and alleviate them from your environment, you are taking the necessary steps to rid yourself of the symptoms of eczema.

What Is Eczema

In this chapter, we'll talk about what eczema is, eczema is difficult to diagnose, any dermatologist will look for a combination of symptoms. Eczema always involves a rash which can appear on any part of the body. The rash is red in color and is usually covered with white scaly skin. The scales are due to inflammation caused by constant scratching. It's the constant scratching that causes the skin to shed skin cells, which results in the white scales that cover the red rash. Ultimately, scratching can change the actual color of your skin. A rash is just the first clue for a dermatologist. There are, after all, many types of rashes with eczema. There are other specific symptoms for which to watch. Lack of moisture can actually cause the skin to crack.

These cracks just make the itch worse, which causes you to scratch more. Eczema can be a vicious cycle most of the time. Eczema rashes also have blisters. If these blisters grow large enough, they can become infectious. Another sign of eczema or dry, brittle nails or nails with fungus. The redness that shows up on the skin can also frequently be seen when the eyes are reddish and when the tongue has red patches and eczema flare up can make the eyes look swollen. Some of this is caused by rubbing the itchy, infected eyes. A good dermatologist will look beyond the red, scaly skin. When eczema becomes chronic, the resulting symptoms can be quite serious. Lymph nodes filter the body against foreign invaders such as germs.

Swollen lymph nodes can mean they are busy fighting eczema flare ups. This is something your dermatologist will check when the body is fighting the symptoms of eczema. It is using precious nutritional resources. That means that adults with eczema are frequently malnourished and children with eczema are often small for their age. When treated, the body immediately begins to process nutrition more efficiently. The effect on children who almost immediately show signs of growth is remarkable. Adults and children with eczema frequently develop asthma and hay fever as well. As a matter of fact, eczema is often associated with allergies. So maintaining an allergy free environment becomes a critical tool in fighting eczema the natural way.

In addition to chronic eczema, there are different types of eczema when properly diagnosed. Most of these are actually treatable. Dermatitis eczema is caused by soaps and other cleaning products. These can leave the skin dry and deprived of necessary oils, resulting in red itchy skin. Since this most frequently affects the hands, it can cause a lot of embarrassment. Fortunately, once the culprits have been identified and eliminated, the rash will debate and the skin will return back to normal. Some people develop rashes due to allergies to substances like Nicole and jewelry. A dermatologist can do patch tests to determine the allergy ones. The substance in question is removed.

The rash should disappear. This type of eczema usually develops in young people and is the result of developing hormones causing flaky dandruff to appear on the scalp and surrounding areas and anteaters shampoo. It can be very beneficial in helping with this type of eczema. Healing your eczema symptoms requires proper diagnosis. You need to see a dermatologist. But not all dermatologists specialize in eczema. It's important that you consult with a specialist who is knowledgeable about eczema, its signs and what can be done to alleviate the uncomfortable itch that is always a part of any eczema. This type of eczema is common in children. If at least one parent suffers from eczema, the child might get it as well. Atopic eczema can be anywhere from mild to severe children with a topic.

Eczema are at a greater risk for asthma and food allergies, so testing should be done for those symptoms as well. Many children do outgrow this type of eczema, but not all signs of atopic dermatitis in children are the usual patches of dry skin that turn red and inflamed. The most likely places for these patches to appear is on the face and neck as well as the elbows and knees. Scratching always makes eczema worse, since children aren't able to understand the need not to scratch, it is important to seek treatment as soon as possible. People with atopic dermatitis usually experience flare ups. A period when the eczema gets worse for a time. Flare ups can occur due to irritants such as soaps, dust mites, dog and cat fur and surján fabrics.

Stress and other emotions can also trigger eczema, flare ups. Varicose eczema occurs in older adults who have varicose veins. Standing can become more difficult as people age, which can bring on both varicose veins and varicose eczema, which can result in dry, itchy patches around the ankle area. Skin in general becomes less moist and drier as people age.

As with any other form of eczema, it's important not to estimate the problem by scratching. This type of eczema can worsen in cold weather.

So keeping your skin moist during the winter is an important part of reducing the constant itching your treatment should. Lifestyle changes, elimination of stress and a diet that removes potential allergens from your diet, all of these treatments will be discussed in this chapter. Ask your doctor how these treatments can best be applied to your eczema, then follow his advice. With proper diagnosis and treatment, you'll be itch free and living the life you are now only dreaming about. There is no reason for you to suffer from eczema. The sooner you act, the sooner your skin will be back to normal.

Beating The Eczema Itch

In this chapter, we'll learn about eczema, which anyone suffering from eczema knows is the constant unabated itching that is the most difficult to endure. While the dry patches may appear unsightly, the itching can become unbearable. To conquer the itch, it's important to know what happens to the skin during an eczema flare up. It's a fact that everyone with eczema suffers from incessant itching. There is no eczema without itching. In extreme cases, the agony can persist all day and all night with little or no relief. Of course, scratching always leads to more itching. The itch begins when nerve fibers located in the top epidermis are triggered. The triggers can be dry skin allergies or emotional stress.

When triggered by drying skin, the nerves become alarmed and send an itch message to the brain. The brain is always ready and eager to respond to a cry for help when it receives the itch message it immediately sends in order to scratch. This is done on a subconscious level, since you actually never consciously told yourself to scratch. Telling yourself to stop scratching doesn't work. The epidermis or the skin's top layer is constantly changing. New skin cells are always being produced. Normal skin is protected by barriers in the epidermis that shields the skin from the itch stimuli that makes it feel dry. Or put another way, these barriers help the skin retain natural moisture.

Skin suffering from eczema lacks that protection. The skin is unable to hold moisture and becomes dryer faster. This causes skin cells to shrink and let irritants into the body. This can happen any time, but it seems to occur most frequently at night when the body is at rest. This accounts for why much of the itching becomes intensified at night. Every fiber of your being just wants to scratch. Our brain is always at work. It can awaken us from a deep sleep with its order to scratch. The scratching feels extremely good and brings some needed relief. As a result, the brain thinks it has done its job in looking out for our general welfare. It rewards our scratching by temporarily lessening the itch.

As most everyone knows, when behavior is rewarded, it becomes intensified and continues. In other words, the brain will simply continue to send scratch messages whenever we feel itchy. A large part of the problem is the brain's eagerness to protect and help us when we feel distressed, when it senses that something is wrong with the skin, it expands the red blood cells to allow immune cells into the fray and protect the skin from invaders. It's these enlarged red blood cells that cause the redness and inflammation of eczema. It is the job of our immune cells to protect us from invaders in normal bodies. That works out very well when we suffer from eczema, however, the immune cells are unable to distinguish between good and bad cells.

This means the attack is directed indiscriminately at any and all cells. Good cells become damaged in the process, which weakens our immune system. When the skin is being attacked, the itching spirals out of control and its defense mechanisms are being destroyed from within. The itch scratch cycle becomes automated. It's a learned behavior to familiar stimuli. Even infants suffering from eczema will respond automatically by scratching. Telling anyone with eczema to just stop scratching is useless. The brain, with all of its complexities, is transmitting different orders. We have seen how the brain, in an attempt to be helpful, will exacerbate the itch.

Scratch cycle scratching becomes a subconscious defense that we do without being totally aware. We simply respond automatically by scratching. The good news is that the brain will always be eager to help us. We just need to send it the correct messages. Studies have shown that stress is not only one of the major triggers for eczema, but the same stress prevents eczema medication from working, creating a double whammy situation. This requires eczema sufferers to become aware of emotional triggers. Does it get worse at work, at home with one spouse? When bills start coming at the beginning of the month, emotional triggers usually have a very specific cause. Unless you pinpoint the triggers, stress will only worsen and create a new cycle of anxiety and depression.

Anxiety will lead to even greater anxiety. A recent survey has found that more than 30 percent of people suffering from anxiety and depression also suffer from eczema. It's good to know that your emotions can be controlled, thereby putting you in charge of your eczema healing process. When we experience stress, we enter a fight or flight state of mind. This causes the body to increase stress hormones. But these hormones can attack the immune system and cause the skin to become inflamed. Stress cannot be entirely eliminated from our lives, and the lack of stress won't totally get rid of eczema. But identifying and eliminating stress will go a long way in.

Making eczema less painful, there is no cure for eczema. You can, however, rid yourself of most of the symptoms. Being proactive begins when you pay attention to your emotions. Ask yourself, have you been feeling sad or anxious for no discernible reason? Does your life seem hopeless? Do you have less energy than you used to? Have you lost interest in activities you used to enjoy? If you've ever blushed, you know how strong the mind skin connection is. The following chapter will take a close look at how we can control the symptoms of eczema with a few changes in our lifestyle.

Eczema & Your Emotions

In this chapter, we'll discuss eczema and your emotions. We wouldn't be human if we didn't have emotions both positive and negative. When we suffer from eczema, however, our unresolved emotional life can cause havoc. Taking care of the self becomes critical to our skin health. Every person is different, and every self-help method may not work for every person. But it is worth the time to experiment and determine what methods work best at elevating your positive feeling and eliminating the negative. Triggering emotions is one of the best ways to relieve stress. You don't need to join a gym, although that is one way of getting some exercise. You can simply walk, swim, play tennis or engage in any other physical activity.

Try climbing the stairs instead of taking the elevator. Two hours of exercise a week is highly recommended. More than that is even better. Exercise provides an added boost to the immune system, which is important for eczema control. The only problem with exercising when you have eczema is that sweating can deprive the body of much needed moisture that can be very drying for the skin and it can start an itch cycle. That does not mean you should be avoiding exercise, simply do low impact exercises that won't have you sweating. Be sure to apply plenty of body lotion after your shower.

Speaking of showers, lukewarm showers dry out the skin, far less than hot showers. If you jog, do so during the early morning or evening hours when the sun is less intense and you will sweat less. Wearing loose clothing while exercising spandex may look sexy if you have curves, but it can irritate your skin. Lose cutting clothes are the best next to the skin. The connection between eczema and diet is still ongoing and will be discussed at greater length in another chapter. But it helps to remember that eczema can be triggered by allergies and glutens. Nuts and dairy are the worst culprits. Many people have found that processed foods can worsen the eczema system.

To ensure that you are allergy free, have your doctor perform the standard patch tests. There is great value in daydreaming. First of all, when you daydream, you are actually focused on your inner fantasy. The more your mind is focused, the less negative anxiety producing thoughts will enter. In addition, this is the state of mind that allows solutions to problems to flow naturally, thus providing you with answers to problems that have been causing anxiety therapy, especially cognitive behavioral therapy, has proven extremely successful in treating anxiety and depression. While you should be consulting with a dermatologist, consider also seeing a psychotherapist.

Therapy can be a very effective way of discovering the emotional triggers that cause eczema to flare up. Sometimes getting at the root of these triggers can be difficult, and a trained therapist can help you with some insight. We've already made the connection between skin and emotions such as anxiety and depression. However, sometimes emotions are repressed. There are thoughts we don't want to face, such as anger. So it's easier to pretend these thoughts don't exist. Unfortunately, these emotions don't simply disappear because we refuse to acknowledge them. For many who suffer from repressed anger, the emotions go straight to the skin.

In a hospital study involving 128 patients, it was found that the 27 patients who had eczema experienced worsening of symptoms whenever they were faced with frustration. As an eczema sufferer, ask yourself, do you frequently feel numb? Shut off from your feelings? Did you frequently pretend to be happy when you're really feeling down? Do you rarely or never share your feelings with another person? Do you become easily irritated at the smallest things? Do you passively agree with people rather than expressing your own opinion? Do you keep busy every moment of the day? Make work? Busyness can keep feelings repressed.

If you answered yes to any or more of the above questions, chances are excellent you are suffering from repressed anger. The good news is you can do something about it and release the emotional triggers. You'll see the results on your skin. Repressed anger is like excess baggage you've been carrying around while striding uphill. It's a heavy load to carry. At some point, your body will make its displeasure known. And one of the ways it lets you know something is wrong is by attacking the skin with eczema. We have mentioned the importance of pinpointing your emotional triggers when we are in denial.

Psychotherapy can be extremely helpful with this, but one clue may be that you insist you never get angry. The fact is we all get angry at times. This is normal. Chances are if you never get angry, your anger is being repressed and fueling your skin with toxins. Forget for a moment what repressed anger does to relationships before it affects another person. It can ruin your health in general and your skin in particular. Anger can be the result of childhood abuse from thirty years ago, or your current work situation involving a nasty boss. The anger may be perfectly normal and justified, but we are. Frequently taught at an early age that anger is inappropriate, all too often parents will tell a child, how dare you get angry with grandma? So anger gets repressed until it becomes a habit and our skin may well be paying the price.

Begin by being totally honest with yourself. This can be harder than it seems. Allow yourself to be open to any thoughts that may come into your head. We all have emotional needs, especially as children. When these needs aren't met, we become angry. But as children we don't feel strong enough to express those emotions. So they become buried. You are no longer a helpless child, so it's OK to express any feeling as it arises. Then once you have gotten in touch with some or all of the repressed anger, you need to release it. It is necessary or sometimes advisable to confront the source of your anger directly.

You don't want to get fired from a job before you have another one lined up.If you're repressed, anger goes back to childhood. The culprit may actually be dead at this point, but acknowledging the anger is crucial. You cannot change that which remains unacknowledged, then work toward forgiveness. This means accepting and moving on with your life. Your life matters. The other person has been made inconsequential. Removing repressed anger from your life is a gift you give yourself, and your skin will surely reap the benefits.

Eczema & The Magic Of Meditation

In this chapter, we'll learn about eczema and meditation. Meditation has been used for thousands of years to alleviate depression and anxiety, with depression and anxiety being an active trigger for an eczema flare up. Many people have found relief from itching through meditation. It is difficult to say whether anxiety and depression causes eczema or whether eczema causes anxiety and depression, but the link has been unequivocally established. Just 15 minutes a day can re-establish improved communication between the mind and body. Find a comfortable place to sit and close your eyes, inhale deeply and slowly, then exhale. Concentrate on each intake of breath and each release of breath.

It's as simple as that. Keep your focus on your breathing when your mind wanders and it will simply bring it back into focus. Researchers have studied the neurons between the prefrontal cortex and the part of the brain that deals with emotional distress. They have found that increased activity in the left prefrontal helped patients heal more quickly from anxiety. This led to the conclusion that communication within the brain can be important to skin health. Below is a meditation specifically to relieve itchy skin. You can record it and listen to it while you meditate. You might find it very helpful to listen to it before you go to sleep. With regular practice, you will see amazing results on your skin. Each time I breathe, I am grateful for my body.

I respect and honor my body. I relieve my body of all stress. I relieve myself of all the tension in my body and especially my skin. I relieve myself of all the anxiety that is in my body and skin. I relieve myself of all fears that I experience with my body. I give my skin permission to deal with my anxieties and fears. I give my skin permission to release all irritation and inflammation that I am holding inside. I take full responsibility for my skin. I take full responsibility for my insecurities. I give myself permission to rid my skin of any anger that it holds. I give my skin permission to rid my body of frustration and irritation. I regard my skin of all anger and shame. I take full responsibility for all of my emotions.

I treasure my emotions. I give my skin permission to feel confident. I give myself permission to move forward with my life. I give myself permission to communicate clearly with others. I take responsibility for my pain and give myself permission to rid my body of all pain. I am learning to accept myself just the way I am. I accept any emotions and anger that may lie deep within me. I acknowledge my anger and release it. I refuse to allow anyone to get under my skin. I give myself permission to feel intimacy. I am learning to express my feelings in a clear way. I am learning not to jump to conclusions. I acknowledge and honor my needs. I am learning to love myself.

I am learning not to let my skin hold me back. I think my skin is doing the best it can to help me. I enjoy the relaxation my body is feeling. I feel at peace with myself. I accept my skin. No matter what its condition. I am deserving of love. I can face the world without anxiety. I can feel my skin becoming nourished. I can feel my skin becoming healthy. I enjoy having beautiful skin. I feel beautiful. This is a lengthy but powerful meditation that can help realign your brain and your skin like meditation. Yoga is an ancient practice. As a matter of fact, yoga philosophy began with meditation and didn't evolve into physical exercise until later. Yoga, especially when used in conjunction with meditation, has been proven to strengthen the mind-body connection, which can get so misaligned for eczema sufferers.

As an added benefit, yoga promoted intense relaxation. This helps calm the mind and the body, which includes the skin. There are a number of yoga disciplines. Any one of them will promote a healthier body and ease the suffering of eczema. Specifically, there are poses that placed the head beneath the heart, such as the downward dog. These poses boost the flow of blood to the head to reduce red, patchy skin poses that involve Twist's help the liver rid itself of toxins and allows less invaders into the skin. Yoga is all about focus. When you focus on the various poses, your mind is less focused on your struggling immune system that is irritating your skin. When rules, your brain irritants lose their power. It gives your skin a chance to relax and heal itself.

Eczema & Skin Hydration

In this chapter, we'll learn about eczema and skin hydration, we know the importance of keeping hydrated. It becomes especially important if you are suffering from eczema. Did you know that your body consists of approximately 75 percent water? Our blood is 90 percent water and our brain consists of 80 percent water. That's a lot of water. Without proper hydration, even a normal body suffers and performs at less than optimal capacity. Even a four percent decrease in hydration will affect our thinking and energy level. Needless to say, dehydration can serve as a quick trigger for eczema, flare ups.

Eczema is dry skin, and when you aren't properly hydrated, you are immediately setting the itch scratch cycle into motion. Please note that water is the best hydrating agent. Alcohol, coffee and energy drinks may be liquid, but they dehydrate and rob the body of needed hydration. Fruit juices are OK, but if possible, water them down. So if you have eczema, always keep a bottle of water at your side. You may not have heard of these, but wet wraps drenched your skin and water and lessened the severity of eczema by up to 75 percent when applied. Along with your topical ointment, this can bring huge relief during a major flare up.

Wet wraps are bandages soaked in water which are wrapped around the affected area after it has been treated with ointment or cream. The wraps help reduce inflammation and soreness while they help the skin absorb the moisture for a more lasting effect. If you are using a steroid cream, the wet wrap will help deeper layers of skin absorb the steroid for greater benefit. A side benefit of the is that your inflammation is under wraps and preventing you from scratching if a large part of the body is being treated, indulge in a hydrating bath infused with bath oils before applying the wet wrap for children or large patches of adult eczema, there are garments that can be purchased for a total wet wrap.

These wet can be used for several days until the redness disappears. Topical creams should be applied on a regular basis each day. Benefits of wet wraps include less itching and scratching, less inflammation, greater hydration, improved sleep. If applied at night, there is a direct correlation between cold weather and dry eczema skin. Everyone knows how the winter cold and dry out normal skin. It can cause serious flare ups to skin with eczema, making it easier and more inflamed. Studies have shown that the colder the weather, the more severe eczema can become. Moving to a warmer climate is an excellent solution and can make eczema all but disappear.

But it may not always be feasible. So it becomes especially critical to moisturize the skin several times every day and keep well hydrated, bathe daily in warm, not hot bath water that has plenty of oils. Consider this an indulgence. There is an overwhelming amount of eczema products on the market. It can be difficult to make sense of it all, but a discussion with your dermatologist can help. Then there are some surprising lubricants the doctor may not even think of. Vegetable shortening, such as Cresco, contains palm oils that can be very soothing to dry skin. Vegetable shortening is thick and helps the skin retain moisture, apply the shortening to moist skin following a shower and let the skin absorb it before getting dressed.

A benefit to using vegetable shortening is that it is inexpensive and you can use a lot of it without spending a fortune. Vaseline Jelly is another soothing product that can lock in moisture. Since it can be messy, you can apply it to infected areas such as hands and feet and wear protective cotton gloves and feet. Any cream or lotion is better than no moisturizer when you have eczema. However, when choosing a cream, look for one containing colloidal oatmeal, which is an ingredient that is known to soothe eczema. As mentioned earlier, even ancient Egyptians bathed in oatmeal. Other excellent ingredients to look for are shea butter and jeremiads, ingredients that specifically relieve itching, avoid creams that contain perfumes or alcohol, as these may cause an allergic reaction and trigger a flare up.

Eczema on the face can be especially frustrating and uncomfortable to handle. Many of these steroid based creams on the market can be too harsh for sensitive facial skin if the rash proves stubborn. Ask your dermatologist about a weaker steroid cream or a non steroid prescription medication. Luckily, there are a number of safe over-the-counter products specially formulated for eczema. So begin to check labels or ask your doctor for a recommendation. Look for creams containing zinc oxide and beeswax, both of which create a safe barrier for sensitive skin. Every skin is different, and you may need to experiment with a few brand names to determine which works best for you.

Wearing makeup can actually be beneficial since it allows you to cover up any red rashes and flaking. But you need to choose your products with care. Your first step is to moisten. Your eyes, your face thoroughly to prevent the makeup from drying out and becoming scaly, avoid makeup with additives such as Butel Paraffin and methyl parathion, these can dry your skin even more and lead to increased irritation. The best makeup for eczema sufferers should contain natural oils to increase moisture when applying makeup. Use your freshly washed fingers to gently dab on makeup instead of a makeup brush. Even brushes that are regularly cleaned can contain bacteria. Complete your makeup routine with a facial mist to seal in moisture.

There is a light therapy that can be extremely effective as an eczema treatment, especially for facial skin. The treatment consists of ultraviolet light that recreates natural sunlight. Approximately 70 percent of eczema sufferers who try phototherapy see improvement on their skin. It takes about two months to see any difference. Phototherapy can reduce annoying itches, reduce inflammation, and increase the number of bacteria fighting cells. If the treatment is successful, patients can reduce their visits to once a week to maintain their state of remission.

Great Home Remedies For Eczema

In this chapter, we'll discover home remedies if you have eczema. People with eczema are quick to look at creams to remedy the problem and these can be very helpful. However, the good news for eczema sufferers is there are a number of great products right in your home that can help with the treatment of itchy skin and reduce inflammation. Discuss any home treatment with your dermatologist before beginning. This chapter contains references to a number of healing baths. This refers to warm or lukewarm baths. Only hot water can irritate and dry out the skin. The healing properties of aloe vera have been known for thousands of years. It is especially soothing for the skin.

Modern research has found that Oliviera is specifically helpful in reducing skin bacteria that can cause infection. As we have discussed, frequent itching and scratching can cause the skin to become infected. Aloe vera is excellent at relieving the itch scratch cycle. Aloe vera is a medicinal plant and people can get the healing gel directly from the aloe vera leaves. It is also available at health, food and specialty stores. When purchasing aloe vera, read the label and make sure it contains no perfumes, alcohol or other additives which can irritate the skin. Apple cider vinegar has so many excellent properties, some consider it a miracle liquid. It has been used since Epocrates as a disinfectant.

Its effect on eczema has not yet been confirmed. Its effect on eczema has not yet been confirmed. However, it is believed to have potential. The fact is, normal skin has an acidic barrier with a level of below 5.0. The level of eczema sufferers is generally higher. This means that the acid barrier isn't working properly to protect the skin against moisture loss and the invasion of foreign organisms. Some people believe apple cider vinegar may be useful in restoring the skin's natural balance. Before beginning any apple cider vinegar treatment on your skin, you should consult with your dermatologist who can perform a patch test with your doctor's approval.

Here are some ways that apple cider vinegar can fit into your eczema curing regime. Take an apple cider vinegar bath, fill your bathtub with water and add two cups of ACTV. Soak in the tub for at least 20 minutes, rinse and follow up with a moisturizer. We have discussed using what wraps soaked in water to enhance the absorption of moisture into the skin. You can add a tablespoon of ACV to the wrap for added healing properties, protect the wet wrap with a dry bandage and leave on overnight. This may sound like a strange eczema remedy, but it has been studied at the Mayo Clinic. Adding just one fourth cup of bleach to your bath can help improve the symptoms of eczema. Bleach kills bacteria.

Imagine where your hands have been when you give in to the urge to scratch. It's a bacteria army invading your inflamed skin the way General Sherman invaded Georgia. Bleach gets rid of harmful bacteria, soaks in the bleach bath for ten minutes, then dries and moisturizes. Well, bleach is drying, so you want plenty of moisture sealed into your skin. Don't take more than two bleach baths a week. Oatmeal as a remedy of skin diseases, anxiety and sleep goes back to ancient times. More than 3000 years ago, it was used by Egyptians and Romans. During the 19th century, oatmeal baths were used in the treatment of skin inflammation.

Colloidal oatmeal is regular oatmeal ground to a fine powder, which is made with water. A 2012 study revealed how colloidal oatmeal can bring needed relief to itchy skin. The study also showed that colloidal oatmeal can be helpful in maintaining the skin's normal level. Stir a cup of colloidal oatmeal into your bathwater, soak for approximately 10 minutes, rinse off with regular water and immediately apply moisturizer. Colloidal Oatmeal is available at health food stores. Or you can use regular oatmeal and grind it to a powder in a food processor. It won't mix with water unless ground to a very fine consistency. Also look for creams and moisturizers containing colloidal oatmeal. Coconut oil has a great many uses and one of them is as a moisturizer to relieve symptoms of dry skin and itching.

While many creams and lotions have additives, coconut oil is pure and natural. It's filled with a fatty acid that is extremely helpful for your entire body, including your skin. A 2014 study showed that using coconut oil for two months proved especially hydrating for children suffering from eczema. The natural oil has anti inflammatory properties to help heal red and infected skin areas. It also decreases bacteria. This is important since eczema rashes can easily become infected. You can apply solid coconut oil directly to the skin, as you would any cream. Do this twice each day or whenever you feel itchy for a scaly scalp.

Melnikova. Oil and rub into the scalp, as you would any conditioner leave on the scalp for about five minutes. Then Rentz, a 2004 study in the Journal of Wound Care confirmed a mixture of equal parts. Honey, olive oil and beeswax makes an excellent A.H. cream for eczema. This treatment is not recommended for children under the age of one. Unprocessed honey fights, bacteria and inflammation, two large triggers for eczema. This natural oil is derived from leaves of the Australian tea tree. It has been found to be more effective in treating eczema than the zinc oxide found in many eczema ointments.

Its antiinflammatory properties are extremely soothing to irritated skin and can reduce the redness and itching that is at the heart of eczema. Allergy serves as a trigger for eczema and tea tree oil decreases the effects of allergic reactions, and has been found that while high doses of tea tree oil produce excellent results in abating the symptoms of eczema, small doses have not been proven as effective. When using tea tree oil, it's important to mix it with a few drops of carrier oil, such as coconut oil. Tea tree oil is very potent, so use a low dosage whenever possible.

Coping With Eczema

In this chapter, we'll talk about coping with eczema every day. We've discussed the role that emotions and stress play in itchy skin and eczema flare ups. We've also reviewed the best natural remedies to control the symptoms of eczema. You desperately want to live a normal life like everyone else. This chapter should certainly help you reach that goal. There are certain things you can do daily to help put eczema behind you, develop good sleep habits. Eczema is constant. Itching makes getting a good night's sleep difficult, which only adds to your overall stress for a better night's sleep. Daily meditation can have a relaxing effect on the brain and lull you into a deep sleep. Apply your favorite A.H.

Cream right before going to bed to prevent overnight scratching. Many people find that listening to Sue the music helps them fall asleep and stay asleep more easily. Of course you want to dress with style. You can, but you need to take your skin into consideration. Don't wear tight clothes that will end up irritating your skin. Avoid scratchy fabrics and wool, which is a natural fabric, can cause a great deal of itching. In addition, many children are allergic to wool and it can trigger a rash on their skin. Cotton is considered the top fabric for eczema sufferers. It is lightweight and doesn't cause allergies. Cotton is soft and won't irritate your sensitive skin.

Best yet, just about any clothing can be found made out of cotton, from underwear to heavy outer garments to other natural fabrics that are safe for eczema. Sufferers are linen and silk. Both are lightweight, breathable and soft enough not to irritate your skin. Just about any synthetic fiber will keep your skin from breathing, so those should be avoided. They also contain chemicals that can trigger an eczema allergy. Keep in mind that poly cotton blend does not mean pure cotton. It always contains polyester. You can also find specific eczema, friendly clothing online which are highly recommended for children.

Avoid any cleaner or detergent with fragrances, alcohol or other additives. That includes face creams, soaps and bath products. Read your labels very carefully. Household cleaners can be harsh and filled with chemicals if you purchase a cleaner look for the National Eczema Association seal of approval. In addition, learn more about the cleaning power of apple cider vinegar. ACV can be used to clean tiles, linoleum counters, blinds can add it to your laundry when you wash your clothes, chemicals and additives in soaps, detergents and cleaners can severely irritate and cause eczema rash, especially on the hand. The frequent wetting and drying of hands during cleaning plays havoc with the skin's protective barrier.

When you do wash, use lukewarm water instead of hot, dry your hands gently instead of rubbing harshly with a towel and always apply moisturizer. It's a great idea to keep a jar of moisturizer by each sink that you use. Keep a travel size moisturizer handy for when you are away from home. Beware of antibacterial sanitizers. They don't use water, but they do contain harsh chemicals that can worsen your dry skin while working around the house yard or preparing food. Use protective white gloves to keep your hands clean. These gloves can be washed and reused and protect your hands from harsh outside invaders such as bacteria and germs. Cover the white gloves with latex gloves when doing dishes.

Don't wear the latex gloves on their own because they can irritate the skin. Each day will bring some type of stress. It is unavoidable. But when you suffer from eczema, stress can cause horrible flare ups. Quite simply, stress can be defined as the way the mind and body respond to daily stressful stimuli. If you have eczema, you need to indulge in self care. You matter. So learn to listen to your own needs instead of putting the needs of others ahead of your own. There's a whole world out there happy to claim a stake in your day. Your spouse wants you to prepare a special dinner. Your children insist on a ride to the mall. Your neighbor wants you to take care of her pets while she is away and your boss keeps piling on the work.

A short word can greatly reduce your daily stress level. Know many people have difficulty with that little word. So practice until you become more assertive. Remember, you have a choice. You can always politely refuse a request even from those closest to you. And remember to assert your own needs. Tell your spouse you'd like to go out to dinner rather than cook. Self care means being comfortable when acknowledging your own needs. Do so and watch your stress level decrease rapidly while your skin clears up. No stress equals no rash. Perfectionism is at the root of a lot of stress. You go through your day wanting everything to be perfect.

That puts a heavy burden on your emotions and inevitably causes tremendous anxiety, which in turn will cause your skin to justifiably .

Except that you have nothing to prove to anyone. Sometimes good is good enough. Usually the need for perfectionism signals a need to avoid failure rather than a desire to succeed. There was no need to overwhelm your brain with demands for absolute perfection. Do your best. The rest will follow. As if dating weren't stressful enough, dating when you have eczema can be a unique challenge. Many potential relationships are destroyed because eczema sufferers are too embarrassed by their condition. It's easier to push someone away and out of your life than to discuss eczema.

The simple act of opening yourself to love has incredible emotional benefits. Discuss the situation and your fears with your potential partner. Explain that there may be flare ups in your future. Any partner who doesn't understand isn't worth having in your life. On the other hand, a partner who is willing to stand beside you on this journey is a treasure. It means he or she genuinely cares about you. How's that for a natural stress reducer? Love automatically brings joy and laughter into your life. Embrace the possibilities instead of avoiding them. It may be difficult at first, but acknowledge your own worth and keep trying. You control your eczema. It does not control you.

Allergy-Proof Your Home

In this chapter, we'll talk about allergy proof in your home. If you are suffering from eczema, common household allergens can make your life a misery. There are triggers literally around your house. The following is a plan to rid your home of allergens and potential eczema triggers forever. Don't turn your bedroom into a dust mite paradise. Wash your bedding once a week. Make sure you rid yourself of any skin. Irritating wool blankets, cover your mattress and box springs and dust mite proof. Wrap's Let's face it, carpets are a lure for every imaginable allergen from dander, mold spores and dust mites. You may not be aware of it, but there's a party happening in your carpets all the time.

The deeper your carpet, the happier the festivities, wherever possible. Replace your carpets with hardwood tiles or linoleum. If you must have carpeting in an area of your home, at least ensure it is low pile and ready vacuum able vacuum once a day to rid yourself of the worst carpet allergens. Make sure your curtains and blinds are made of washable material and clean them at least once a month. Or blinds should have wide slats for easy dusting and cleaning. Fresh air is great. Unfortunately, open windows are an invitation for pollen to enter your home, keep your windows closed and use air conditioning when needed. Upholstering can harbor dust mites, instead opt for furniture made of wood, leather and other materials that are easy to clean.

Unless you live a minimalist lifestyle, there will be clutter. That's especially true if you have children, dust, books and knick knacks at least once a week. Place children's toys in a bin, wipe down all surfaces at least once a day. You love them, but they come with allergens. If you are considering getting a pet, discuss your allergy free option with the veterinarian. Once you have your pet, bathe it once a week. Make sure your stove has a vent fan to handle the cooking fumes, wash your dishes after you use them and wipe down the faucet an entire sink to remove any germs and mold. Remove old food as they can create mold cleaning your refrigerator every month or every two months.

Wallpaper can attract dirt and mold, use enamel paint to color and decorate your walls. A humidifier will keep the air from becoming too dry during the winter months. You should keep the all around temperature of your home at around 72 degrees. Certain house plants are great for removing particular allergens from the air or best plant choices are bamboo, palm and other palm trees. English IVY, peace, lily, gerbera, Dazy. Pests are annoying enough, but they also leave a residue that can trigger allergies. It's a good idea to have a professional exterminator fumigate your house. Cockroaches. Unfortunately, a common household pest thrives on water and moisture. Ensure that your kitchen and bathrooms are leak proof and all of your containers are tightly sealed.

There should be no smoking in your entire house, no exceptions like cockroaches. Mold grows with moisture, remove damp clothes from your washing machine as soon as they are done. Washing machines can be a great breeding ground for mold. You love your yard and you should be able to enjoy it. However, it can cause sneezing and allergies that can trigger your eczema with proper care. However, you can enjoy your yard, ensure that you mow your grass regularly to keep it short. Regular fertilization of your soil will choke out allergy producers such as Nestle's and Dandelion do your yard work after it is rained. Dry days account for the highest pollen levels. So those are the days to avoid your yard. If you can wear long sleeves and gloves while you garden, this will keep pollen from reaching your skin and creating a rash.

Keep an eye wash in your pocket when you venture outside. This will prevent redness in the event your eyes get hit with pollen. Also wearing sunglasses is an excellent idea. When you are done with your yard work, remove your clothes immediately and place them in the laundry. This will prevent pollen on your clothes from spreading. It's also a good idea to shower and shampoo. When you get back inside, you won't be able to control the pollen from your neighbor's garden. But you can't minimize pollen on your own by planting flora that are less likely to cause an allergic rash. Azalea fir and dogwood trees are an excellent choice. You can also plant begonias, tulips, daffodils, hanzi and nasturtium to cut down on the pollen. With the right plants, your garden will become a source of pleasure instead of a trigger for an annoying rash.

Eczema & Children

In this chapter, we'll discuss eczema and children. While children who have eczema do suffer, parents need to be aware of the stress that this can cause for them when a child suffers from eczema. The entire family is affected. In a study including 38 families, it was reported that when children suffered from moderate to severe eczema, family dynamics were severely impacted. These families reported a significantly lower quality of life than families who had children without eczema. They felt it also affected their relationship. For these parents, self care and attention to their relationship is critical to their survival. It is also important for the children that the parents deal with the stress. Parents are very likely to increase the stress level of children.

The majority of children with eczema develop symptoms before they are one year old, some as early as a month. The first step is to have the child diagnosed by a dermatologist to determine the exact type of eczema the child has. With a small child suffering from itchiness and inflammation, everyone can be on edge. Sleeping through the night is difficult enough for infants and the itch factor and the night can turn into a nightmare for both parents and child. By the time a child reaches the age of four or five years old, it becomes aware that he or she is different. The rash is very visible and the child is aware.

When people comment on the child's condition, parents need to reassure the child that this rash is not their fault as it can severely affect his or her self-esteem. It is important that children learn not to scratch, which means parents need to remain ever vigilant. Applying a moisturizer at the first sign of itching can help the child cope. Older children should be taught to moisturize as soon as they are able to do so with a doctor's approval, an antihistamine can help the child sleep through the night. A daily routine is important to help the child cope with the persistent itching. He or she should bathe daily in lukewarm water with a soap that is fragrance free, gently pat the child dry.

Instead of rubbing the skin, the bath should be followed immediately with a moisturizing cream. Fortunately, most children do outgrow their childhood eczema when parents provide the proper treatment. All too often, however, treatments will improve the symptoms and parents become laxer in maintaining the same care. This then leads to a renewal of the itch cycle. Even if the symptoms slowly abate. The proper treatment needs to continue to help your child overcome the symptoms of eczema. Try to do the following, keep baths as cool and lukewarm as possible scents. Hot water can have a drying effect on the skin, always clean with non allergenic soaps that do not contain perfumes or other additives.

Make sure you towel dry very gently without harsh rubbing against the skin. Never bathe your child without moisturizing afterward. Petroleum jelly is especially effective. Remember to apply the moisturizer several times each day.

Dress your child in cotton clothing or in special clothes designed for eczema sufferers snip your child's fingernails to prevent him or her from scratching and infecting the skin. Ensure that your child drinks enough water every day to keep moisturized. Help your child establish a skin care regime so that he or she can care for him or herself. Recognizing at school and exams, can present eczema triggers for your child and be proactive in helping your child cope.

Researchers have been studying the connection between eczema and food allergies. At times, eczema symptoms can be heightened by certain foods and other cases. The foods themselves can trigger eczema. In either case, there is a direct link between foods and allergies related to eczema. Eczema, hay fever and asthma frequently occur at the same time and within the same families. Studies have determined that over 80 percent of eczema sufferers also have food allergies. 30 percent of children are found to have both eczema and food allergies. It is believed that food allergies weaken the immune system and skin barriers, thus creating an environment for eczema to thrive.

Any food can cause an allergy, but there are certain foods most commonly associated with allergies and eczema symptoms: eggs, dairy, sugar, wheat, nuts, especially peanuts, processed foods, white pasta and breads. Many doctors suggest doing an allergy patch test for children suffering from eczema. This can help eliminate certain food culprits. As a parent, you need to be careful of hidden ingredients such as sugar and ketchup. Reading labels is a must because many foods contain hidden triggers. Discuss your child's diet with a certified nutritionist. Usually fish and lots of fresh fruits and vegetables are highly recommended foods. High end probiotics such as Kiffer and sauerkraut should also be consumed on a regular basis.

Final Ideas & Tips

Eczema is a skin condition caused by a weakened immune system. The symptoms are redness, inflammation and white scaly patches of skin that can occur anywhere on the body. There is no cure for eczema, nor is it contagious. You cannot catch eczema from another person. The symptoms, however, can be contained with the proper treatment. Here are some important points about eczema and how to deal with the symptoms. Naturally, effectively, in long term eczema, flare ups are caused by a vicious itch scratch cycle. Stop the itch and you can break the cycle. Itches are usually brought on by certain triggers. These triggers can be environmental, emotional or both. There's a direct tie between emotions and skin. That is why it is important to get at the root of negative feelings such as anxiety, depression or repressed anger.

This isn't always easy if a trained therapist can be of invaluable help. Stress is debilitating for all of us, yet it is close to unavoidable. Stress is a part of life, but it can be much harder on those suffering from eczema for the simple reason that it will inevitably trigger a skin rash. It's important to understand exactly what triggers your stress. Then you need to find ways of calming the stress factor. Exercise, yoga, meditation are all proven ways to release negative feelings and embrace more positive emotions. They have been proven beneficial to eczema sufferers by calming both the brain and the skin. They have the added benefit of improving your overall quality of life on a daily basis, while dermatologists usually treat eczema with a steroid based ointment.

There are so many other, perhaps even more effective ingredients you can use on your skin. You probably have many of them in your home. So try the suggestions in this chapter on your rash. Special moisturizers and baths can perform wonders on your dry skin and tone down the itching, which will result in less scratching and inflammation. Special moisturizers and baths can perform wonders on your dry skin and tone down the itching, which will result in less scratching and inflammation. Eczema is all about dry, itchy skin and proper hydration. Inside and out is essential. Creams can help keep your skin moist with water and lots of it will help hydrate the entire body. Consider water your anti eczema trump card while you are checking your home for a few special ingredients.

Check every day for possible allergens. Rugs, bedding, pests, dust and dry air. Play havoc with your system as they easily trigger allergies. Dust mites and pests can hide anywhere and frequently do. In some cases, this can mean doing an overhaul of major offenders, such as replacing rugs with easy to clean hardwood floors and wallpaper with paint. It may take some effort, but your skin will notice the difference. At the same time, you can make your garden close to allergen free by keeping your grass low and planting non pollinating plants. These changes will eliminate many allergy triggers from your home and you will be able to enjoy your garden without fear. Parents with children face a special problem. They need to attend to their child's needs while living with constant stress.

This can affect their relationship. These parents need to deal with both their child and their own quality of life. Even if these parents do not suffer from eczema, their situation will be greatly helped. If they practice some or all of the anti stress suggestions in this chapter, their stress is real. It's good news that the majority of children with eczema will outgrow their symptoms as they age. In the interim, they need to learn how to handle their flare ups as best they can. Eczema is stressful and irritating, especially since there is no cure. Nor is there one specific cause. Many factors can work together in creating the skin disorder. That is why every part of your life, from your emotions, stressors and home, need to be examined thoroughly and regularly. These elements work in unison. This can necessitate a few major lifestyle changes. It is

It is important that you handle this one day at a time. Everyone is different. So handle your eczema free journey at your own pace. The last thing a person with eczema needs is additional stress. Discuss specific difficulties with your dermatologist for the best and quickest results. Be assured, however, that the suggestions for natural elimination of eczema symptoms will eventually work and the effort will be worth your while, since it entails a significant improvement in your overall lifestyle. Less stress, more exercise and a healthier body without an irritating rash await you at the end. Eczema can disrupt and control your entire life in so many ways. This is the chance for you to take control and enjoy everything life has to offer. Imagine your life without rashes, inflammation and cracking on. Sightly skin, then go and make it happen.

Insomnia

This chapter Book contains proven steps and strategies on how to handle all the areas of insomnia from the causes to the steps on how to cure it, all the information in this chapter Book will help you to overcome the process of insomnia. All of the nights staying awake and all of the days constantly feeling exhausted will fade away. After reading this chapter Book, you will not only learn about where insomnia comes from, but you will also know how to cure any part of it. Thanks again, and I hope that you'll enjoy this chapter Book and benefit immensely from it.

The Science Behind Insomnia

In this chapter, we'll talk about the science behind insomnia. The basic idea of insomnia is that people will be staying awake at night without any reason. People think that it's caused by stress or simply not being able to get to sleep. Sometimes they will not be able to rest because of eating at different points of the day, no matter what the reason is. The fact is that there are times when people are not able to get back to sleep. Insomnia, by definition, is the difficulty of falling asleep, or it could be the difficulty of staying asleep. Both of these definitions have to do with the fact that the person is having trouble getting sleep since they are facing another kind of troubling situation.

Mentally, a person will know that they have insomnia when they are not satisfied with the amount of sleep that they have been getting. They will naturally feel as if they have a low level of energy throughout the day, fatigue at different moments of the day, a large difficulty in concentrating on tasks, and a large amount of mood disturbances. And lastly, there might be a drop in performance level in the workplace. Any of these symptoms are possible to have when it comes to staying awake all throughout the night. It is simply because the mind and body both need to have rest. If one or both of them do not get rest, then the person will feel lower than usual. They will feel exhausted and they will feel the annoyance of wanting to sleep without actually being able to sleep.

When it comes to seeing if you have insomnia or not, it's best to see that there are two different types of insomnia. If you have a couple of nights where you cannot get to sleep, but then you begin to sleep right after on the following night, you might not think that you have insomnia when you might actually have acute insomnia. This kind of insomnia comes from the basic levels of stress that the person is facing. They will face a short period of time where they're not able to fall asleep because of the life circumstances happening around them. Commonly, this will happen when a person receives bad news from their boss or they might have gotten a bad grade on a test. Both of these situations can cause the person to have a night or two where they simply cannot get any kind of sleep.

This kind of insomnia lasts for such a short period of time. There is normally no reason to look for any kind of treatment for it. Instead, it normally will be resolved on its own. The second kind of insomnia is called chronic insomnia. This is where the person will not be able to sleep for a few nights every week for a few months. The person might have this happen to them when they are facing a major change in their environment since they may have just moved houses or might be having trouble adapting to a new season of harsher weather. Other reasons why a person might have this kind of insomnia is because they have an unhealthy level of sleep habits where they sleep whenever they want to.

If a person wakes up whenever they want to or if they stay up as late as they want, then the mind will be used to staying awake when it wants to without having a specific schedule.

The body will not be able to function with a small amount of sleep one night and then more sleep later on during the day. While this might seem possible at first for a short amount of time, this is not possible to have happened for a longer period of time. Eventually, the mind and body will force the person to fall asleep and stay asleep until fully rested. It will force the person to have a normal sleep schedule since it will begin to affect their own normal life schedule. Otherwise, it will need to be treated by a doctor or a medical physician who can diagnose you for chronic insomnia.

Normally, it will be linked to another medical or psychiatric issue, meaning that the reason you might be having chronic insomnia will be because of stress or something else on your mind. Even if the situation is not normally stressful to you, or even if you do not feel the stress, your body will feel the stress causing the chronic insomnia. In these two cases of insomnia, they still have the same causes. Both of them can be caused the same way, even though they are healed in different ways. For insomnia, it is a treatable issue that is usually linked to a kind of medical condition.

Some of these medical conditions can be very serious and others will be mild, making it so that most people can have insomnia at some point in their life. Otherwise, the insomnia will come from other common symptoms that people are able to have at any point. These symptoms include nasal allergies, sinus allergies, lower back pain. Overall, chronic pain, gastrointestinal problems, arthritis, asthma and other neurological problems, most of these can occur at any point during a person's lifetime. These can cause stress to the body and cause the mind to stay awake for a longer period of time. While some people have a cold, they will realize that they are staying awake for a majority of the night or they might see that they are waking up constantly in the middle of the night.

Both of these factors caused the person to have a major lack of sleep and rest. They might try to sleep while having a cold, but the insomnia is still able to come. The other pains in the body that cause insomnia are simply from the fact that the body cannot get into a comfortable position to get rest. Do you ever have it where you get into bed and then you're not able to get into a comfortable position? This is the same situation that will happen constantly inside of the body if it's in any kind of pain. In order to have more time healing, the body will stay awake until it's in a position of more rest.

Otherwise it will become a constant battle where the person will need to find a new way to sit, or they'll need to find a new medicine to stop the pain from truly occurring. With all of these different causes in mind, it's just as important to learn and determine the exact factors that hinder your sleep. If you find that some of these risks apply to you, then you simply have a higher chance of having insomnia at some point in your life. So what's the next step? Simply take preventive counter measurements at the same time, look after your own health to make sure that you can always have a restful sleep.

The risk factors involved with insomnia include being a female, being pregnant, or in the period of menopause, an older adult above the age of 40 suffering from more stress, suffering from depression, having a night job, travel long distances where there is a time change or have a family history of insomnia. All of these factors lead a person closer to insomnia. Since the situations listed involve a person's choices, they can choose to take a longer vacation in which they are moving through different time zones. They can choose to go through the hard times of having a job at night where they will need to adapt to a completely different lifestyle. Otherwise they will have a job during the nighttime shift because they were moved into that position or they had no other choice available to them.

At that moment, it's hard to deal with the risk factors of insomnia when a person thinks about all the natural effects that can happen, sometimes life will get in the way where they have relationship problems, family problems or job problems. Not only that, but they might be suffering from financial or personal problems where they are having trouble balancing out work in their life. Things naturally become difficult, and sometimes it causes a person to go through a time of insomnia where the mind and body will stay awake until more of the stress or depression is gone. In some cases, it takes longer. In other cases, people are able to find a solution very quickly. Either way, it is difficult to stop the factors of insomnia from coming.

Since insomnia has many different causes and risk factors, there are many different things that you are able to do to prepare yourself from having more sleepless and restless nights. It is easy to see what the causes are, but other times it's harder to go forward and stop the normal stress factors of life from happening. Life gets hard and sometimes even harder to the point where the person will not know which side is up. The most important part to remember when beginning any preparations for healing from insomnia is not to be afraid. Do not be scared of any outcomes or results that might happen. The more fear you have, the more stress that comes along with it. To make the case of your own insomnia worse, it is important to stay calm and work through the treatment to prevent yourself and heal yourself from the insomnia.

The Brain Of An Insomniac

In this chapter, we'll talk about the brain of an insomniac when it comes to the function of the mind. It's an interesting scientific standpoint that scientists continue to do research and they continue to look towards the functions of all the brain waves and how all the thoughts interact during the day and night. During every hour of the day, the mind is able to adapt itself to any situation, whether the mind is trying to get food, get a drink, get out of the car, walk through a door or just get some rest. The mind constantly will try to find new ways to survive and flourish. It will continue through this cycle of getting enough resources during the day and then have enough energy to heal and rest during the night.

Normally, people will have a normal level of brainwaves where the mind will stop thinking as quickly and will prepare for the night by shutting down parts of the mind's thought process. The farther into the nighttime goes, the more the mind is slowing down and becoming capable of getting another night of full rest. This is the reason why a person will find it harder to get through their job or any kind of work later on in the night. Studies show that the process of the mind will naturally change throughout the day, and sometimes it will cause a major form of anxiety inside the mind. This is where the mind will become stressed enough to the point where the brain waves will not slow down and therefore the mind will not be able to completely relax later on in the night.

Instead, it will go through a period where the brain waves will move faster to cause more thoughts and more energy needed to be consumed. The same amount of resources that are collected during the day will need to be taken in at night. The body will then run through twice the amount of energy and resources and cause the person to have a lack of energy within their own life. As for the mind and how the brain waves respond to the phases of insomnia, there have been three different studies done to see how the mind will react during the night. Scientists have known that the learning and memory functions of the brain have a majority of control with causing a person to go to sleep.

The more a person learns during the day, the more energy they are utilizing that day in, the more energy they're gaining. Overall, the more a person forms memories inside of their own life, the more the mind will have dreams during the night. The ability to have a larger variety of dreams during the night allows for the mind to calm down and use the images to enforce more of a positive image inside of the person. The mind wants the body to be calm during the night, and the best way to do that is by looking through the happy memories that the person has gone through. Whenever you see a loved one inside of your dream, you smile, you are happier and your body relaxes more.

For a person with insomnia, the mind during the night runs faster and has more trouble getting to the same kind of calm and relaxing state, the mind will be just as active during the day as it is at night in one of the studies about brain waves during insomnia. Scientists were able to see that the neurons inside of the mind are more active at night. Inside the mind of a person who has chronic insomnia, the neurons travel around the mind faster and cause more thoughts to pass through the mind at night. Therefore, the person goes through a period where they are in a constant state of information processing that does not stop at any point during the whole day.

This causes insomnia, since the person will not be able to have enough sleep or rest to remain stable inside of the study. The researchers were telling others that insomnia should not be seen directly as a nighttime disorder. Instead, it's more of a 24 hour brain condition that causes the mind to stay on this small amount of time where the mind does not have enough rest during one night interferes with the memory inside of the brain. It does not affect the memory of the person in the long run. Instead, it makes the next day, after one night of no sleep, much harder. The person will have a harder time concentrating, remembering small facts and remembering information that is told directly to them the same day. To test out this theory, they compared the test scores of students that had a full night of sleep versus students that did not have any sleep the night before.

The students who had more sleep were able to focus on more parts of the question at once, and they were able to remember more of their choices on the test a few hours after it was over. The idea of this experiment was to measure out the amount of the mind that requires rest in order to remain focused throughout the day. When a person has insomnia, they are not able to go through and have the same level of concentration. Some people believe that since their mind will be functioning just as quickly at night when they have insomnia, they believe they can have more focus the next day. The experiment done during this research disproves this thought. Just because the mind is as active at night as it is during the day when it has insomnia does not mean that that is a good idea to rely upon.

Not only does it build up the lack of concentration in the mind, but it will also build up the amount of plasticity inside of the brain. The research on what plasticity is and how it contributes to the state of insomnia is still unknown. They do know that the plasticity of the mind does build up throughout a person's life and it does contribute to other forms of disease later on in a person's life. The more plasticity that exists inside of the mind, the less chance a person has to remember memories overall, not only on a short term basis, but on a long term basis as well. It's harder for the mind to hold on to all the levels of concentration and memory.

When a person has reached an elderly age, the mind during that age will naturally slow down and it will slow down at a faster rate if there's more plasticity inside of the brain. The second area of research in insomnia surrounded the idea of a person constantly having stress or constantly worrying. They were investigating how if a person has a stressful life and then gets insomnia, how the mind will respond at night. The first fact that they were able to see immediately was that the cognitive function of the mind does not change whether a person is suffering from insomnia or if they're sleeping all right. However, they were able to support the idea that the mind with insomnia does not have the same amount of functions throughout the day. The main parts of their research were able to show that the mind wanders throughout the night.

People who have insomnia will be thinking at night, but that does not mean that they will be thinking about a specific subject. The mind not only has trouble concentrating in the next day, but the mind will have trouble concentrating on the different areas of work happening during the nights where the person does not have enough sleep. Not only that, but the mind will continue to use energy during the day that it should be resting, not having the energy to function during the day. It makes it harder for them to perform at a higher level. The next part of the same research compared the memory function to the tasks of efficiency that the person will naturally go through in any part of the day. When a person goes through the troubling states of insomnia, they will not be able to remember a larger portion of memories during the day.

Since the memories could not be immediately remembered, the tasks during their lives were harder. The minds would wander around whenever they had to do simple tasks of the day. The. Minds, brain waves will be slower and will cause the person to move at a slower pace and quickly forget the information in front of them, the brain will attempt to be active, but there will not be enough resources for the brain to go through. Therefore, the mind will exhaust itself every day during the stages of insomnia. The third and last scientific study that occurred to study insomnia was the idea of gray matter inside the brain. The main thing to know is that gray matter exists in the frontal lobe and controls the processes of memory and executive function. When a person does not have enough sleep at night, they will have a large decrease in the amount of gray matter.

Whether the person is suffering from insomnia or if they are having trouble sleeping overall, they will start to slowly develop symptoms of depression or trauma. The person with insomnia will not only have to deal with the exhaustion of not having enough energy, but they will go through the harsh areas of stress in the mind. The best way to resolve this issue is to consult a doctor and see what kind of medicine would be best for your own personal case. Overall, the mind has to gain enough sleep and rest to have a proper amount of concentration. Going through insomnia will simply elongate the amount of time that the body does not get rest. It will cause the brain waves to keep moving faster throughout the brain, and it will cause the mind to slowly lose the purpose of memory. The important thing to remember is to get enough nutrition and to get enough sleep every night. No matter how difficult it is to find a balance, it is important to have a high level of concentration every day to have the most amount of memory function.

Sleep Starvation

In this chapter, we'll talk about sleep starvation, the devil, the mind and body both need to have rest in order to function and to have a full amount of concentration the next day. If there's no rest, then the gray matter, memory and elaborate functions of the mind will result in the person not being able to get through the day. Their mind will wander and they will not think through all the steps needed to get through the day. The first thing to do right now is think about all the things you do the moment you wake up in the morning, think about the first five things that you do. You might turn off the alarm clock, check the phone, stand up, turn on the light and walk to the bathroom. No matter what your normal routine is, all of these things do not require very much thought.

All of these things in the morning are easy to do since they occur every day. When you are facing the troubles of insomnia, you're not nearly as focused as you normally are. The mind is continuing to think as fast as it normally would, but does not have all of the resources to have enough energy to properly function. This means that your first five things you do in the morning may not all be remembered, or they might take longer to complete. It might take you only two minutes to do all of your first five actions in the morning when it might take 10 minutes to complete your first five morning actions.

When having insomnia, you might also forget to do a task or two. You might forget to turn off the alarm and you might forget to check your phone for any updates. Many different things can happen, but overall, this is only the start for what happens when you are struggling with insomnia. After the first night facing insomnia, you might notice a major difference in the amount of energy you have, you might notice how difficult it is to think about the next thing to do during the day. Or you might find it more difficult to remember all the information during the day. Other people around you will not realize all of these things happening to you.

Normally, your day might be to wake up, get ready for work and then go shopping afterwards. At work, you have to be able to function at a very high level of efficiency. No matter how exhausted you might feel, there are only a certain amount of days that you will be given sympathy. There are only a certain amount of sick days that you're allowed to take off. Insomnia cannot take over your life, but it can cause a major portion of it to stop in your own job. You're expected to go forwards and complete a certain amount of work. Whether you are in charge of packing boxes, doing research or writing a paper, you have to be at the top almost every day. You have to perform close to your own highest level in order to truly earn the paycheck.

At the end of the week. Any small amount of rest that is taken away during the night can cause a problem. But it may not be enough to completely take you away from the focus of the job. For example, instead of getting eight hours of sleep, you only get six hours of sleep. Those two hours of sleep are very important, but they will not do as much damage to your life as insomnia. Losing two hours of sleep might make you move slower, but you're still able to focus and get all the tests of the day done to your own fullest potential. Losing an entire night of sleep basically causes a person to stop thinking. They will go through the day struggling with the focus on any task they will go through and have trouble reading a question while thinking about an answer.

The mind will be concentrated on reading each word rather than putting the information together to figure out how to answer the question. Insomnia can affect your work performance. All you're thinking about is to get the task done. You are thinking about the fastest way to get through the day rather than thinking about the best way to get through the day. At first this seems all right to do because you're still completing all the work and getting the job done. The real problem occurs with your own reputation in the job. Your boss will see that you're working at a slower rate, that you're not focusing as much, and that you're not having the right attitude to get through the job. This can really put you in the wrong spot where your boss might stop you from working that day and might even fire you from the job.

Now, while this might not happen, it still has a possibility of happening. Insomnia is a distressing factor to life that not only can cause someone trouble in the workplace, but in their own life at home. When you think about your home, think about all the important parts of your own home. You might think about your wife, husband, children, pets are all these aspects. Some people might also think about their garden or their own remodeling project that they've been working on. There's no right or wrong answer as to what's important inside of your own home. It's your own life and it's a very important factor to keep balanced. Many things that happen every day you probably do not even really think about.

The simple things, such as getting everyone ready for the day, getting into the car, going somewhere to eat, or making sure that everyone has what they need are all things that continuously happen. They become easier as time passes, since everyone works together in a balance to ensure that everyone is ready for their own day. Normally, this is easy to do, but having insomnia makes it much more difficult. The moment a person's family life or their home life starts to get off balance, it becomes very stressful and they begin to question if there is any way to get back to a steady state. It doesn't matter if the stress is coming from not having the groceries in time or waking up late.

A small amount of stress can build to become something that is incredibly difficult to control. Insomnia causes a large amount of exhaustion where the person will not know exactly what should be done. They'll be running through the house not knowing what needs to happen since their own mind will be wandering around, there won't be any specific thoughts that appear in their mind. The same idea happens in the job where the time of not being focused can add up to a bad situation. If you are suffering from insomnia and need to make sure that your kids go to school, you might forget that they need to have their lunches packed. They need you to get enough rest to ensure that they have the proper support in order to get through their own day.

If not, it becomes harder for them as a child and then it becomes harder for you as a parent since you want to be the best for your own child. The moment you are suffering from insomnia, you will not be able to remember things very well and you will have a harder time getting through the routine of your own house. If you miss a day of not cleaning the house, it's not the end of the world. If you start to make a habit of it and you forget to clean up around the house, then it will be harder to maintain your own home. A smell might start to develop and all the plants might be overgrown all around your house. Nothing will be kept at a clean level since insomnia stops you from having the right amount of energy to go through any of these tasks.

The last part of your home life is your relationship. Whether it's your partner, husband, wife, boyfriend or girlfriend, being in a relationship is a job on its own, the moment your own significant other starts to seem different where they are more tired or they're not focusing on you as much things might get strange, strange in the way where one person might start to feel lonelier or they might start to feel as if things are getting complicated. All of these emotions can go very deep to the point where a large talk might need to happen. It's difficult when dealing with insomnia where you do have to figure out how to live life with no actual energy inside of you. You'll feel tired all of the time when you start to care less about things and you will start to think about what should and should not be done in your own life. Think about how hard life is on its own.

Imagine then adding in the fact that you are not getting any kind of rest, which is making you stop focusing and then is forcing you to stop concentrating on the important parts of your life. You might stop doing your job while at work. You might start forgetting about your children and what they need for school. You might start forgetting about all the little things you do for your own romantic partner. Many different things can happen when you are suffering from insomnia, since there are many different outcomes, it's important to protect yourself from it and stop yourself from getting close to it.

The Insomnia Cure

In this chapter, we'll talk about the cure, natural and artificial remedy, there are two basic categories when it comes to insomnia remedies. The first is the artificial remedy. This type of remedy or medicine can be found in the pharmacy and clinic. Artificial remedy usually carries a high cost, but it typically delivers fast results. Most medicines today are toxic, filled with harmful chemicals that are not safe to be consumed for a prolonged period of time. The other kind of remedy is called natural remedy. People have practiced natural medicines for centuries. This type of remedy utilizes the body's natural healing process to cure insomnia.

This remedy is often less expensive, but what makes them stand out is the fact that they're not as toxic as artificial remedies. Being aware of the benefits of natural remedies might cause an increasing number of people to use these resources, regardless of which kind of remedy you choose. The goal is to help you fall asleep and stay asleep. These remedies are meant to aid you to get more rest at night. Most of these remedies will cause drowsiness, so it's best to take them right before bed unless it says otherwise. It's also important to make sure that you talk to a doctor before getting any medication that I'm about to share with you that is applicable for Lunesta. Lunesta helps you fall asleep quickly and studies show people sleep an average of seven to eight hours.

Don't take Lunesta unless you're able to get a full night's sleep as it could cause grogginess because of the risk of impairment. The next day, the FDA recommends the starting dose of Lunesta be no more than one milligram tion. This is a sleep medication that works differently than the others. It works by targeting the sleep wake cycle, not by depressing the central nervous system; it's prescribed for people who have difficulty falling asleep. Rose Arem can be prescribed for long term use and the drug has shown no evidence of abuse or dependence. a plan or Senada of all the new sleeping pills, Senada stays active in the body for the shortest amount of time. That means you can try to fall asleep on your own.

Then if you're still staring at the clock at two a.m., you could take it without feeling drowsy in the morning. However, if you tend to wake up during the night, this might not be the best choice for you. Doc Sipan or Silent or this sleep drug is approved for use in people who have trouble staying asleep. Cislunar may help with sleep maintenance by blocking histamine receptors. Do not take this drug unless you're able to get a full seven or eight hours of sleep dosages based on your health, age and response to therapy. Benzodiazepines, these older sleeping pills try Asalam, which is Halcion, Temazepam or Restoril, Alprazolam or Xanax and others may be useful when you want an insomnia medication that stays in the system longer.

All of these are meant to heal the effects of insomnia by staying in the system longer. They are used to treat sleeping problems such as nightmares and sleepwalking. The main problem with these kinds of medications is that they might force you to feel sleepy during the day. They also cause the body to become dependent on the medication. It's important to get a medical evaluation before you take any sleeping pills. Visit the doctor for a thorough examination. Always ask your doctor about potential side effects before making a decision about which sleeping pills to consider taking. Depending on the type of prescription sleeping pills may include side effects such as headache, severe allergic reaction, prolonged drowsiness to just name a few.

On the other hand, some would prefer to go for natural remedies. Instead, you don't need to resort to pharmaceuticals with dangerous side effects and fatigue upon waking. Use these natural remedies to reset your sleep cycle and end insomnia. One, go camping, having trouble falling asleep, grab a tent and go camping. Throughout most of human history, humans went to bed shortly after the sun went down and woke up in the morning. As it rose, there were candles and later oil lamps, but the light was not very bright, so people went to bed early. According to several studies, campers fell asleep about two hours earlier than usual when denied access to their gadgets and electrical lighting.

It's found that artificial light sources can negatively affect circadian rhythms. When the lure of the TV or fiddling on the phone keeps you up late at night, it's time to grab a tent and go camping. Leave your electronic devices at home, leave your phone in the car, take some time to meditate, write, do some yoga. Most importantly, sleep on the ground, not in your camper, your car or in a cabin. Get grounded. Your goal is to destress to take a break from distractions and efforts to avoid artificial light and to use natural light and magnetic fields to reset your circadian rhythms to music therapy. Listening to music while sleeping does in fact have benefits worth considering for all ages. Music has the unique ability to soothe us, excite us and elicit a wide range of emotions.

The soothing, sweet music helps to re-establish a connection to your sense of inner peace and allows you to feel completely secure and enjoy deeper, more restful sleep. Research has shown that people who listen to calming music before going to bed have improved sleep quality during the night than people who don't. Hence, if you're having trouble falling asleep, this could be a solution. Three Power down for better sleep. Sleep is not an on and off switch. Your body needs time to unwind and ready itself for shut-Eye. Insomniacs will find it very hard to shut down their brain or quiet, anxious and worrying thoughts when they are on the go before bedtime. You have to separate your day from night time. For instance, if you read before heading to bed, your body knows that reading at night signals sleep time.

If you take a warm bath before bed every night, your body recognizes that it's time to slow down and relax during the first twenty minutes, complete any chores that absolutely must get done before bedtime for the last twenty minutes, lie in bed quietly and meditate. Focus on the rhythm of your breathing and shoo away any negative thoughts during this time. The goal of this power down is to relax your body and prime it for sleep. For sleep in a cool room, people with sleep onset insomnia have consistently warmer core body temperature immediately before falling asleep compared to their healthier peers.

Thus, this group of insomniacs needs to wait for two to four hours before their bodies cool down and initiate sleep. Research shows that the optimal temperature for sleep is between 60 to 68 degrees. When you're trying to sleep, your brain loves the cold. Sleeping in a cold bedroom can help release anti-aging hormones. The hormone melatonin is a powerful antioxidant that combats inflammation, protects against cognitive decline and cancers, and strengthens the immune system. It reduces oxidative stress and neurodegeneration, indicating its anti-aging benefits. Sufficient sleep is the key in improving your body's production of melatonin.

Creating a conducive sleeping environment, including lowering the room temperature, can help the hazards of insufficient sleep, can put your health and safety at risk, and make changes in your sleeping habits. Start by creating a bedroom conducive to optimal sleep. Five Break a sweat exercise early. It's no secret that exercise improves sleep and overall health. But a published study about sleep shows that the amount of exercise and time of day it's done makes a difference. Researchers found that women who exercised at a moderate intensity for at least 30 minutes each morning, seven days a week, had less trouble sleeping than women who exercise less or later in the day.

Morning exercise seems to affect body rhythms that affect sleep quality. One of the reasons for this interplay between exercise and sleep may be body temperature. Your body temperature rises during exercise and takes up to six hours to drop back down to normal because cooler body temperatures are linked to better sleep. It's important to give your body time to cool off before bed. Sleep is a crucial part of our health and healing. Take it seriously and seek out the help of a professional medical practitioner. If you can't get your sleep under control, once you get your biological clock reset, your new sleep habits will require discipline, but you'll reap the benefits of a healthy, restful sleep.

Lifestyle Modifications For

In this chapter, we'll learn how to prevent insomnia by making simple lifestyle modifications without further ado, let's get started. It's important to examine your lifestyle and see if any of these adjustments can be made. Simple lifestyle changes can make a world of difference to the quality of your sleep. Although not all insomnia is due to stress, it's undeniable that people who experience ongoing stress are more susceptible to insomnia. And in the case of insomnia related to stress, alleviating the stress should alleviate the insomnia. As mentioned in the Book earlier on, stress affects the quality of one's sleep, which can upset the balance between sleep and wakefulness.

It's important to handle all parts of your own life in the best manner possible. To ensure that you are at a healthy balance, you need to ensure that you are having sufficient sleep on a daily basis. Sleep plays an important role in your physical health. Insufficient sleep for a short time may make you more moody and irritable. More over the long term effects are serious cardiac problems depression, stroke, heart attack, to name a few, according to sleep experts. There are studies that show that when people get sufficient sleep, they will not only feel better, but it will also increase their odds of living healthier, more productive lives to overcome insomnia.

You should stay away from any kind of nicotine, caffeine and alcohol. All of these will cause the mind to naturally become restless. Over time, having a constant amount of caffeine will force the mind to be more active than it is because caffeine is a stimulant, most people will have it early in the morning or to remain alert during the day. Therefore, insomniacs should stay away from these drinks in order to have quality sleep, skip the coffee break, reach for a glass of plain water instead of coffee, which may be the reason why you're having a hard time falling and staying asleep at night. Besides that, setting up a sleep schedule for yourself is one of the best self-help techniques for insomnia.

It's a major step in overcoming insomnia for good. It is so important to go to bed at the same time at night and wake up at the same time every morning because the body needs consistency. The body likes a routine. It thrives on habit. With a regular bedtime and wake up time, your body is more likely to stay on track if you can avoid alternating schedules, late night parties, night shifts or other things that may disrupt your sleep schedule. Next, you should try to limit your bedroom activities if you are constantly watching television or doing work inside of your own bedroom, then your mind will adapt to that being the place where it needs to be the most active, try to work outside of the bedroom and only use your bedroom to fall asleep, take the TV out of your bedroom.

Televisions are a major cause of insomnia. It consists of blue light which suppresses melatonin production and the stimulating nature of some programs make falling asleep difficult. Therefore, finish your Netflix marathon outside your bedroom and then head to sleep. You should condition yourself to know that your bedroom is for sleeping, not for other non sleeping activities. Not only that, you can always adjust your own daily schedule to include time for yoga or meditation. There is an abundance of evidence that yoga and meditation can improve sleep patterns, often dramatically. It is important to have some relaxation time for yourself. These techniques can be done in your own home for both comfort and privacy.

It helps to increase the total flexibility of the body. Relax your mind and distress the body. Try to spend at least 30 minutes a day to either meditate or do yoga. Typically, meditation and yoga are best done in the early morning in a quiet place and with exposure to sunlight for meditation, all you have to do is sit down and clear your mind, try to listen to relaxing music to help calm you down. The moment you start to get used to the idea of meditating throughout the day, the mind will be able to relax faster at night and therefore you will have an easier time falling asleep.

As for yoga, you can either go for yoga classes with a bunch of friends or home practice where you can have more privacy. It will benefit your sleep. In many ways, the practice of certain yoga postures will increase the blood circulation to the sleep center in the brain, which has the effect of normalizing the sleep cycle. Remember, sleep is not a lifestyle choice or luxury. It is natural and necessary. So root out the underlying causes. Change your diet, stop watching TV before bed, set up a sleep schedule, do some yoga and meditate. Follow the advice mentioned above and eventually you'll get your quality sleep.

Switching Off

In this chapter, we'll talk about switching off fighting insomnia is an uphill battle when you are trying to cure insomnia, you are actually trying to stop your own mind from being too active at night. There's no reason to be afraid of staying up for countless nights in a row and wondering if this is all going to end. Worrying will only bring about sleepless nights. So stop battling insomnia in your head. All that you need to do is switch off your monkey brain at night. You want your own mind to slow down to the point where you can easily fall asleep.

Even if someone is not suffering from insomnia, they still might want to know what they can do in order to have better control of themselves and fall asleep whenever they want to. The truth is, having a proper amount of sleep not only helps you to be fully alert the next day, but it also helps the person to rest at night. One of the reasons why people struggle to fall asleep is that once they lay down in bed, they will start to think about their day and life in general. More often than not, they start thinking about useless things that serve no purpose but only hinder them from falling asleep. Switching off definitely needs practice for many busy adults, the only time they actually have to reflect upon their lives and what they're doing is during bedtime.

While it's not a big deal to reflect, don't do it during bedtime. Oftentimes this is the biggest culprit that stops you from falling asleep. So for those who want to reflect on their lives, consider waking up earlier to have time in the morning to do so or even schedule some time in the evening to do some reflection. Another reason why people fail to switch off is that they have many activities at night that are overstimulating, causing them to stay awake instead of feeling tired. Some even love to have caffeine at night as a routine. No wonder why people are struggling to fall asleep. So stay away from coffee from your mobile phones, laptops, televisions.

When it's bedtime, avoid activities that force you to think and require physical exertion at night and most importantly, avoid bluescreen from electronic devices. Another key to falling asleep is to schedule your sleep. Most people don't do that. Instead, they choose to fall asleep only when they're tired. But what they should do instead is to set up their own routine and schedule their bedtime upon repetition. Your mind will be conditioned to switch off when the clock hits the usual hour to fall asleep schedule and set a routine and make sure that falling asleep is a habit. How you schedule your evening till bedtime varies and there are many ways to do it and there won't be a one size fits all solution.

But the general rule of thumb is the same. How to switch off at night. The first thing you should do after you've eaten dinner and cleaned up for the night is turn off any of your electronic devices. Having your phone or computer switched on when you are getting ready for bed will stimulate your brain and it will eventually hinder your sleep. Admittedly, your electronic devices are addictive and you won't know when to stop. The light by itself will interfere with your sleep pattern and cause you to stay wide awake. So when it's one or two hours before bedtime, avoid your gadgets at all costs. If you want to have a restful sleep, reading before sleep is fine, but not through your electronic devices.

Reading a physical book as a hobby before bed actually helps you in getting ready to sleep. Also, it's better not to read in your bedroom. You're encouraged to read in another room, since you do not want your mind to be active in the room that you need to fall asleep in again to condition your mind to switch off the moment you step into your bedroom. If you are able to completely relax when reading a book, then it's fine to go through and read a book while laying down in bed. Otherwise try to do it only in another room. The next thing you can do is listen to music and write down any kind of reminders that you will need for the next day, the music by itself will help you to calm your mind and clear your stress away.

Try to listen to music that is smoother and slower in rhythm. Listening to anything that is loud or exciting will stimulate the mind, and it will be harder for you to get to sleep at that point. For example, you will find yourself in a much relaxed state. When you listen to classical music, then rock music. Another tip is to plan your days ahead before sleep. Writing down reminders for the next day helps to clear out your mind, since you will stop thinking about every single detail that you need to remember the next day. Staying awake in bed while constantly reminding yourself that you need to remember something will keep your mind active. Think of your notepad as a Dommett and forget it.

Vault simply grabbing a piece of paper and scribbling down a few notes will definitely help you calm down faster and get some rest in return. Another thing that you can do is have a relaxation drink such as tea right before bed. However, make sure you stay away from caffeine, alcohol and drinks with a high amount of sugar. A nice cup of tea can calm your mind and help your body to relax. This is also a great way to create time for yourself, a time to quiet down and relax. You can do this while either reading or listening to music. If you don't find pleasure in drinking tea, consider having a light snack before bed. Do not consume anything that is too high in calories and difficult to digest. Regardless, a light snack is good because sometimes the reason why you're having trouble getting to sleep is simply because of hunger.

The last thing you can do is bring down your room temperature, the best way to do this is to set your bedroom thermostat to be a bit cooler. Our body is conditioned in a way that when it enters a cooler environment, it will get a signal that it's time to rest. Also want to take a quick shower right before bed, preferably a cold shower to immediately cool down. Otherwise you can try to get a bed fan, a cooler mattress or go for a short walk before bed. All of the things mentioned can be part of your own personal bedtime routine. Go ahead and try them and figure out what works best for you and your schedule. In no time at all, you won't have any trouble falling asleep and staying asleep.

Thoughts & Tips

I hope this chapter Book is able to serve and guide you in stopping or preventing insomnia. You're free to try any tips and strategies mentioned in this chapter Book to ensure restful sleep. After all, restful sleep is the foundation for your mental and physical well-being, whether it's artificial or natural remedy, lifestyle changes or setting up a routine.

All these contribute in preventing insomnia. So what to do next? It's time to take action today, find out which of these methods works best for you and implement them into your daily routine. Write them down and imagine what your normal day looks like when you add these strategies to your routine.

Any five or ten minutes that you have open, think about what you could do to help relax your mind, to help you get to sleep later on during the night. Only by trying them out can you find the best way for you to fall asleep and stay fast asleep. Everyone is born unique, so don't be afraid to experiment with your body and soon you'll never suffer from insomnia again.

Keto Diet

The Keto diet is rapidly gaining in popularity, although it's been around for almost a century. There is a reason why Quito is so highly regarded. It's not a fad diet. It actually works and it has tremendous health benefits. In addition to weight loss, when on the keto diet, you are feeding your body exactly what it needs and are eliminating toxins that will slow it down. The keto diet focuses on low carbohydrates, which the body converts into energy to help speed up weight loss.

What Is The Ketogenic Diet

In this chapter, we'll talk about what the ketogenic diet is, the key to diet is a low carbohydrate diet, but it differs from other low carb diets such as paleo, in that it deliberately manipulates the ratios of carbs, fats and protein to change fat into the body's primary source of fuel. Our bodies are used to turning carbohydrates into insulin to use as fuel. That means the extra fat is stored and keeps adding on the pounds. The ketogenic diet uses fats for fuel, which means it gets used instead of stored. Thus, weight loss becomes easy. In addition to weight loss, the ketogenic diet is known as the healing diet. The lack of sugar intake has been proven to help and prevent many diseases from heart disease, high blood pressure, cancers, epilepsy and many symptoms of aging. The manipulation of carbs, fats and proteins is called ketosis.

It's a state when the body, deprived of the usual carbohydrates and sugar, is forced to use fat as its primary fuel. Of course, turning insulin into fat also means lowering the amount of insulin in your body. That's why the keto diet has been so successful in helping people deal with diabetes. It adjusts the sugar level. Naturally, the ratio of carbs, fats and protein can vary. Many people allow themselves up to 50 grams of carbohydrates a day and still lose weight on a stricter regime. The carb intake can be between 15 and 20 grams daily. The less carbs, the quicker the weight loss. But the diet is very flexible. On the Keto diet, you don't count calories.

You count carbohydrates and adjust the intake of carbs versus fat and protein. A typical keto diet will get 60 percent of its calories from fat, 15 to 25 percent of calories from protein and twenty five percent of calories from carbohydrates. The only limitation on the diet is sugar. What you need to avoid the ketogenic diet is not a fad. Many scientific studies have shown the benefits and healing effects of ketosis. Discuss the ketogenic diet with your doctor if you're interested in consuming less sugar, losing weight or preventing diseases from occurring.

Benefits Of The Keto Diet

In this chapter, we'll talk about the benefits of the keto diet, weight loss and higher energy levels are only a side effect of the keto diet, a kind of bonus. As a matter of fact, it's been scientifically proven that a low carbohydrate diet is the fastest and easiest way to lose weight. But the keto diet has many additional medical benefits. Let's begin by stating that a high carbohydrate diet with its many processed ingredients and sugars has absolutely no health benefits. These are merely empty calories, and most processed foods ultimately serve only to rob your body of the nutrients it needs to remain healthy.

Here's a list of actual benefits for lowering your carbohydrates and eating fats that convert to energy control of blood sugar. Keeping blood sugar at a low level is critical to manage and prevent diabetes. This kind of diet has been proven to be extremely effective in preventing symptoms of diabetes. Many people suffering from diabetes are also overweight. That makes an easy weight loss regime a natural. But the keto diet does more carbohydrates get converted to sugar, which for diabetics can result in a sugar spike. A diet low in carbohydrates prevents these spikes and allows more control over blood sugar levels. Mental focus. The keto diet is based on protein, fats and low carbohydrates.

As we've discussed, this forces fat to become the primary source of energy. This is not the normal Western diet, which can be quite deficient in nutrients, particularly fatty acids, which are needed for proper brain function. When people suffer from cognitive diseases such as Alzheimer's, the brain isn't using enough glucose, thus becoming lacking in energy and the brain has difficulty functioning at a high level. The keto diet provides an additional energy source for the brain. A study by the American Diabetes Association found that Type one diabetics improved their brain function after eating coconut oil, which we'll see is an important part of the keto diet.

That same study indicated that people who suffer from Alzheimer's may experience improved memory capacity on Akito diet. Those with Alzheimer's have seen improved memory scores that might correlate with the amount of ketone levels present. What does this study mean to the average person? With the emphasis on fatty acids such as a Big Three and a Mega Six found in seafood? The Ketut diet is likely to fuel the brain with additional nutrients to help achieve a healthier mental state. The brain tissue is made up largely of fatty acids. You've heard fish referred to as brain food, and the increased consumption of those fatty acids will logically lead to improved brain health. Our body does not produce fatty acids on its own.

We can only obtain it through our diet. And the keto diet is rich in fatty acids. A diet high in carbohydrates can lead to a foggy brain where you have difficulty in focusing. Focusing becomes easier with the increased energy provided by the keto diet. In fact, many people who have no need or desire to lose weight use the keto diet to improve and enhance brain functions, increase their energy. It's not unusual and has become almost normal to feel tired and drained at the end of a day as a result of a poor carbohydrate laden diet, fat is a more efficient source of energy, leaving you feeling more vitalized than you would on a sugar rush acne. While most of the benefits of Akito diet are well documented, one benefit catches some people by surprise, better skin and less acne. Acne is fairly common.

90 percent of teens suffer from it, and many adults do as well. While it was always thought that acne was at least exacerbated by poor diet, controlled research is still being conducted. However, many people on the Keiter diet have reported clearer skin. There may be a logical reason. A 1972 study found that high levels of insulin can cause the eruption of acne. Since the Akito diet keeps insulin at a low and healthy level, it may very well affect skin health. In addition, acne thrives on inflammation. The ketogenic diet eases and reduces inflammation, thus enabling the body to decrease acne. Eruption's fatty acids, which are found in abundance in fish, are known as anti-inflammatory.

While research is still being done, it seems likely that the Akito diet has beneficial effects for a clearer, healthier and more glowing skin. Kitto and anti-aging. Many diseases are a natural result of the aging process. While there have not been studies done on humans, studies on mice have shown brain cell improvement on a keto diet. Several studies have shown a positive effect of the keto diet on patients with Alzheimer's disease. What we do know is that a diet filled with good nutrients and antioxidants, low and sugar. Are high in protein and healthy fats, while low in carbohydrates enhances our overall health, it protects us from the toxins of a poor diet.

There's also research indicating that using fatty acids for fuel instead of sugar may slow down the aging process, possibly because of the negative effects that sugar has on our overall well-being. In addition, the simple act of eating less and consuming fewer calories is a matter of basic health as it prevents obesity and its inherent side effects. So far, studies have been limited. However, considering the powerful positive effects of the ketogenic diet on our health. It's logical to assume this diet will help us grow older in a more natural way while delaying the natural effect of aging.

A normal Western diet laden with sugars and processed foods are certainly detrimental to warding off the signs of aging Quito and hunger. One of the major reasons diets fail is hunger. People who diet feel hungry and deprived and simply give up a low carbohydrate diet naturally leaves people feeling full and satisfied. Less hunger means people will actually remain on the diet longer while consuming fewer calories. Kito and eyesight. Diabetics are aware that high blood sugar can lead to a higher risk of developing cataracts.

Since the keto diet controls sugar levels, it can help retain eyesight and help prevent cataracts. This has been proven in several studies involving diabetic patients KITO and autism. We know the keto diet affects brain functions in a study on autism. It was found that it also has a positive effect on autism. 30 autistic children were placed on the keto diet. All showed improved and autistic behavior, especially those on the milder autistic spectrum, while more studies are needed. The results were extremely positive.

Keto Diet & Cancer

In this chapter, we'll talk about the keto diet and cancer. Cancer has turned into a serious disease in our modern society. While cancer was not a large factor before the 20th century, it did exist. Of course, our modern diet and sedentary lifestyle have made cancer the second primary cause of death, with six hundred Americans dying from this disease every day. It appears that our bodies do not react well to being exposed to daily toxins, while any cancer treatment must be guided by your physician. It's a good idea to discuss the keto diet and what it can do to help the treatment of this disease. A cancer specific keto diet may consist of as much as 90 percent fat. There's a very good reason for that. What doctors do know is that cancer cells feed off carbohydrates and sugar.

That's what helps them grow and multiply a number. As we've seen, the Keiter diet dramatically reduces our carbohydrate and sugar consumption as our metabolism is altered with the keto diet, in essence, it removes the food on which the cancer cells feed and starves them. The result is that the cancer cells may die, multiply at a slower rate or decrease. Another reason why a HITO diet is able to slow down the growth of cancer cells is that by reducing calories, cancer cells have less energy to develop and grow in the first place. Insulin also helps cells grow. Since the keto diet lowers insulin levels, it slows down the growth of tumor cells that went on the Keto diet. The body produces ketones while the body is fueled by ketones.

Cancerous cells are not. Therefore, a state of ketosis may help reduce the size and growth of cancer cells. One study monitored the growth of tumors in patients suffering from cancer of the digestive tract. Of those patients who received a high carbohydrate diet, the tumor showed a thirty two point two percent in growth. Patients on a keto diet showed a twenty four point three percent growth in their tumor. The difference is quite significant. Another study involves five patients who combined chemotherapy with a keto diet. Three of these patients went into remission. Two patients showed a progression of the disease when they went off the keto diet.

More studies are needed, but these numbers are encouraging. The keto diet may help prevent cancer from occurring in diabetic patients in the first place. People with diabetes have a higher risk level to develop cancer due to elevated blood sugar levels, since the ketogenic diet is extremely effective at decreasing the levels of blood sugar. It may prevent the initial onset of cancer from what research has discovered so far, the ketogenic diet may stop the growth of cancer cells, help replace cancerous cells with healthy cells, change the body's metabolism and enable the body to starve cancer cells by depriving them of needed nutrition.

By lowering the body's insulin level, the ketogenic body may prevent the onset of cancer cells on a ketogenic diet, specifically for cancer. Your fat should be at 75 to 90 percent protein, 15 to 20 percent and less than five percent. Carbohydrates, foods to eat eggs, including yolks, all green leafy vegetables, as well as cauliflower, avocado, mushrooms, peppers, cucumbers and tomatoes. When choosing dairy, opt for a full fat version of cheeses, butter, sour cream, yogurt and milk. Eat nuts such as walnuts, almonds, filberts and sunflower and pumpkin seeds. Foods to eat in moderation have one helping of root vegetables such as yams, parsnips, carrots and turnips.

Every day fruits contain sugar, so treat them like candy. One small piece per day, a glass of wine, vodka, whiskey and brandy once a week, no cocktails with sugars, a small piece of chocolate with seventy five percent or higher cocoa content once a week. Foods to avoid any food containing sugar, including cereals, soft drinks, juices and sports drinks, candies and chocolate limit artificial sweeteners as much as possible. Starchy foods such as pasta and potatoes, breads, potato chips and French fries, cooking oils and margarine.

Keto Diet & Epilepsy

In this chapter, we'll talk about the keto diet and epilepsy. The initial use of the keto diet has nothing to do with weight loss or diabetes management for which it is now so well known. Instead, the diet was created by a doctor in nineteen twenty four to help his patients suffering from epilepsy. Epilepsy is a nervous system disorder that can bring on recurrent seizures at any time. The symptoms can be spasms and convulsions or an unusual psychological view of the world. In any case, it's caused by abnormal brain activity. The severity of the symptoms varies from person to person, but a person is diagnosed with epilepsy if he or she suffers from more than two seizures in one full day.

Anyone can suffer from this disorder, but it seems to affect young children the most, perhaps because the young brain is still in a state of development. Seizures are frequently managed by drugs. Sometimes they work, sometimes they don't. As far back as nineteen twenty four, however, Dr. Russell, of the Mayo Clinic, conducted groundbreaking research and created the ketogenic diet to help children suffering from epilepsy. It was remarkably effective, but doctors lost interest. When the new anti seizure medications came on the market, it was easier for them to prescribe medication than to discuss diet.

However, people who use the Kitto Diet to treat seizures continued seeing remarkable success. Today, doctors are returning to using low carbohydrate, high fat diets to treat their patients. The results have been extremely promising. In 1998, the Journal of Pediatrics published a study involving 150 children who experience seizures despite taking popular anti seizure medications. The children were placed on the ketogenic diet for one year, which the researchers assessed their progress. 83 percent of the subjects were still in the study. After three months, over one third of the children showed a 90 percent decrease in seizures. At the end of the year, slightly more than half of the subjects had remained on the diet, and a quarter of them experienced a 90 percent decrease in seizures.

The numbers indicate that the keto diet has a tremendously positive effect on children who suffer from seizures. The researchers consider it more effective than medication in many cases. For anyone with children who experience seizures, the inclusion of Akito diet in the child's treatment should be discussed with his or her physician. Another research on the effects of the keto diet on childhood epilepsy involved 145 children. The children were divided into two groups, with one group being treated with medication. While the other group received a ketogenic diet, 74 percent of the ketogenic diet group were successful in reducing seizures. There have been more studies of childhood epilepsy and the keto diet. These have sparked new and considerable interest within the medical profession.

Keto Diet & Blood Pressure

In this chapter, we'll learn about keto diet and blood pressure. One third of American adults suffer from high blood pressure. It is a serious health problem that can lead to heart attacks and strokes. Obviously, the higher the blood pressure, the greater the risk. Aging and obesity greatly increase the chances of developing high blood pressure. Blood pressure is usually treated with a variety of medications, some of which can have side effects. The best blood pressure is 120 over 80. High blood pressure is the result of hypertension and the causes aren't always clear. But we live in an increasingly tense world, and more and more people are dealing with high blood pressure to a known fact that people suffering from high blood pressure frequently carry excess belly fat and can become at risk for Type two diabetes.

To get at the root of all these problems may require a change in lifestyle. The symptoms of high blood pressure can be caused by an overload of carbohydrates in the diet more than the body is able to handle. As we've discussed, carbohydrates are converted into sugars, which raises the body's blood sugar level, forcing the body to create additional insulin. Insulin stores, fat and an excess of insulin can lead to obesity. All of this can have a negative effect on your blood pressure. Consuming fewer carbohydrates decreases both the level of insulin and the blood pressure level. This simple dietary change can make a huge difference in your blood pressure.

An interesting study released in the Archives of Internal Medicine. Forty six overweight people took part in a weight loss experiment in which people were divided into two groups. One group was put on a ketogenic diet containing a maximum of 20 grams of carbohydrates while the other group was given the weight loss drug Orlistat, in addition to being counseled to follow a low fat regimen. Both groups showed similar weight loss. What surprised the researchers was that half of the keto group showed a decrease in blood pressure, while only 21 percent of the low fat diet group had any decrease in blood pressure, while weight loss itself would bring about a lowering of blood pressure.

The study suggests that a decrease in carbohydrate intake can help lower blood pressure even more. It was found that potassium specifically had a huge effect on lower hypertension. Doctors recommend at least 4700 milligrams of potassium each day for anyone wishing to lower his or her blood pressure. Foods high in potassium or avocado, acorn, squash, bananas, coconut water, dried apricots, pomegranates, salmon, spinach, sweet potato, white beans. While all these foods are permitted on the ketogenic diet, limit your intake of sweet potato and beans, which are starchy and can contain a high level of carbs.

What To Eat On Keto Diet

In this chapter, we'll discover what to eat on a keto diet. Some people associate the Keto Diet with the bad word fat and are quick to dismiss it. Nothing could be further from the truth. Fat is allowed because it's converted into energy. Our body needs healthy fats to thrive. Other foods on the diet could not be healthier. When you're eating ketogenic, you're filling your body with nutrition. Let's take a look at the foods you'll be eating. As this chapter, Of course, is already pointed out, the elimination of processed foods and sugar is one of the best things you can do for your health in general. Processed foods are filled with toxic preservatives that do nothing for you but rob you of your good health.

Fresh is always better when purchasing anything at the market and getting into the habit of reading labels. They can be very sneaky and revealing. Keep your carbohydrates under 50 grams a day and you'll feel the difference. A stricter ketogenic diet will contain approximately 20 grams of carbs a day. Foods to eat on a ketogenic diet. One seafood everybody knows about the healthful fatty acids, vitamins and minerals and seafood. Very few of us eat enough. The key to diet encourages the consumption of all things from the sea. Shrimp and crabs are carb free, and other shellfish contain only a low amount of carbohydrates. Fatty fish, such as salmon and sardines, are highly recommended because of their high omega fatty acid content.

Fish truly is brain food. Enjoy at least two servings or more of seafood a week. On the keto diet, simple canned tuna counts as seafood. Two vegetables can. A diet that recommends unlimited green leafy vegetables be anything but healthy. They are extremely low in carbohydrates and bursting with vitamins, antioxidants and the fiber we need. Daily green vegetables such as broccoli, spinach and kale are believed to decrease the risk of heart disease and cancer. Cauliflower and turnips can be prepared to look and taste like rice or mashed potatoes with much less starch and carbohydrates. Starchy vegetables such as potatoes or beets do have carbs and should be limited on the keto diet.

Three dairy foods. There are cheeses to satisfy everyone's taste. They are high in fat content for energy, high in protein and calcium, and low in carbohydrates. Yogurt and cottage cheese are a great source of protein and calcium. They are low carb and fit well into the ketogenic lifestyle. Be sure to stick with plain yogurt as the flavor types contain a lot of sugar, as are the so-called low fat versions of yogurt. You can flavor yogurt and cottage cheese yourself with a few berries and nuts for avocados. Avocados are truly a superfood. They are high and important vitamins and minerals, including potassium.

According to a study. Avocados are also believed to help lower cholesterol by 22 percent, loaded with nutrients and delicious taste. Avocados only have two grams of net carbohydrates. Use them in salads and sandwiches, five meat and poultry. The key to a diet is to eat plenty of meat. Meat contains very few carbs and is high in protein to help you build muscles whenever possible. Choose healthy grass fed meats which are higher in fatty acids. Six eggs are high in protein and contain a mere one gram of carbohydrates as they are also inexpensive. They're ideal for anyone on a ketogenic diet.

Eggs also make you feel full, thereby helping you eat less. Many people take pride in consuming only the whites of eggs, but the true nutrition lies in the yolk, so be sure to eat the egg in its entirety. Seven Coconut Oil. Too many people are unfamiliar with coconut oil, another superfood. It is perfect for people dealing with diabetes and it's been used with Alzheimer's patients. Coconut oil can be used in most recipes in place of butter or oil. You can also use it for Frying and Tang eight dark chocolate. Did you know that dark chocolate has a high amount of antioxidants? As a matter of fact, dark chocolate is reaching superfood status. Chocolate with 80 percent or higher real cocoa powder can lower your blood pressure. An ounce of eighty percent.

Dark chocolate contains 10 grams of carbohydrates, so it definitely counts as a healthy snack. Keep in mind, the lower the cocoa content, the less healthy the chocolate will be. Milk chocolate does not count as healthy chocolate foods to avoid on a ketogenic diet. The keto diet has a lot less restricted foods than many other diets. Sugar, Of course, should be avoided. That doesn't mean you can't enjoy sweet desserts. There are many keto-friendly recipes that substitute unsweetened applesauce for sugar and baked goods. Substitute sweeteners such as. KVIA can also be used in moderation.

Keep in mind that fruits are healthful, but they do contain a great deal of sugar. So limit the amount you eat to just a few slices a day. Fruit juices are concentrates that have vitamins but lack fiber and their sugar content is extremely high. Read the label on any bottle of juice before buying the best juices that are green with just a hint of fruit for flavoring. Be careful with cereals. Most are packed with sugar and robbed of any nutrients. Many claim nutrition was added. But all that means is that all the nutrition has been removed and they have returned a small amount 100 percent. Bran cereal will fit into your keto diet and you can sweeten it with a handful of berries. Just be sure to examine all the labels in the cereal aisle. This can be very tricky.

Also, remember that honey too is a sugar that totally white starches from your diet. They're nothing but empty calories. This includes white bread, pasta and rice by the wholegrain version instead and enjoy in moderation. Legumes and beans are healthy for you, but they are high in carbohydrates. You can have them occasionally. Just make sure you keep it within your daily 20 to 50 carb gram count. Alcohols tend to be empty calories, but certain spirits will be better for you than others. Beer is filled with carbs and should be off your keto diet. The expression beer belly exists for a reason.

Enjoy a glass of wine instead. Of course, there are variances in different types. Wines, dry wines contain a minimum amount of sugar, while sweet dessert wines contain much more pure alcohol, such as whiskey and vodka or carb free. But they do contain calories, so have a care. Mixing alcohol for fancy cocktails usually creates a haven for sugar. So avoid those. Wine coolers may be a tasty treat, but in reality they're just sugary sodas with some added alcohol. They should definitely not be on your keto diet at any time.

How Keto Diet Works For Weight Loss

In this chapter, we'll learn how the keto diet works for weight loss. Many people confuse the ketogenic diet with low carb diets or paleo diets. However, there are considerable differences in what you should be aware of. Quito versus low carb. A low carb diet can be anything it wants to be as long as it is low in carbohydrates and low is rarely defined on a low carb diet. You simply make random food choices that curb your carb intake arbitrarily. Since there's no real number, you might still be consuming too many carbs. Most importantly, what the low carb diet lacks is that all critical key tonic state that turns carbs into fats and provides your body with a new and effective source of fuel.

This can leave you very hungry and tired. The ketogenic diet has a specific ratio of carbs to fats to protein. This manipulation is critical, and it's why a low carb diet won't work as well, if at all. Kito versus Paleo. Paleo is also a low carb type diet. It's based on the assumption that eating the way our caveman ancestors did i.e. meat and no carbs, sugars or grains is the healthiest type of diet. There are problems with this reasoning. First, our ancestors never experienced the kind of diseases that we face. The ketogenic diet is specifically a healing diet that is meant to benefit the body in many ways and help prevent diseases.

The paleo diet does not do that. Also, the paleo diet is based on eating meat instead of manipulating the ratio of fats, carbohydrates and protein to achieve a catatonic state that uses fat as fuel. Basically ketogenic is low carb, but it's much more. There's a reason the ketogenic diet has become so popular it helps improve your overall well-being. In addition to helping you lose weight, you have more energy during the day and you feel sated and full, thereby reducing the cravings for unhealthy snacks. In essence, you're eating less but better. That's what makes the keto diet so unique and successful. The ketogenic diet is not magic.

It is a scientifically proven method that balances your body's fat intake to help you achieve optimal weight loss by using fat instead of sugars as your primary source of energy. The key to diet induces a state of ketosis, which is achieved when your body stops receiving carbohydrates to turn into glucose. The fewer carbohydrates you consume, the more you force your body to burn fat for energy instead of storing it. That's why it's possible to lose weight so quickly on the keto diet. It counts carbohydrates instead of calories. Using fats as an additional energy source is what ketosis is all about. It's a natural state that helped our hunter gatherer ancestors survive.

They feasted on low carb foods when they could and fasted when food was scarce, fat was stored and converted into energy during the scarce times. The ketogenic state is a natural human state, which makes the ketogenic diet so powerful and successful. In addition to the benefits of the diet, most people simply enjoy the way it makes them feel better. Weight loss results on the keto diet differ among individuals, depending on their specific body composition.

But weight loss has been the consistent result of people who've been on the keto diet. The keto diet is known as the best weight loss diet, as well as the healthiest twenty seventeen study divided cross fit training subjects into two groups, with both groups following the physical training. But only one group combined the ketogenic diet.

With the training, the results showed that those on the keto diet decreased their fat mass and weight far more than the other group. The Keto Diet Group showed an average of three point five kilo weight loss, two point six percent of body fat and two point eight three kilos in fat mass, while the other group lost no weight, body fat or fat mass, both groups showed similar athletic performance ability. A 2012 study divided overweight children and adolescents into two groups. One was put on a diet, the other put on a low calorie diet. As in other Quito's studies, the children on the keto diet decreased their weight and fat mass and lowered their insulin levels considerably more than the lower calorie group.

Besides more rapid weight loss, a decided advantage of the Ketso diet over a low calorie diet is that people actually stick to the keto diet. A lower calorie diet will help you lose weight, but you may constantly be feeling hungry and deprived. That's the main reason most diets fail. Hunger and deprivation are not part of the ketogenic lifestyle. What is ketosis? As we stated earlier, the keto diet isn't magic, it's proven science ketosis is a natural occurrence that happens when you don't feed your body enough carbohydrates and it's forced to look for energy elsewhere. You have undoubtedly experienced ketosis when you've missed a meal or have exhausted your body with vigorous exercise.

Whenever these things happen, your body helps you out by raising its level of ketones. However, most people eat enough sugar and carbs to keep ketosis from happening. We love our sugar and carbs, no matter how bad they are for us, and our bodies will happily use them as fuel. And since our bodies want to help us out, it turns any excess glucose into fat and stores it for future use stored fat translated into bigger and bigger sizes at the clothing shop. The more you restrict your carbohydrate consumption, the more your body will produce ketones. It really has no other options. When we restrict the amount of carbohydrates that we eat, our body will still provide us with energy.

But it must turn to another source and that alternate source is that fat that it has so thoughtfully stored for emergencies. The result is a state of ketosis. It happens when our body breaks down the fat in the fatty acids and glycerol researchers have discovered most of what they know about ketosis from people who fast, thereby depriving them of all sources of energy. After two days of fasting, the body is starting to produce ketones and it breaks down the available protein and begins to use stored fat for fuel. Ketosis is the natural process the body goes through when deprived of other sources of energy. Obviously, going on a ketogenic diet is healthier than fasting.

Ketogenic should become a lifestyle, not a quick weight loss method. One of the reasons it's so beneficial is that ketones offer protection against diseases and damages that can affect the body. We have already discussed how the Keto Diet is an excellent tool to prevent many diseases and maintain health and strength longer. Planning your keto meals will depend largely on your goals. Are you trying to lose weight or are you on the Keiter diet to alleviate the symptoms of some disease? The average keto diet will consist of four meals per day, with a total of 100 grams of protein, 20 to 50 grams of carbohydrates and one hundred and forty to one hundred and sixty grams of fat. This can, Of course, be adjusted to your personal needs.

For example, if you're on Akito diet to improve cognitive functions, you may want to raise your fat intake to ninety grams a day for optimal results. Benefits of intermittent fasting on keto. The science behind the ketogenic diet is that the body burns fat when deprived of other sources of fuel. Intermittent fasting is a deliberate deprivation of food and takes the concept a step further. We're not talking about long term fasting. Intermittent fasting while on Keto diet means having two meals a day or fasting for one day a week. The fasting time gives the body a chance to rest and rid itself of toxins. It provides an extra boost to the weight loss benefits of Quito, and it's a great way to jump start the diet for weight loss. The keto diet, combined with intermittent fasting, will help you reach your goal faster and easier.

Getting Started On The Keto Diet

In this chapter, we'll discuss how to get started on the keto diet. Congratulations, you're ready for a new and improved you. There are so many wonderful benefits to the ketogenic diet. You can expect many positive changes, both physical and mental. So let's not delay and get the journey started. Clear your pantry. We're sure you have plenty of willpower, but there's no need to confront a kitchen filled with tempting sugars and carbohydrates, make a clean sweep and pack the offending items in a box, then donate the loot to a needy neighbor or soup kitchen. They will appreciate your gesture and you're on your way to a key lifestyle. If you have a family, try to get them involved. And if they refuse to refrain from eating carbs and sugar, at least insist they do so away from home. It's a fair request.

Weigh yourself, the keto diet does not require you to live by the tyranny of the scale, it's a matter of fact, as you build up healthy muscles, you might notice a slight initial gain. That's great. So don't worry. You should, however, have an idea of what your starting point is. If you opted for the Ketut diet solely to lose weight, you'll be able to track your progress. But don't become a slave to the scale. The occasional way in perhaps once a week is enough. What about your favorite meals? Perhaps the very thought of giving up your favorite foods has prevented you from getting started on the Keiter way of life. Relax.

The truth is, for every dish that you love and can't live without. Yes, that includes cheesecake and mashed potatoes. You can easily find a low carb substitute that's just as tasty. First, let's consider items that your market labeled low carbohydrate labels are frustratingly deceiving and you'd have to be a nutritional expert to understand them all too frequently. Off the shelf, low carb products have simply substituted sugars for carbs. So don't fall for that bit of deceit. You need to learn to read labels with the diligence that you read. Your wealthy uncles will, but your best bet is to stay away from all these products and simply find healthier substitutes.

Same goes for anything labeled low fat, which inevitably means added sugars, craving a taco, using a lettuce wrap instead of a taco shell. Do you want rice or mashed potatoes? Great. Or rice, a cauliflower and you won't be able to tell the difference. Can't give up your favorite pasta dish, turn a zucchini into Zardoz by slicing it or using a spiral cutter and enjoy your pasta. You absolutely have to have your favorite dessert on the keto diet. You can just bake it with almond flour and use unsweetened applesauce and or avocado to create some sweet smoothness. Learn about coconut oil, which can be used as a butter substitute and Satsang frying and baking coconut oil has incredible health benefits, especially for Type two diabetes.

On the keto diet, you'll be able to enjoy all your favorite meals only better. Always stay hydrated. Keto diet tends to lower your insulin levels so your kidneys may be excreting more liquid than usual. Be sure to drink plenty of water.

Condiments can be the enemy. Don't assume condiments don't count on a diet on the Keiter diet. They most certainly do. Ketchup is filled with sugar. Not all salad dressings are equal. Read the label and never opt for the fat free version. They have merely substituted sugar for fat. Ordering salads when eating out is one of your best options. But beware of the dressing that that restaurant serves. Either ask about the ingredients or better bring your own salad dressing.

Don't hesitate to do that. Even in a posh eatery where the maitre d might become spastic at the sight of you pulling salad dressing out of your bag, explained to the server without apologies. Do you have a special dietary need and you will be using your own. Thank you very much. No further explanation is required. Keep track of your ketone level. It's especially important to remain aware of how your body is responding to the Keto diet at the start of the diet, and you could do so by a simple urine test. You can also purchase a blood ketone meter test early in the morning before your exercise has the opportunity to fluctuate your ketone level. Friends and family can be annoying.

Bless their hearts, those nearest and dearest. You may not always understand what you are doing when eating as a group. They may put subtle pressure on you to just try a bite or one slice of cake won't kill you or worse. But I cooked it especially for you. It will take resolve to stick to your diet. It may help to fill up on keto friendly snacks before you sit down and eat. Enjoy some nuts and avocado or just a leg of chicken before you eat and you will be less tempted. Celebrating occasions, especially if you're the guest of honor, can be a huge hurdle when the gang at the office or your parents enter a room with a cake yelling surprise on your birthday, it's hard to refuse. So try being a bit sneaky.

Instead, by all means, gush over the offering. You're expected to do that. You can even help cut slices, then discover a sudden and irresistible urge for coffee. Would you verbalize loudly and clearly, gently remove yourself from the center of activity to get coffee for yourself and anyone else? By the time anyone notices, hopefully they've missed the fact that you haven't eaten anything. Traveling, traveling while on the keto diet can be a challenge. So be prepared. Pack a personal blender with some avocados and bananas for a few quick and healthful smoothies. Paxman Gervais's or tuna for protein. Eating out. Eating out isn't as difficult as you may think. Even fast food places have salads these days in any restaurant.

Stick to meat and vegetables and for potatoes and. Noodles, you can even navigate the tricky maze in a Chinese restaurant while abstaining from rice, you can enjoy the following clear soups, steamed fish with vegetables, egg foo yung, stir fry dishes, moo shu without the wrappers are just a few suggestions. Ask your server if your meal can be prepared without the cornstarch that's frequently used as a thickener. Even if you end up in a fast food place that doesn't have a salad, simply toss the bun from your burger and just eat the meat. You can do the same at a friend's house or at a barbecue exercise. Keto diet will build muscle mass and give you added energy.

Don't forget to incorporate exercise into your daily routine. It could be as simple as walking more, taking the stairs or joining a gym. How long should I stay on a ketogenic diet? While the amount of time you spend on the diet can vary and should be discussed with your doctor, many people who use the ketogenic diet for weight loss remain on the diet for several weeks until they've achieved a goal and then they turn to a paleo diet or other maintenance eating. We have listed several options in the conclusion of this chapter. Book, you do not want to lose weight only to return to your old eating habits. If you are on the ketogenic diet for medical or therapeutic reasons, check with your doctor to ascertain if you should remain on the diet for a longer period of time.

Great Keto Recipes

In this chapter, we'll learn about keto recipes, you can take your favorite recipes and turn them into Kitto. Let's look into a few recipes to see how easy it is. Might be an excellent idea to buy an Iquito cookbook for your kitchen. Two of the most important Keiter recipes are the simple cauliflower, rice and Zardoz. They couldn't be easier to prepare. People can get frustrated on the diet when they crave pasta and rice, and these two recipes definitely satisfy those cravings. They taste just like the real thing. The Zardoz can be used for any pasta dish. Invest in a calorie counter as you will need it. Omelet muffins make plenty of these ahead of time.

They'll use fast ingredients, one tablespoon of butter, 10 eggs, salt and pepper to taste a half cup diced ham, a quarter cup drained spinach, a quarter cup diced onion, a quarter cup chopped red bell pepper, a quarter cup shredded pepper jack cheese directions. Preheat the oven to three hundred and fifty degrees. A muffin pan with nonstick spray, whisk the eggs, then stir in the remaining ingredients, fill the muffin pan with the mixture and bake for twenty five minutes. Nutritional facts calories. One hundred and fifty five carbs. Two grams fat 10 grams protein twelve point five grams breakfast casserole. This is a delicious casserole everyone can enjoy. It will leave you satisfied until lunch ingredients.

Ten eggs, quarter cup of whipping cream, one cup ricotta cheese, one diced onion, salt and pepper to taste, one package of thawed frozen spinach, one cup of sliced mushrooms, one pound of crumbled sausage meat directions. Preheat the oven to three hundred and fifty degrees. Whisk the eggs, whipping cream, ricotta cheese and onion. Well, season with salt and pepper. Add the spinach, mushrooms and crumbled sausage. Bake for thirty minutes and serve these pancakes with butter and sugar free syrup or with berries ingredients.

One and a quarter cup of almond flour, two tablespoons of honey, a dash of salt, one teaspoon of baking powder, a teaspoon of cinnamon, six beaten eggs, a quarter cup of plain Greek yogurt, three tablespoons melted butter, one teaspoon of lemon extract directions, stir the flour, baking powder and cinnamon in a bowl, combine the eggs, honey, yogurt, lemon extract and butter in another bowl, slowly stir the egg mixture into the flour mixture, use two tablespoons of batter and drop on a hot griddle cook for four minutes, then flip and cook for another two minutes. Continue until all batter has been used. Nutritional information. Four hundred and thirteen calories. Thirty four grams of fat. Eighteen point four grams of carbohydrates.

Sixteen point three grams of protein. Apple red cabbage. Cabbage is a great vegetable to have on Kaido. This red cabbage side dish has yummy ingredients. Eight slices of bacon cut into pieces, one large diced onion, one peeled and sliced apple, two cups of chicken broth, three tablespoons, red cider vinegar, two tablespoons, coconut, palm sugar or sugar substitutes such as Splenda, one teaspoon, ground cloves, a half a teaspoon allspice, a half a teaspoon, nutmeg, salt and pepper to taste and one shredded red cabbage directions. Fry the bacon in a skillet until crispy. Add the onion and saute for five or six minutes. Stir in the broth, sugar vinegar, spices, salt and pepper. Add the cabbage and cook on low for forty five minutes.

Nutrition facts. 160 calories. Seven point eight grams of fat. Sixteen grams of carbohydrates, four grams of protein. Cinnamon, granola, and storbeck granola usually have a high sugar content. Try this instead: ingredients: one cup of chopped walnuts, a half cup, shredded coconut, a quarter cup sliced almonds, two tablespoons, sunflower seeds, half teaspoon cinnamon, one tablespoon coconut palm sugar, one tablespoon, melted butter directions. Preheat the oven to three hundred and seventy five degrees. Combine the walnuts, shredded coconut, sliced almonds and sunflower seeds. Add cinnamon and coconut palm sugar and stir into the nut mixture. Spread the mixture in a single layer on a baking sheet, drizzle with the melted butter and bake for twenty minutes.

Nutrition facts. One hundred and eighty calories, 19 grams of fat, four point one grams of carbohydrates, four grams of protein, herbed omelet with smoked salmon. You can enjoy this omelet any time, but a breakfast of protein and fatty acids gets the day. Started right ingredients, two tablespoons, butter to beat and eggs, one teaspoon tarragon, a teaspoon of time, salt and pepper to taste a tablespoon of butter, two tablespoons of chopped onions for very thin tomato slices, two smoked salmon sliced and one teaspoon of capers. Whisk the eggs and add the tarragon, thyme, salt and pepper, melt the butter in a skillet and add the beaten eggs and chopped onions. Cook for three or four minutes until the eggs begin to set.

Transfer them to a plate and top with the tomato and salmon slices. Sprinkle with the capers, nutrition facts, and calories. Two hundred and thirty nine fat. 15 grams. Carbohydrates four grams. Protein 22 grams. Cheeseburger salad, this is your favorite cheeseburger without the bun ingredients, one pound of ground beef, salt and pepper to taste three cups, chopped lettuce, one small diced onion, one sliced tomato, a quarter cup of shredded cheddar cheese, four tablespoons, oil and vinegar dressing directions, fry the ground beef in a skillet for four minutes, add the onion and cook for another five minutes. Place the beef and onions in a bowl and add the remaining ingredients except the dressing coat with the salad dressing, nutrition facts.

Calories, 290 fat, 14 grams carbohydrates, six protein. Twenty five grams, cauliflower, and rice. This very simple recipe is for basic rice. You can dress it up with vegetables, spices or stir fry it. Use this any time you need rice as a side dish or in a recipe. Ingredients one cauliflower head directions, chop the cauliflower into florets, place the florets in a food processor and pulse. Until you have a rice-like consistency. Cook the rice in a pan of salted water for five minutes. Nutritional facts. Calories. Twenty one. Carbohydrates five. Fat zero. Protein zero. Zardoz, these noodles made from zucchini taste like noodles. A spiral Isar is the easiest way to create noodles, but you can also use a mandoline.

Zardoz get soggy very easily, so do not cook for more than a minute, seasoned with butter or shredded cheese ingredients. One Zucchini Directions uses a spiral to create pasta strands, bring a pot of salt water to boil and cook the Zardoz for one minute bacon wrapped chicken. A very decadent and delicious way to enjoy chicken ingredients. Two pounds, boneless, skinless chicken breast, two cups, chopped spinach, one cup sliced mushrooms, one cup cream cheese, half cup cottage cheese, salt and pepper to taste 12 slices of bacon directions. Preheat the oven to three hundred and seventy five degrees.

Combine the spinach, mushroom cream cheese and cottage cheese in a bowl season, the mixture with salt and pepper use a mallet to flatten the chicken pieces to a half inch thickness. Use a sharp knife to cut pocket's into one end, spoon the mixture into the pockets. Wrap two bacon slices around each chicken piece, brown the wrap chicken in a skillet, five minutes on each side and place the chicken pieces in a baking dish. Bake the chicken for 45 minutes. The bacon should be crispy and the chicken done. Nutrition facts calories. Three hundred ninety fat. Twenty two grams carbs. Three point nine grams protein.

Forty one grams cobb salad. The salad is very high in protein. Enjoy ingredients for dressing. One tablespoon, olive oil, one tablespoon, white vinegar, one teaspoon Dijon mustard, two tablespoons diced onion, salt and pepper to taste ingredients for Cobb salad. Three quarters of a cup cubed cook chicken, a half cup diced tomatoes, a half cup blue cheese, two tablespoons, blue cheese, one sliced hard boiled egg, two cups chopped greens, one sliced avocado, four cooked and sliced bacon slices directions arranged the greens on a plate, arrange rows of chicken, diced tomatoes, blue cheese, egg slices, avocado slices and bacon pieces on top of the greens.

Combine all the dressing ingredients, drizzle the dressing over the salad. Nutrition facts calories. Two ninety five fat. Eleven grams carbs four grams protein. Twenty two grams slow cooker pot roast. This pot roast is prepared without potatoes or carrots. If you add them, adjust the carbs accordingly. Ingredients two pounds chuck roast salt and pepper to taste one tablespoon of olive oil to minced garlic cloves, one chopped onion, two and a half cups of beef broth, one half cup dry red wine directions season the roast with salt and pepper, salt and pepper, the roast heat, the olive oil in a skillet and brown.

The roast on all sides placed the roast and remaining ingredients in a slow cooker. Stir the ingredients to combine and cook on low for six hours. Nutrition facts calories 242 fat twelve grams carbs nine point eight grams protein 21 grams spinach and sausage soup. The soup is loaded with flavor while remaining very low in carbs ingredients. One pound of spicy crumbled Italian sausage, one tablespoon of olive oil, one chopped onion to slice carrots, one minced garlic clove, two tablespoons, red wine vinegar, a half teaspoon of oregano, dash of hot sauce, four cups of chicken broth, one half cup whipping cream, two cups, baby spinach, salt and pepper to taste directions, heat, the olive oil in a skillet, saute the crumble sausage for five minutes until it's no longer pink. Transfer the sausage to a plate and drain on a paper towel.

Saute the onion, garlic and carrot in the same pan. Deglaze the pan with the red wine vinegar. Add the chicken stock, whipping cream, oregano and hot sauce and stir well seasoned with salt and pepper. Simmer the soup for five minutes, transfer the sausage back into the pan and stir in the spinach. Cook for one minute to allow the spinach to wilt. Nutrition facts calories one thirty seven fat seven point eight grams carbs two grams protein eleven grams tandoori chicken. Tandoori chicken is all about the spice marinade.

Serve it with some cauliflower rice ingredients, two pounds, chicken thighs, ingredients for marinade, one cup, plain yogurt, two teaspoons of lemon juice, salt and pepper to taste two tablespoons of olive oil to minced garlic cloves, one teaspoon of chili powder, one teaspoon grated fresh ginger, one teaspoon garam masala, one half teaspoon cumin directions with a sharp knife cut several slits into the chicken thighs, seasoned the chicken with salt and pepper and drizzle with lemon juice. Find the remaining ingredients in a large bowl, place the chicken in the bowl and coat thoroughly, refrigerate for up to 24 hours.

The longer you marinate, the more flavor is absorbed. Preheat the oven to three hundred and seventy five degrees, line a baking sheet with aluminum foil and layer the chicken on top. Bake for about 45 to 50 minutes until the skin is nice and crispy. Nutrition facts calories 145 fat five point eight grams carbs two point three grams protein 17 grams curried lamb filled with exotic spices. This curry dish is perfect with Ketel Rice, ingredients, two pounds of lamb meat, a tablespoon of olive oil, one diced onion, three minced garlic cloves, a half teaspoon grated ginger, a half teaspoon turmeric, one half teaspoon curry powder, a half teaspoon.

Massawa, two cups of beef stock, one cup, plain Greek yogurt, one teaspoon lemon juice directions. Cut the lamb meat into small pieces, saute the onion in the olive oil for five minutes, then add the garlic, ginger, turmeric, curry powder and garam masala stir for another five minutes. Add the meat and brown it for ten minutes. Pour in the beef stock and simmer for forty minutes, remove from heat and stir in the yogurt and lemon juice. Nutrition facts calories. Three twenty nine fat. Seventeen grams carbs. Nine point one grams protein. Thirty six grams cheddar biscuits. These tasty biscuits are great any time they freeze well so keep them handy. Ingredients.

Two cups, almond flour, one cup shredded cheddar cheese. One cup coconut oil. One cup cream cheese. Three eggs, two teaspoons baking powder, one teaspoon baking soda. Dash of salt directions. Preheat the oven to three hundred and twenty five degrees, cover a baking sheet with aluminum foil and place the flour and the cheese in a food processor and pulse to a grainy consistency. Add the baking powder and baking soda, heat the cream cheese and coconut oil in a small pan and warm until they melt. Stir it into a creamy smoothness, whisk the eggs and add the salt, stir the flour mixture into the egg mixture and stir until the dough forms using a tablespoon to drop the dough onto the baking sheet.

Bake for twenty five minutes. Allow the biscuits to cool for slicing nutrition facts. Calories one hundred and six fat. Eleven point one grams carbs. Two grams of protein. Three point nine grams.

Final Thoughts & Tips

Congratulations, you've mastered the ketogenic diet, you've lost weight, feel better, look fabulous, and are enjoying an abundance of energy. You've put a lot of effort into improving your health. So what happens when you've reached your goal and it's time to abandon the keto diet? It's a hard fact that maintaining your weight loss can actually be more difficult than losing that weight in the first place. Returning to your old bad eating habits may be all too tempting. In addition, when you discontinue the keto diet, your metabolism is likely to slow down, making weight maintenance more difficult. You certainly don't want to lose momentum and return to the unhealthy all-American sugar and carbohydrates swamp.

With your lost weight returning, the options below are undoubtedly best at maintaining your current state of health. Consider your options before you stop the Keto Diet. Have a plan in place and know where you're going. Since the keto diet provides you with many options, it'll be easier to adjust to a maintenance style. Continue on the Keiter diet that's been successful for you, but consume more food, not different high carb foods, but the same foods you ate on the diet. In somewhat larger quantities, you'll be eating more calories. This will allow you to eat more protein and fats, but keep the carbohydrate level low.

Now this can be a hit and miss process. Simply add more calories to your diet and see how your body reacts and adjust accordingly. This option ensures that carbohydrates are no longer running your life as you won't suffer from the cravings you might have had when you started the Keiter diet shift from losing weight to gaining muscles. With the increasing energy you enjoy on the keto diet, you may wish to focus on improving your muscle tone. Many athletes are fans of the keto diet. This means retaining your low body fat, but adding muscles and defining strong muscles helps strengthen bone density and keep you strong as you age. The best way to gain strong muscles is to consume more calories in the form of lean proteins.

This option is difficult to maintain unless you include a resistance training exercise program. Remain on low carb but not on keto. When you use the keto diet to lose weight, your carbohydrate restrictions are fairly strict. You can still maintain your weight with a low carb diet, but not as rigid as Kitto. There are many healthy beans and legumes you can enjoy by adding a few more carbs to your diet. How much more carbs are very individual because everybody is different at a few cups of beans, lentils or another helping of carrots to your diet each week. See how your body reacts. If you continue to maintain your goal weight, you're right on track.

Add 10 grams of carbohydrates a week until you are satisfied with the results. The advantage of this option is that it allows you to eat good, healthy foods that were off limits on the keto diet. Having a greater variety of foods from which to choose will make it easier to maintain your weight if you find yourself gaining weight. Simply cut down on the added carbs just a bit. Use intermittent fasting. Intermittent fasting gives you additional options. Remember that fasting forces your body to burn fat.

Here are some ways you can fast, intermittently eat what you want for five days, then fast for two days, eat two meals a day instead of three, providing for a longer period where you are not consuming food. When you begin to embrace keto, you will be enjoying all the benefits of healthy eating. By continuing to consume fewer carbohydrates as a lifestyle, your body will remain sleek and strong. You will also be providing it with ammunition to ward off many chronic diseases.

Beginners Guide To Juicing

In this chapter, we'll talk about the beginner's guide to juicing, juicing has a lot to offer that will benefit your health and wellbeing. Juicing can make you feel better in so many ways. Your mom probably told you repeatedly, eat your vegetables. Maybe you hid the spinach beneath the mashed potatoes. Kids do that now. However, you know how important eating more fruits and vegetables is to your optimal health. They're known to reduce the risk of certain cancers, heart disease, high cholesterol and high blood pressure. They are filled with vitamins and minerals. You need to remain healthy and full of energy. It's a simple fact that the more fruits and vegetables you eat, the more you enjoy the benefits.

You should be eating more than five servings every day. That sounds close to impossible, doesn't it? This is where juicing comes in. We can't always consume all the fruits and vegetables we need. Juicing concentrates the produce so that one glass can serve as the equivalent of several pieces of fruit and vegetables. Juicing makes it easier to enjoy the benefits of fruit and vegetables. Here's how it works. A juicer extracts all the liquid and discards everything else. So what you're left with is highly concentrated fruit and vegetable juice. A blender mashes the whole fruits and vegetables, but leaves the fiber.

We'll talk more about the difference between juicing and blending later because they both have their benefits. This chapter will show you how to incorporate juicing into your healthy lifestyle. Juices can serve as a vibrant meal replacement, but you need solid foods as well. We'll discuss why and how to go about enjoying a juice cleanse, juicing versus blending. These days, people are becoming more aware of the effects that the foods they consume have on their body and entire life. This is definitely a step in the right direction. Every study over the past few decades indicates that many of us are overfed and undernourished. We are eating all the wrong foods. As the current juicing craze gains momentum, it's important to discuss the difference between juicing and blending.

Juicing, as we discuss, separates the juice from fiber, leaving you with a heavy concentration of plant based nutrients. Your body gets a heavy shot of vitamins and minerals. Not surprisingly, you need a juicer to extract juice from fruits and vegetables, blending processes, the entire fruit or vegetable, simply creating a different form of the same thing. You blend a carrot. You get a carrot, albeit in a liquid smoothie form. It's not concentrated like juicing. It does, however, retain all the needed fiber that juicing removes. Juicing provides more concentrated nutrition. You use more produce to get that glass of juice so it's more expensive.

Blending gives you all the benefits of produce along with the fiber. Both have their uses depending on what you're trying to achieve. As a general rule of thumb, the amount of fruits and vegetables needed for one glass of juice will provide you three glasses of blended smoothies. Since blending retains fiber, which slows down the absorption of sugar into the bloodstream, blending might be an excellent option if you're watching your sugar intake. When you blend, you can also add different types of food to the blender, such as yogurt or nuts. Both juicing and blending are an excellent way to consume more fruits and vegetables.

If you're feeling sneaky, it's a great opportunity to get some vegetables and fruits into your finicky little eaters. Actually, if they help with the process of juicing, they're likely to become more interested in eating the whole thing. Juicing and blending let you use up produce that is ready to wilt. However, one or the other may be better for certain types of fruits and vegetables. Let's take a look at what type of produce is best or blended. Either method will give you some inherently superior goodness, but there are times one method is better.

Although all fruits and vegetables can be juiced, producing fruits try papaya, all citrus fruits, apples, pineapples and grapes for blending less juicy fruits work best such as avocados, bananas, peaches, all berries and mangoes. Of course, you can pick more than one for a heavenly blend for juicing vegetables. Try tomatoes, cucumbers, celery, green leafy vegetables and cabbage. Use vegetables with lots of fiber for blending such as kale, spinach and any squash. Adding some citrus fruit to your kale or spinach can remove some of the bitterness whenever you blend. Remember to add water, coconut milk or yogurt.

The Science Of Juicing

In this chapter, we'll talk about the science of juicing. Juicing is one of the fastest growing and most popular health trends. We know that fresh vegetables and fruits are necessary to our health. They contain the vitamins and enzymes that our bodies need to thrive. Fresh juice is an excellent way to counteract our nutrition challenged Western diet, processed sugars and flours, unhealthy fats and cholesterol laden foods have turned our once healthy bodies into weak shadows of their former selves. Instead of sustaining our health, our modern diet is increasing our vulnerability to diseases and is depleting us of energy. When you add lack of exercise and environmental toxins to the equation, juicing certainly provides a much needed weapon against today's lifestyle.

Fresh vegetables and fruits can help get our health back on track. They should be the mainstay of our diet, enjoyed in different ways. Each day we can all benefit from increasing our intake of fresh produce. The good news is that juicing provides us with concentrated wholesomeness. We get more health benefits and a glass of juice than we could possibly get by eating an apple or orange. What is not immediately evident is that juicing our produce robs them and us of the fibers we need to stay healthy. Nature intended for us to bite into its rich bounty. Juicing removes fiber from produce, an effect that separates all those glorious vitamins and antioxidants from the fiber and fiber is an important part of a healthy diet.

The importance of fiber nature packages the energy and nutrients in fresh foods with fiber. Fiber plays many important roles in our health. What role does fiber play in our health? Quite an important one. As it turns out, fiber removes toxic waste from our colon. It keeps cholesterol from getting into our bloodstream. It makes us feel full after eating, thus helping us eat less and lose weight. It slows down sugar absorption into our bloodstream, a serious problem for pre diabetics or diabetics. It improves overall digestive functions. So fruits, vegetables and fiber are all a good thing. But juicing separates them as a juicer pulverizes the produced into a contracted juice, it strips away much of the fiber.

In a way, the juicer can process produce in much the same way processed foods have their nutrients removed, which means the juicer is processing the food instead of our own digestive system. Fruit juice, Of course, contains fructose and natural sugar. However, our body can't distinguish between natural and unnatural sugars, so a constant craving for sweet juice can actually lead to weight gain instead of weight loss. There is no denying that juices provide nutrient dense calories that our bodies crave. That's why juicing is so beneficial. It especially lets us enjoy the benefits of healthy vegetables we otherwise might not touch. For instance, you may not enjoy the taste of Caylor spinach and thus avoid eating these important vegetables.

However, when they are juiced along with other ingredients, you derive the benefit of these power foods in a very pleasant way. Blending different fruits and vegetables is very much a part of juicing. However, unless you're doing a short term cleanse will be discussing cleanses in another chapter. Be aware that juicing should become a part of a healthier, more robust lifestyle. It should not replace every meal for any length of time. It's one of the best ways of getting all the nutrition we need for maximum health and energy. For example, two cups of carrot juice, very doable, has the nutritional equivalent of eight pounds of carrots. You surely don't want to eat those eight pounds of carrots in one sitting, whereas you can enjoy two cups easily.

However, you still need fiber when you're juicing. That means that along with juicing, you should be eating foods high in fiber such as whole fresh fruits and vegetables, oatmeal and legumes such as lentils and beans. These foods are the perfect complement to your juicing diet. Juicing is wonderful when used as a fast food, a quick, very potent and nutritious meal with all the juicers on the market. We'll discuss them in a later chapter as well. You'll be juicing it in no time and loving it. Why? Juicing. Juicing extracts juices from vegetables and fruits. Instead of eating your produce, you're left with only the liquid to drink. Remember that little citrus reamer your grandmother used to squeeze you a glass of fresh orange juice. Grandma was juicing.

Of course juicers have come a long way since then, although Grandma's little gadget can still come in handy. Why is juicing more important today than ever? Because it's unfortunate. A typical Western diet consists of up to 60 percent processed foods, that's more than half, 30 percent of our diet is meats and dairy, which provides needed protein.

But we need more than protein to thrive. You may notice that leaves exactly 10 percent for fruits and vegetables, not nearly enough. Our bodies lack the proper food balance. That may be fine when you're 12 years old and are made up of pure energy, but by the time you reach the northern part of your 20s, your body starts paying a heavy price.

How juicing helps your body. Plant based foods consist of micronutrients, the vitamins and minerals you need to act and feel your best. These micronutrients help protect you against disease and warding off infections. Even if you inherited divine genes, you still need to maintain them. Your parents may have handed you sheer gold, but it'll turn to rust if you don't give your body the fuel that requires juicing that lets you reboot to better health no matter what condition you're in. The time to start is now. Juicing is the best way to detox your body, improve your immune system, start losing weight, ease any gut problems and enjoy more energy than you'd ever thought possible. Juicing and detoxing.

Our bodies try to detox every day when we use the bathroom or sweat, it knows what to do. But when you don't give it the fuel it needs, it can't do a proper job. The skin, liver and kidney are all tools for eliminating toxins. But an unhealthy lifestyle can make it difficult. Pollution, drugs, alcohol and a poor diet can create an overload of toxins inside of us. And when our body can't eliminate toxins, naturally, it starts to store them where they nibble away at our immune system. Tissues and organs causing serious health problems. We are natural plant eaters. Our forefathers gathered whatever plants and berries they could every day. Hunting down some meat happened a lot less often and nothing was processed.

Today, we've turned from a mostly plant based diet to consuming more and more processed foods, meats and fats. Over 30 percent of American men and women suffer from obesity while still lacking vital nutrients. As we pointed out, they are overfed and undernourished. We crave sugars and fats and that's OK. We celebrate with cake and commiserate with a pint of ice cream. An occasional slice of cheesecake does no harm. However, junk food can become a habit and we don't even realize it. We order pizza because everyone else does. This leaves our health at serious risk. Juicing will not only give our bodies a fighting chance.

As we get used to the taste of various fruit and vegetable juices, we will start craving them. We get the similar feeling of satisfaction from drinking delicious juices that we used to get from chomping down on a potato chip. That's when we start to feel and look better. You can start slow. As the great Chinese philosopher Lao Tzu said, a journey of a thousand miles begins with a single step. Start your journey by juicing a glass in the morning to go with your breakfast and eat well for the rest of the day. When you feel ready, you can have a glass of juice, replacing an entire meal. You still need fiber and protein, so don't rely on juice for all your nutrients unless you're doing a short term cleanse. We will discuss that separately.

What if you're not ready to start juicing? Perhaps you don't feel ready for juicing. You may like the concept, but you aren't quite willing to forgo the fast food burger at lunch, the pizza delivery when you get home and those nachos while watching the game. That's OK. It's your decision. However, this is when you might need a glass of juice the most. While you're consuming all those toxins, your energy is lagging. You aren't feeling as well as you could. Why not give your body the ammunition it needs and a fighting chance with at least one glass of concentrated juice a day, preferably more. The additional nutrition can help counteract some of the toxins. So if you must have that pizza but have a glass of concentrated juice as well.

Juice Cleanse

In this chapter, we'll learn about juice cleanses, a juice cleanse is a way to detoxify the body by solely consuming juices for up to 10 days. Solid foods are not part of most juice cleanses if you embark on a cleanse for more than three days. Check with your doctor first. A 2009 study published by Proceedings of the Nutrition Society found that people consuming five servings of fruit or vegetables in the form of juice concentrated over eight hours did increase their bodies. Antioxidants and other micronutrients, however, consuming nothing but juice concentrate can lead to sugar spikes. Also, such a cleanse lacks fiber and can leave the person feeling perpetually hungry.

A cleanse, Of course, lacks any form of animal protein. Several days of a pure juice cleanse can cause severe fatigue. So limit the total days. You consume nothing but pure juice, juicing and gut health. The advantage of a three day juice cleanse has improved gut health. Two thousand years ago, the father of medicine, Hippocrates, said all disease begins in the gut. Modern research shows that he could not have been more correct and impaired. Gut can lead to obesity, chronic fatigue and other diseases. The fact is, the connection between body and brain is strong. When our gut is not functioning properly, it can affect our brain or mood.

Juicing sweeps through a messy gut and tidies it up. A 2014 study at UCLA found that a mere three day cleanse increases good bacteria and decreases bad bacteria in our gut. People who go through a juice cleanse report simply feeling better. A cleanse returns the body to its natural state without all those dangerous toxins before starting a juice cleanse. Check with your doctor if he or she gives the go ahead. Here's what you can do to maximize the benefits. One, don't just jump into a cleanse. You wouldn't start a running plan with a marathon schedule, you would prepare your body a few days prior to the cleanse, and start drinking more water. B reduce the amount of caffeine you usually consume. Use this time to start incorporating green tea into your diet.

See, for a week or so prior to your cleanse, include more raw fruits and vegetables into your diet every day. An excellent way to do this is by preparing at least one green smoothie per day and one or two days prior to your cleanse, eliminating meats and dairy from your diet entirely. If you're used to consuming meat and dairy with every meal starting a few days earlier, this will help your digestive system accept the plant based cleanse quicker. E If you're still consuming processed foods, just stop processed foods, provide you with no benefits and could be responsible for many health problems.

Start to examine labels. If you aren't familiar with an ingredient, you shouldn't be consuming it. Be aware of hidden sugars, even in foods labeled natural. After preparing your cleanse, decide which cleanse is most suited to your goals. The best and healthiest cleanse will be five days or less kidney cleanse. All cleanses are beneficial, but the role of the kidneys is to detoxify our entire body. If they do not function properly, your health suffers the consequences.

Clean health begins with clean kidneys. A kidney cleanse removes toxic waste that can accumulate and make you feel sluggish. If you're on a special diet, consult your doctor about incorporating kidney cleanse into your lifestyle.

Start your kidney cleanse. Slowly substitute just one meal with a glass of healing juice. This will help you determine which ingredients work best for you. Benefits of a kidney cleanse. When toxins remain stored in your kidneys, you can become uncomfortably bloated as they aren't being flushed out. Toxins in your kidneys can lead to excessive fatigue. If foods aren't being processed properly, your body won't absorb the nutrients. As a result, you'll have less energy and are more likely to tire quickly. If the kidneys aren't flushed properly, you may be susceptible to kidney infections. A good kidney cleanse can help. Bladder problems are the result of toxins or bacteria in the urinary tract. The urinary tract is located partially in the kidneys.

Symptoms of a urinary tract infection is the need to urinate frequently. This can occur especially during times of stress or a weakened immune system. The best way to rid your kidneys of toxins is by consuming a large amount of liquids. Cranberry and orange juice is especially helpful in cleaning out the kidneys as they are naturally unfriendly towards bacteria. We'll have several juice recipes. These are especially effective in flushing out kidney impurities by regularly cleansing your kidney of impurities, you lower the risk of developing kidney stones considerably. Recipes for a kidney cleanse, watermelon juice, ingredients, three cups, chopped watermelon, one cucumber, parsley and basil leaves, one lemon, one cup chopped kale, a one inch knob of ginger directions.

Cut the watermelon and cucumber into pieces and feed all into the juicer. A cabbage cleanse ingredients, half a cabbage, one cup broccoli florets, one lemon, one cucumber directions, chopped the cabbage and add all the ingredients to the juicer. Cranberry juice, ingredients, one cup, cranberries, one cup, sparkling water, two tablespoons , green tea powder, two tablespoons, honey, one tablespoon, apple cider vinegar, place all the ingredients in the juicer and process carrot juice, ingredients, two carrots, two cucumbers, a half cup sparkling water directions, cut the vegetables in chunks and place in the juicer along with the sparkling water.

Beets and cabbage juice ingredients, two beets, one cucumber, a half a cabbage, a bunch of parsley directions, roughly chop all the vegetables, place the ingredients in a juicer with enough water to help blend cucumber and celery ingredients. Three celery stalks, one small cucumber, a half cup cilantro, a one inch knob of ginger directions chopped the ingredients needed and fed into the juicer.

Juicing & Anti-Aging

In this chapter, we'll talk about juicing and anti-aging; aging is a natural part of life. When we're 13, we can't wait to grow older. When we hit fifty three, aging starts to look a bit different. Our skin has begun to sag. We're fighting wrinkles instead of acne, and our body doesn't always obey us. Most of us want to stem the aging process in order to look and feel better. That's perfectly normal and desirable, especially at a time when we are gaining so much knowledge about the harm we do to ourselves by consuming toxins and generally indulging in an unhealthy lifestyle, aging is inevitable. The negative side effects of aging are not. Here's the truth. Our lifestyle contributes much more to our own aging process than father time.

While a certain Hollywood contingency has clung to youth with the use of surgery and Botox, many have ended up looking like young throat facelifts and injections aren't the answer to graceful aging. Aging has little to do with wrinkles, which are the result of aging, not the cause of aging. And the related damages are the logical consequence of cellular damage and the body's inability to fight these changes. With enough antioxidants, we simply use up what we have during our lifetime. See Denim Harmon. This is where a diet filled with antioxidants comes in.

Optimal diet, regime and juicing helps combat the onset of sagging skin, hair loss, osteoporosis and other signs of aging. It doesn't stop the aging process, but it can slow down the worst effects and let us enjoy excellent health well into our older years. Juicing, along with a healthy diet, keeps us more vital for a longer period of time. Here are some recipes that are very useful in providing anti aging antioxidants, glowing skin juice, ingredients, three carrots, two apples, one cup blueberries, one cup green tea directions, roughly chop the carrots and apples, place the carrots, apples and blueberries in the juicer and process in a glass, combine the juice and the green tea and serve over ice, glowing greens, juice, ingredients, bunch of baby spinach, one small avocado, three celery stalks, one cup of strawberries directions place the ingredients in the juicer and process.

Beauty elixir ingredients, one cup, cranberries, one cup blueberries, one tablespoon, sesame seeds and one cup of black tea directions. Add all ingredients except the sesame seeds to the juicer and process. Stir the seeds into the juice. Green sunshine juice ingredients, kale leaves, collard greens, parsley, one cucumber, one lemon, one inch grated ginger knob directions. Process the ingredients and the juicer. Pour in a glass and sprinkle with cayenne pepper and turmeric.

Juicing & Energy

In this chapter, we'll talk about juicing and energy. One of the most amazing aspects of juicing is how it can boost your energy to new heights. This is especially important as we grow older, all those fruits and veggies know how to do their job. These days, we live in a high energy world, with many of us trying to fit twenty six hours into a 24 hour day. It's exhausting. Many people have developed the habit of consuming toxic so-called energy drinks to get an added energy boost. We all want to feel more energetic, but at what cost? The dangerous side effects of these energy drinks are well known and as follows: energy drinks. Drinking too many caffeinated energy drinks can prove lethal. These drinks force the heart to work harder, which can lead to serious health problems. People with chronic heart conditions are especially at risk.

A study revealed that over 4500 calls were made to poison control centers by people who consumed too many of these toxic drinks, even at their most benign. Studies show that drinking energy drinks affect cardiac rhythm in a significant way. Drinking energy drinks every day causes migraine headaches due to caffeine withdrawal. When the drinker tries to stop this daily habit, the body becomes addicted to caffeine. Large quantities of the energy drink can cause panic attacks and anxiety. This can lead to bad performance and emotional issues. The purpose of energy drinks is to rev up the brain, which leads to insomnia and other sleep problems. Sleep deprivation can cause additional problems, such as difficulty in concentrating.

Energy drinks have a high sugar content which can exacerbate or cause Type two diabetes conditions. An abundance of energy drinks can cause serious dehydration. Energy drinks deplete the body of needed liquid. Instead of replenishing it, energy drinks can elevate blood pressure to an abnormally high level. Those who are experiencing high blood pressure are placed at risk for possible strokes due to the high caffeine content. More energy is a worthwhile goal. But why rely on toxic energy drinks and suffer the consequences? Fruit juices provide an abundance of energy by providing the body with the healthy nutrients it needs.

If you are serious about boosting your energy, tost the energy, drink and reach for the juice, juices for energy, homemade juice ingredients, three tomatoes, one onion, two celery stalks, two carrots, a half a green bell pepper, one garlic clove, two cups of water, lemon juice and horseradish to taste directions, roughly chop the vegetables and garlic and process all ingredients through the juicer pineapple juice, boost ingredients, two cups, chopped pineapple, one orange, one inch nub of grated ginger directions, peel the orange in place. All the ingredients in the juicer are served over ice kale boost ingredients, a bunch of kale, one cup coconut milk or coconut water. One chopped apple, one tablespoon, melted coconut oil.

A half a cup of groundnuts directions process the kale, coconut oil, chopped apple and coconut milk through the juicer. If your juicer is powerful enough, add the groundnuts. If not, simply stir them into the juice. Beet and apple juice ingredients, one beet, one apple, three celery stalks, one inch grated ginger nub directions, chunk the vegetables and add all ingredients to the juicer. Apple plus juice, ingredients, two apples, four carrots, one cup spinach, one cup broccoli florets, direction's chunky apples and vegetables and all ingredients to a juicer and serve over ice power, vegetable juice, ingredients, three carrots, two celery stalks, one green pepper, one apple directions cut up and processed the ingredients through a juicer.

Store Bought Or Homemade - Pros & Cons

In this chapter, we'll discuss store bought and homemade juices. OK, perhaps you're convinced that consuming more juice can have a tremendously positive effect on your health. You're determined to make juices a daily habit. That's great. But what about all those beautifully bottled juices lining the shelves at the supermarket? Why not simply stock up and avoid all the juicing hassle? Yes, those processed juices are certainly convenient, but they are pasteurized and depleted of nutrients. Consider this. If you found out carrots were good for you, would you opt for fresh carrots or a chicken pot pie filled with processed carrots? Bottled juices are processed much like all other processed foods.

This is exactly what fresh juicing is designed to avoid possible problems with bottled juices. One, the process of bottling these juices can decrease the amount of important juice nutrition so you have no control over the fruits and vegetables being processed. These bottled juices may contain pesticides or other chemicals for juicing organic, fresh off the farm as best three, you can't even be certain the produce has been cleaned properly. For if you are purchasing fruit concentrates, you may be buying little more than sugar water.

Five for juice is sold in cans. These cans add acids and other chemicals that can blend into the juices. Six bottled juices lose potency as it sits on the shelf. Exactly how many nutrients are left in that juice that may have been shelved for a month, you simply don't know. Since some juice bottlers add artificial flavorings, bottled juice will forever remain mystery juice. Eight bottled juices are expensive. You're paying around three dollars for one helping of juice. Juice is made in your juicer, compare the bottled juices with juices prepared, fresh in your kitchen. One homemade juice contains all the natural vitamins and enzymes of the original fruit.

Nothing is lost, too. You can mix and match fruits and vegetables according to your taste. If you want to add juice to your life, make sure the juice is as fresh and uncontaminated as possible by fresh types of juicers once you've decided to incorporate juicing into your life. You'll need to determine what type of juicer is best for you. A juicer is a machine that extracts juice from fruits and vegetables. You'll want to pick the right one for your needs. Size and ease of cleaning should be a consideration. Juicers can vary in cost, and the initial outlay may be a financial burden, while usually you get what you pay for.

We recommend getting started on your juice regimen as soon as possible and buying an inexpensive juicer to start saving up for a better, costlier juicer. And you'll be ready by the time your inexpensive machine falls apart as an alternative to a full sized juicer. There are many less expensive travel sized users available, such as the magic bullet. This is an excellent machine that makes one cup of juice at a time. We'll discuss it in detail later. First, understand that the juicer and a blender are two different machines. As we've discussed, a juicer extracts juice while removing fiber while a blender creates a pulp like smoothie. With all the original ingredients intact, both machines have their uses.

And in this chapter we'll be discussing juicers only. By the way, juicers are frequently given as wedding gifts to people who have no interest in using them. Check with your friends and family to see if someone has a juicer gathering dust. They may be happy to get it off their hands and you could end up with a free juicer. Centrifugal juicers. These are one of the less expensive types of juicers and perhaps do less than an optimal job. They process the produce by disposing of the pope and straining the juice relatively fast. But they don't always get all the juice, thus making for moisture pulp. It may not be the best use or type for low liquid fruits like bananas and avocados.

Hürrem, a slow juicer, definitely one of the most expensive juicers at just under seven hundred dollars. What makes the Hürrem HHC unique is its slowness. The juicer rotates slowly, much like grandma's orange squeezer, thus getting all the pure flavor. It gets every drop of juice from the produce and leaves nothing but extra dry pulp. It has an internal brush for self-cleaning. Breville B.G. for 30 the juice fountain cold. This is a top of the line centrifugal juicer at under two hundred dollars. It does have some great features. Other centrifugal juices do not and its legion of fans swear by it. The Breville BJP for twenty ACL has a low and a high speed. It's a super wide three and shoot lets you insert large chunks of produce without chopping.

Best of all, it makes up to 70 ounces of juice. Its handy juice jug can store juice in the refrigerator for up to three days. This means you get more juices in less time since you don't need to juice as often. Breville J.E. Ninety eight juice fountains plus eight hundred and fifty. What juice extractor? This little powerhouse costs under one hundred and fifty dollars. Has a wide feeding chute, stainless steel cutting blades and we'll get you eight ounces of juice in five seconds. It provides thirty percent more juice than most others in Terrifico juicers and comes with a cup and cleaning brush of 750 wide mouth fruits and terrifico juicer 850 watt juice extractor.

The Gourami GE 750 has an extra wide opening for large pieces of fruit and vegetables, saving you, cutting and chopping time. It can make two cups of juice at once and it's very easy to clean. It comes with a free juicing recipe book at under fifty dollars. It's an excellent buy. Masticating juicers, masticating juicers or cold pressed juicers. Press the juice through a strainer. They have a lower speed than centrifugal juicers and as a result extract more juice and retain more nutrients. They tend to work better for leafy vegetables. They're more expensive, but they end up providing more juice. They can save you money in the long run. Omega J.

Eight thousand six Nutrition Center masticating dual stage juicer juice extractor. This is a slow juicer that yields a high volume of juice. It's worth the just under three hundred dollar price tag. The slow speed preserves most of the. Nutrients and allows you to store the juice for up to three days can also chop nuts into peanut butter. Prepare baby food, grind coffee and make fresh pasta with an attachment. It's hard work at any price. The Aycock three slow juicer extractor, the 150 999 Aycock is compact and can be stored easily. It can also be cleaned in the dishwasher. Its large feeder lets you insert whole fruit, saving you from chopping and cutting. It really extracts the juice from the fruit and is an excellent buy for the money.

Omega VRT 350, heavy duty, dual stage vertical single orgo, low speed juicer not cheap, over four hundred dollars. The Amiga works at a very low speed to retain maximum nutrition. The Pope is injected automatically, making the cleanup easier. Its small size doesn't take up much counter space and as a bonus, it juices nuts without a problem. Personal juicers are an excellent way to save money on juicers to buy a small personal juicer. They're much less expensive than larger juicers, easier to clean, and you could take them on your commute. Magic Bullet MJB 080 one juice bullet at under fifty dollars. This little beauty uses a 700 watt motor to create the perfect eight ounce glass of juice with only three parts.

It disassembles quickly and easily cleans Nutribullet. The Nutribullet is a bit more powerful than the magic bullet and costs about twenty dollars more juicer or blender decisions. Decisions both a juicer and a blender can provide healthy drinks, but the following two blenders have juicing options, providing you with the best of both worlds. They are costly but made of the top of the line quality material that will last for years. Blendtec total blender, the Blendtec is available for just under five hundred dollars. This powerful machine has a juicer option to extract more juice from the produce. Weida mixes a thirty five hundred divided mix. Eight thirty five hundred is a slightly stronger blender and chops produce very fine. You can strain the small bits through a cheesecloth and end up with a perfect juice.

The Many Benefits Of Juicing

In this chapter, we'll talk about the benefits of juicing. As we've already mentioned, it's difficult to consume the amount of fruits and vegetables we need to stay healthy. Juicing provides us with a concentrated burst of power that eating the produce cannot. It's a struggle most of us face. Does anyone really eat three pounds of produce every day? Let's see how juicing can fill that gap. The many advantages of juicing. One, since juice contains no fiber to digest, it becomes absorbed into the bloodstream more quickly. You feel the effects immediately. Juicing lets you enjoy greens.

You never eat in a lifetime like kale, perhaps by mixing the kale with other vegetables and fruits, such as an apple or an orange or both, you create a palatable juice that suits your taste. Keep in mind that fruit contains a lot of sugar, one of the pitfalls of juicing and could lead to weight gain. Therefore, try to keep the vegetable to fruit ratio around 80 to 20 percent juice and give you the opportunity to try out a lot of healthy, exotic vegetables that you've probably walked past in the produce aisle of your local market without giving them a glance. Imagine the variety of vegetables you can try if you juice before every meal using two vegetables that gives you six different vegetables on any given day.

Our digestive system needs good bacteria called probiotics, vegetables and fruits. Rich and probiotics are leeks, leafy greens, carrots and bananas. Be sure to include those in your juicing regimen. Ginger isn't a product, but it's definitely gut friendly, so be sure to add some to your juicer. Can juice and cure cancer? Studies are still being done, but we know one thing for certain. Juicing can arm the body with enough ammunition to help with side effects of chemotherapy. It can deliver that tsunami of nutrients when the body needs it most, since it lets you absorb more nutrition, ammunition for your body quicker. Keep in mind that this is an adjunct to regular cancer treatment that should be discussed with your doctor.

We can be reasonably sure that juicing can do much to prevent cancer. The increased nutrients you consume with juicing are your best defense against this terrible disease. The best cancer fighting foods are leafy greens, asparagus, carrots, beets and broccoli. One reason juicing is a better way to defend yourself against cancer is that cooking those same vegetables will kill a lot of the enzymes. Think raw. To lower your cholesterol, you need to consume less meat and fats and increase your intake of fruits and vegetables. Juicing, with its high density juice content can provide you with the most fruits and vegetables in the shortest time. Meat and saturated fats should be reduced as a matter Of course.

At the very least, eat more chicken and nutritious seafood. Our lives are more stressful and faster than ever. Gone are the days when you went home to a healthy homemade dinner. Most of us simply don't have the time or the inclination. This means we rely more on fast foods, takeout and delivery. That pizza may taste good, but what is it doing to your health? Drinking more juice and regular juice cleanses can eliminate the daily and accumulated toxins. We feed our bodies and revitalize our digestive system. Our skin needs nutrients to look its best. A

a diet of junk food can and probably will result in acne and dull, lifeless skin. By eating less chips and fried foods and eating more fruits and vegetables, we give our skin what it needs to glow. Incorporating one or two glasses of juice into your day will give you a smoother, healthier complexion. A glass of juice before your meal will help suppress your appetite. You'll be consuming less bad foods, which is very good for you. Best fruits and vegetables for juicing while all fruits and vegetables are good for you. Let's say that some are more equal than others. There are certain power vegetables you don't want to miss. Let's look at the best vegetables and fruits to use in juicing. You want a good mixture of taste and nutrition as a rule of thumb vegetables add more nutrition while fruits add the flavor.

Don't forget the 80 percent 20 percent ratio of vegetables to fruit. It's OK to have pure fruit juice, but be careful not to overload on sugar. Also, you should add water based vegetables such as cucumbers as often as you can. The produce chapter of your local market is your oyster's best vegetables for juicing. One cucumber has a high water content containing potassium and antiinflammatory ingredients. Don't peel the cucumber before juicing because the skin contains a lot of nutrients. Carrots, in addition to adding color, carrots are filled with vitamins such as a C. Minerals such as manganese, potassium and iron grade for lowering blood pressure and improving your immune system.

A true powerhouse, carrot's also improve eyesight and help you get glowing skin. Brockley, another powerhouse known to reduce cholesterol and help in the prevention of some cancers. It's bursting with antioxidants and vitamins. D, B, C and E also contain iron and calcium, yams, a high vitamin content, iron and magnesium and lots of sweet taste to make yams the perfect juicing vegetable cabbage, another high water content vegetable that blends beautifully with apples. Cabbage is great for weight loss, purifying the digestive system and boosting a weak immune system. Celery, high water content and lots of vitamins, folate and potassium make celery a great base for juicing.

It's wonderfully refreshing and blends well with just about all other produce celery as a source for vitamin C, B1 and B6, it can help fight cancer and lower blood pressure. Kale is high in vitamin K and loaded with crucial minerals, kale is being studied as a possible aid in cancer prevention. Another powerhouse, spinach, has lots of vitamins, A, C and E, as well as protein, potassium, COLENE and iron. Even if you hate the taste of spinach, you'll love it blended with sweet carrots and apples. Best fruits for juicing apples, an apple a day keeps, you know, the rest. Apple is the fruit powerhouse and you should be eating or drinking some every day. Besides removing toxins from your body, apples can reduce the risk of Alzheimer's, cancer and diabetes as well as lower your cholesterol.

Most of the nutrients in apples are right beneath the skin, so don't peel them before juicing pineapples. These have a high sugar content, but just a little goes a long way in brightening up vegetables you might not otherwise use blueberries. These are great for detoxing the digestive system. It's also thought that blueberries may protect the brain against the onset of Alzheimer's. Strawberries. They are high in vitamin C, just wash them and juice with the stems. Citrus fruit, grapefruit, oranges and lemons are high in vitamin C and help with the absorption of iron. They're also filled with disease fighting antioxidants, cherrie's contain anti inflammatory and disease fighting properties. They also sweeten any vegetable juice. You do need to put them before juicing.

They have a high sugar content, so only use a few. Sometimes you just don't have the needed ingredients handy and you really don't want to take another trip to the market. That's perfectly fine. Most fruits and vegetables have logical substitutes, so don't hesitate to use one instead of another. Juicing is not rigid. Instead, its purpose is to help you consume as great a variety of fresh, healthy juices as possible. Best substitutions reducing apples and pears can be substituted for each other. Coconut or bananas are an excellent substitute for avocado. Vegetables such as carrots, yams, beets or radish can provide the same nutrients.

Celery, zucchini and cucumbers all add water and flavor. Green such as kale, spinach, Swiss chard and arugula are very nutrient dense. Watermelon has a high water content, but it can be exchanged for any other melon. Add half a cup of sparkling water if you like. You can substitute berries for one another. Tropical fruit such as mango and pineapple can be exchanged. Citrus fruits can be used in place of mangoes. Go ahead and experiment for the best flavor combinations.

Great Recipes For Juicing

In this chapter, we'll talk about recipes for juicing, always scrub your produce thoroughly, investing in a brush is a good idea as repealing most of the nutrients in fruits and vegetables is just beneath the skin. If possible, avoid peeling and simply toss everything into the juicer as is. You need to peel oranges, but use other peels and rinds as much as possible. And there's no need to throw out the pulp. Save it for the next time you make a vegetable broth. This chapter has a few recipes that provide a perfect use for that healthy pulp, carrot and orange juice ingredients.

One pound peeled and sliced carrots, three peeled oranges, one cup pineapple, a half inch piece of ginger and a bunch of parsley directions process the carrots, pineapples and oranges in the juice first. Then add the ginger and parsley, watermelon, smoothie ingredients, three cups chunked watermelon, three cups, ice, one banana, one cup chunked cantaloupe, a half cup, apple juice, two tablespoons, agave nectar directions. Combine all ingredients in a blender, green juice. This is a great juice any time, but it's an especially good detox when you've overdone the fun, such as on vacations or during the holidays.

Ingredients, two apples, one peach, one cucumber, one bunch of collard greens directions. Cut up the fruit, peach, cucumber and greens and process in the juicer rise and shine juice ingredients to apples, to carrots, to oranges, directions slice but don't peel the apples, peel the oranges, process all the ingredients through the juicer beet cleanse ingredients. Two beets, two oranges, one lemon, one bun spinach, a half a piece of ginger directions. Cut up the fruits and vegetables and process them through the juicer. Add the ginger. Last raspberry surprise ingredients. One cup raspberries, one cup spinach, half cup pineapple, three carrots directions feed all ingredients into your juicer.

Merry peach berry. Asparagus is a very mild vegetable, so it'll blend easily with the fruits and berries. You don't have to, but it's probably better to remove the tough stems from the asparagus before juicing ingredients for asparagus. One pitted peach, one cup blueberries, one cup spinach, trim the asparagus and process the fruits and vegetables through the juicer pineapple delight. The fruit helps sweeten the Swiss chard ingredients. One apple, one cup strawberries, eight chard leaves, one cup pineapple. Handful of parsley directions process all ingredients in the juicer sweet spinach. This is perfect.

If you don't like spinach because you'll barely taste it, you'll just enjoy the benefits. Ingredients. One apple, one cup spinach, one orange, a bunch of parsley directions process the ingredients in the juicer, turnip and carrots. The turnip is a much underrated vegetable. With these two vegetables, you're getting plenty of vitamin ANC ingredients. Three carrots, one half turnip, one cup strawberries, directions, peel the turnip before processing the ingredients in the juicer digestive rescue juice. The prunes are a gentle way to clear the digestive system. Ingredients for prunes, half cup grapes, one diced apple directions place the ingredients in the juicer and process.

Going Beyond Juicing

In this chapter, we'll be talking about going beyond juicing. Let's talk pulp. That's the stuff that the juicer extracts from the juice and is meant to be thrown out. What a waste of good money and excellent nutrients. Fresh produce, especially organic, are quite expensive. Then think of all the fiber enzymes in flavor in that pulp instead of tossing the pulp. There are quite a few ways you can put it to good, healthy and flavorful use. How to use pulp use pope to make extraordinary homemade vegetable broth, tossed the pulp into the pot for extra flavor and nutrition. Use the pulp in vegetable soups along with your other chopped vegetables. Use the pulp and vegetable soups along with your other chopped vegetables. Most pasta sauces have onions, tomatoes and green peppers.

Blend your homemade or store bought sauce with some pulp to give it an additional taste boost. Let the Pope dry and use it to top your salad as you would. Croutons or bacon bits have more fiber in your greens. Simply add the Pope to the Greens already in your smoothie. If you're preparing a veggie burger, you're likely using mushrooms or a legume as the main ingredient. Add the pulp to bind the burger and add extra flavor. If your diet is paleo or vegan, you already know about using veggies for healthy sugar free baking pulp can be used in bread, zucchini bread and muffins, carrot muffins, recipes using pulp vegetable quiche ingredients.

One frozen pie shell, two cups milk, four eggs, two cups, shredded cheese of choice, one half cup, veggie pulp, half cups, spinach, half teaspoon, cinnamon, salt and pepper to taste directions, preheat the oven to three hundred and fifty degrees. Bake the pie shell for ten minutes to prevent sogginess while the pie shells baking whisk together the milk and eggs add salt, pepper and cinnamon fold in the spinach in pulp. Remove the pie shell from the oven and add the shredded cheese. Pour the egg mixture over the cheese and return the pie shell to the oven and bake for thirty minutes. Carrot muffins, ingredients, one half cup pulp, mostly carrots, half cup applesauce.

One and three quarter cups, white flour, two eggs, two tablespoons, brown sugar, a half teaspoon of baking powder, three quarter cups chopped nuts. Preheat the oven to three hundred and fifty degrees. Coat a muffin pan with nonstick spray, combine the eggs, sugar pulp and applesauce in a bowl. Mix together the remaining ingredients except the nuts in a second bowl. Add the flour mixture to the egg mixture and stir well, then stir in the chopped nuts, transfer the batter to the muffin pan and bake for twenty five to thirty minutes. Veggieburger ingredients.

One cup pulp, one cup, black beans, a chopped onion, one tablespoon soy sauce, one cup chopped portobello mushrooms, a quarter cup ground almonds, a cup of breadcrumbs, a teaspoon of coriander with salt and pepper to taste place the pulp beans, onions, mushrooms, almond soy sauce and breadcrumbs in a blender and process. Add the coriander, salt and pepper if needed. Add water to the ingredients, create veggie patties, place the patties on a baking sheet and bake at three hundred and fifty degrees for twenty five minutes. Serve on buns with sliced tomatoes and sliced avocados.

Minestrone soup ingredients. One medium onion to cloves, garlic, two tablespoons, olive oil, one chopped onion, two chopped celery stalks, one cup tomato and carrot based pulp to chopped tomatoes. One cup each slice string beans and zucchini, eight cups of chicken broth, three cups, canned cannellini beans, a half teaspoon oregano, half teaspoon thyme, half teaspoon basil, salt and pepper to taste three cups of small cooked elbow macaroni directions, heat the olive oil on a large soup pot, saute the onions and garlic for five minutes, add the pope and stir. Let that simmer for five minutes. Add the remaining ingredients except the beans and pasta and simmer for thirty five to forty minutes.

Add the remaining ingredients except the beans and pasta and simmer for thirty five to forty minutes. Add the beans and pasta and simmer for an additional fifteen minutes. Juicing has so many benefits it's difficult to believe it can be made even better. So get ready for the best news since juicing. You can add some super foods to your juices that will elevate the taste and add some powerful health benefits. So-called superfoods are dense in nutrients and fight diseases in a bold way. This is truly taking juicing to another level. Take care because just a little of these foods go a long way. Let's look at some of these super foods.

Some of them may surprise you. You can use these ads in both a juicer and a blender when juicing nuts, soak them overnight prior to juicing. Acai berries contain a powerhouse of antioxidants for your immune system. These are difficult to find fresh. So check the freezer section at your local market. Aloe vera is known for its skin soothing properties. It also has antioxidants for your immune system. You can purchase aloe vera in juice form. Apple cider vinegar is known for its ability to detox the gut, add a tablespoon to any juice and reap the benefits, especially a sweet juice. Your best bet is to buy raw apple cider vinegar. Avocados are high in fatty omega three acids.

Bee pollen is loaded with valuable nutrients such as amino acids and vitamins. It will sweeten any juice by simply adding a spoonful. Cacao nibs are the unrefined seed from the cacao tree and can help against heart diseases. Cacao nibs come in either nut or powder form. Mix some with your favorite berries. Cayenne pepper is a known antiinflammatory spice. It's very hot, so use just a little. It can give your juices a kick experiment for the best taste combination. Cinnamon is another spice with wonderful health boosting properties. It can help control blood sugar levels, protect against health diseases and can fight the onset of cognitive decline.

Any fruit can be sweetened with cinnamon. Coconut oil filled with antioxidants is a must have ingredient to regulate blood sugar. Coconut oil is solid and it's best to melt it before adding it to a juicer. Coconut oil adds subtle sweetness to your drinks. Flax seeds, hemp seeds and chia seeds are not only nutritious, but they are filled with fiber, which is important when you are drinking Fiberglas juices, grind the seeds in a grinder and stir a tablespoon into your juice. It'll add a nice nutty taste. Goji berries are high in vitamins A and C soak them before adding them to the juicer.

They taste tangy and are a great addition to sweet juices. Turmeric powder has lots of antioxidants added to your carrot juice for an exotic flavor, nuts in general, and especially almonds and walnuts, provide lots of nutrients, soak the shelled nuts overnight and add them to the juicer. These are some of the major powerhouse add ons for your juices. They add both great flavor and nutrition, so use them as often as you can.

Why Your Healthy Lifestyle Is Important

In this chapter, we'll discuss why a healthy lifestyle is important. If you're interested in juicing and having more energy, this chapter can put you on the right track for optimal energy. However, you can go even further. The healthy juicing lifestyle goes beyond what you put into your body and includes what you do with your body. Lifestyle is all about the habits we've developed or have failed to develop. Habits are those little things we do each day that add up to the sum of who we are. Juicing is a great start and an excellent habit to get into. Good nutrition is the key to living well, but why stop there, sit back for a minute and consider how many other habits affect how you look and feel when we want to change for the better.

Sometimes we need to change our mindset. You won't get out of the starting gate if your thoughts revolve around everyone's going to die at some point. So why go crazy with all the good stuff or I'm too old to change or I'll just have a glass of juice. I'm too busy for other things. I'm sure you can come up with creative excuses of your own. Everyone has an Uncle Herb who smokes like a chimney, a pizza every other day and never moved from the couch and he lived to see his 90 ninth birthday. Good for Uncle Herbie. What about the hundreds of thousands of others who suffered years of chronic ill health before leaving a spouse and children years before their time? A healthy lifestyle does more than just adding years to your life.

It elevates the quality of your life every single day. It makes you feel better, happier and more competent. You function on an optimal level, not only physically, but emotionally and mentally as well. It can take willpower to break some bad habits, but these habits have become an integral part of who we are. So if you want to upgrade to a better version of yourself, take it slowly but get started. Every step you take counts. Manage your weight to improve your heart health and immune system and lower your cholesterol and blood pressure. Substituting a glass of concentrated juice for one meal each day will help you reach your weight goal.

Start moving your body. You don't have to turn into an athlete or join a gym, although those will certainly help you develop healthier habits. Take the stairs instead of the elevator walk instead of driving to a park a few blocks from your destination. If you do drive, get off your chair and do jumping jacks. Your toe touches every hour or so. Staying active isn't quite the same as exercise. Exercise is a deliberate routine to strengthen your body. Staying active means you keep moving. If you sit behind a desk every day, commute to work and relax in front of the television in the evening, you're living a sedentary lifestyle. Even while spending an hour or so at the gym.

Our bodies were designed for movement, so get into the habit of creating movements throughout the day. Walk to the copier and make your own copies instead of having your assistant do it. Take hourly breaks for five minutes of jumping jacks, knee bends, auto touches. If your office doesn't allow for privacy, use the restroom. If your office is multi storeyed, take the stairs instead of the elevator. Enjoy a well-balanced diet in addition to juices, eat plenty of fresh produce, lean meats, beans, nuts, whole grains and legumes. Avoid unhealthy fats and anything that's been processed, including white sugar and flour as a piece of fruit to your diet each day. Learn to broil or braise instead of frying. A healthy lifestyle includes a healthy disposition.

Everyone faces challenges in life, but positive people deal with them and move on. Negative thoughts do affect how we feel, so strive for positivity that will stimulate your endorphins. Exercising is an excellent way to improve your mood. In addition, find an interest that you enjoy pursuing. Be more approachable to meeting new people, join a club, meet others with mutual interest. Living in isolation is bad for your physical and mental health. Poor sleeping habits can cause fatigue and irritability. Even worse, it can lead to heart disease, high blood pressure and other chronic problems for a better night's sleep.

Reduce your caffeine intake and develop a bedtime routine at the same time every night. Don't nap during the day. Keep hydrated. Sure, you're juicing, but don't forget to drink eight to ten glasses of water each day. Lack of fluids can lead to serious fatigue. Did you know that eighty percent of the doctor's visits are stress related? Stress impacts every aspect of our health. Develop a habit to help you distress taichi. Yoga and or meditation are proven. Stress reducers in hundreds of studies start for a few minutes each day and increase your time until it becomes a habit. The results will surprise you. You know, smoking threatens your health in addition to everything, it saps your energy. We know it's a difficult habit to break, however.

If you want more health and energy in your life, you need to try to talk to your doctor about various smoking cessation techniques. Most experts recommend replacing cigarettes with something healthier. Consider taking a walk, meditating or grabbing for a piece of fruit instead of a cigarette. You have nothing to gain but your life. Change is not always easy and it rarely happens quickly. You need to start by developing a healthier mindset each day. The helpful thing about juicing is that when you juice three times a day before a meal, the active juicing will keep you more focused on creating a better lifestyle. It will give you the reminders you need to keep on track. So just yourself to a healthier you each and every day.

Intermittent Fasting

Why is intermittent fasting so popular? Obesity is becoming an increasing problem, so it's no wonder that many people are looking for a better way to lose weight. Traditional diets that restrict calories often fail to work. For many people, it's difficult to follow this type of diet in the long term. This often leads to yo-yo dieting, an endless cycle of weight loss and gain. Not only does this often result in mental health issues, it can also lead to even more weight gain overall. It comes as no surprise then that many people have been searching for a diet that can be maintained long term. Intermittent fasting is one such diet, more of a lifestyle change than eating plan.

It is different from regular diets. Many followers of intermittent fasting find it easy to follow for extended periods. Even better, it helps them to lose weight effectively. However, this type of eating plan also offers benefits beyond weight loss. Many people believe that it can offer other health and wellness benefits. Some of those benefits are even said to stretch further. Some say it makes them more productive and focused. As a result, they become more successful in the workplace. There have been recent stories in the media of CEOs who claim their success is all down to intermittent fasting.

Yet the benefits don't stop there. There is some evidence to show that intermittent fasting or IAFF helps wellness in other ways, too. It has been said to improve blood sugar levels and immunity. It may boost brain function, decrease inflammation and repair cells in the body, too. With all this in mind, it's easy to see why this way of eating is becoming more popular here. We'll take a closer look at why intermittent fasting works to promote weight loss. We'll examine the benefits of this lifestyle change and we'll show you how to get started with this diet protocol.

What Is Intermittent Fasting

In this chapter, we'll talk about what intermittent fasting is. Intermittent fasting is rapidly becoming a popular choice amongst those trying to lose weight. However, it's also popular with many other people, too, who want to reap its health and wellness benefits. So what is intermittent fasting all about? How is intermittent fasting different from other diets? Essentially, intermittent fasting or idea for short is a pattern of eating rather than a regular diet. Standard diets focus on what you're eating. Dieters are restricted to a certain number of calories or specific types of food. This leads to dieters thinking constantly about what they are and aren't allowed to eat.

Fatty and sugary foods are absolutely forbidden. There's a strong focus on vegetables, fruit and low fat, low sugar meals. Those following these ways of eating often end up fantasizing about treats and snacks. While they may lose weight, they may struggle to stick to their eating plan. In the long term, intermittent fasting is different. It is a lifestyle rather than a diet. It involves eating patterns during which you cycle between windows of fasting and eating. Unlike other diets, it doesn't focus on what you're eating. Instead, it focuses on when you should eat. Some dieters enjoy the greater freedom this gives them. They can eat the foods they enjoy without guilt. Many people also find that it fits better into their lifestyles.

However, there are some potential pitfalls when it comes to IVF for weight loss. The origins of intermittent fasting, intermittent fasting as a lifestyle choice, is relatively new. However, the concept of fasting certainly isn't. There are verses in the Bible and Quran about fasting for religious purposes. Many religious people still fast today for religious reasons. The month of Ramadan remains a time when Muslims refrain from eating from sunup to sundown. Therefore, it's easy to see where the idea of intermittent fasting originates. Even during ancient Greek civilizations, fasting was practiced in many primitive cultures. Fasting was part of many rituals.

It has also formed the basis of political protest, for example, by the suffragettes. During the early 20th century, therapeutic fasting became a trend during the eighteen hundreds as a way of preventing or treating poor health carried out under a doctor's supervision. This type of fasting was adopted to treat many conditions from hypertension to headaches. Each face was tailored to the individual's needs. It could be just a day or up to three months, although fasting fell out of favor as new medications were developed. It has recently reemerged in 2019. Intermittent fasting was one of the most commonly searched terms. So what should you know about it? The most popular types of intermittent fasting.

There are plenty of different kinds of intermittent fasting. Each one has its own following and all follow the same principle of restricted food intake for a certain period of time. However, the length of time and the gap between eating windows varies. Perhaps the most popular I-F method is the 16 aid fast. This involves an eating window of eight hours, followed by 16 hours of fasting. Many people find this the most convenient option for them. If they skip breakfast or dinner, they can fit it easily into their lifestyle. Another popular I-F option is the 24 hour fast. This is sometimes known as the Eat, Stop Eat method. It involves eating normally one day and then avoiding food for the following 24 hours.

The gaps in between fast could be as short as 24 hours or up to 72 hours. The five to fasting method is also popular. This involves eating normally for five days of the week. The other two consecutive days, the dieters should restrict their calorie consumption to around 500 to 600 calories. Some dieters choose the 24 method. This involves concentrating, all eating each day into a four hour window. During the other 20 hours of the day, the dieters should eat no calories. There are several other types of fasting diets. Some people follow extended fasts of up to 48 or 36 hours, others fast for even more extended periods. If you're considering trying, if you need to choose the right method for you, why do people prefer intermittent fasting to other ways of dieting? Unlike other types of dieting.

If you allow dieters to eat pretty much what they want, they can eat the sugary or fatty foods they crave. They can go out to eat and not worry about calorie counting. They don't have to eat foods they don't enjoy. They don't have to feel as if they're depriving themselves of the things they love. It's easy to see why it's such a popular choice. Not only that, but intermittent fasting offers many more benefits than other types of diets. Yes, it promotes rapid weight loss. However, it also helps dieters to feel more focused and be more productive. It helps them to feel healthier and more energetic with the wellness benefits of this way of eating brains. It's no wonder people prefer it to regular diets.

The Many Benefits Of Intermittent Fasting

In this chapter, we'll talk about the benefits of intermittent fasting. There are several benefits that those who follow an intermittent fasting lifestyle report. Here we take a closer look at some of the most common weight loss. Many people who do intermittent fasting do so to lose weight rapidly. There is evidence to show that this way of eating helps you to shed the pounds more quickly. There are several reasons why I help weight loss. It enhances the function of the metabolism for faster fat burning. It also reduces the number of calories you consume in 24 hours. By lowering insulin levels, increasing growth hormone levels and increasing norepinephrine, IAFF speeds up the breakdown of fat. It also facilitates the use of fat to produce energy.

Fasting for short periods of time has been shown to increase metabolic rate by up to 14 percent. This means you'll burn more calories as a result. I can help cause weight loss of up to eight percent over a period of three to 24 weeks. That's an impressive loss for those who try and report a reduction of seven percent in the circumference of their waist. This indicates a loss of belly fat, the most harmful type of fat that results in disease. As an added bonus, I have caused reduced muscle loss when compared to calorie restriction diets, repairing cells. When you fast, your body cells begin a process of removing waste cells. This is known as autophagy.

Autophagy involves the body's cells being broken down. It also involves the portion of dysfunctional and broken proteins that have built up over time in the cells. What is the benefit of autophagy? Well, experts believe that it offers protection from the development of several diseases. These include Alzheimer's disease and cancer. Therefore, if you follow an intermittent fasting regime, you may help to protect yourself from diseases. As a result, you may live a longer and healthier life. Insulin sensitivity. More people than ever before have Type two diabetes.

The disease is becoming more common due to increasing obesity. The primary feature of diabetes is increased levels of sugar in the blood due to insulin resistance. If you can reduce insulin, your blood sugar levels should decrease. This will offer excellent protection from developing Type two diabetes. Intermittent fasting has been proven to have a major benefit when it comes to insulin resistance. It can reduce blood sugar levels by an impressive amount in studies into intermittent fasting with human participants, blood sugar levels decreased by up to six percent while fasting. As a result, fasting insulin levels can be reduced by as much as 31 percent. This shows that I could offer the benefit of reducing the chance of developing diabetes. Another piece of research carried out amongst diabetic lab rats showed I have protected against damage to the kidneys.

This is a severe complication associated with diabetes. So again, it suggests that intermittent fasting is also a great option for anyone who already has diabetes enhanced brain function. When something is good for your body, it's often good for your brain, too. Intermittent fasting is known to improve several metabolic features. These are vital for good brain health. Intermittent fasting has been shown to reduce oxidative stress. It also reduces inflammation and reduces the level of sugar in the blood. Not only that, it reduces insulin resistance. As we showed earlier, these are all key factors in enhancing brain function.

Studies that have taken place with lab rats have also shown that I can help boost new nerve cell growth. This, too, offers benefits when it comes to brain function. Meanwhile, it also increases the level of BDNF brain derived neurotrophic factor. This is a brain hormone and if you are deficient in it, you may suffer from brain problems and depression. When you try intermittent fasting, you will have better protection from these problems. As an added advantage, studies in animals have shown that I can protect against damage to the brain from strokes. All of this suggests that intermittent fasting offers many brain health benefits, decreased inflammation.

It is known that oxidative stress is a key factor in chronic diseases as well as aging. Oxidative stress involves free radicals, which are unstable molecules reacting with other key molecules such as DNA and protein. The result is damage to those molecules that causes harm in the body. There have been several studies to prove that I can help improve your body's ability to resist oxidative stress. Other studies have also shown it can help to combat inflammation, which also drives many common diseases.

How Intermittent Fasting Really Helps Weight Loss

In this chapter, we'll learn about why intermittent fasting helps to promote weight loss, although intermittent fasting offers many benefits, the greatest one is weight loss. Most people who embark on this lifestyle are hoping to shed pounds and maintain a healthy body weight. So why does intermittent fasting help to promote weight loss? Here we look at the three main reasons for reduced calorie intake. The main reason that I have helped to boost weight loss is because you naturally eat less. When you only have a short eating window, you have less time to eat. Usually you'll miss at least one meal per day in order to accommodate this schedule.

As a result, you'll consume fewer calories within each 24 hour period. As you know, you must maintain a calorie deficit to shed weight. Therefore, it helps you to reach your weight loss goals effectively. It's important to note, though, that some people fail to lose weight when they fast intermittently. This is because they don't reduce their calorie intake during their eating window. They continue to eat as much as they would have if they have been eating normally. Therefore, they don't have the necessary calorie deficit to shed the pounds. As long as you don't eat excessively during your eating window, you'll automatically reduce your calorie intake. Hormonal changes boost metabolism. The human body stores energy in the form of calories in body fat.

If you don't eat, your body changes a number of things so that stored energy can be more accessible. These changes involve the activity of your nervous system. They also include major changes in a number of key hormones. These changes occur in the metabolism. When you're fasting, insulin increases every time you eat. If you fast, your insulin level will dramatically decrease. A lower insulin level facilitates fat burning HGH. Human growth hormone skyrockets. When you fast, it can increase by as much as five times its normal level growth hormone. Ade's muscle gain and fat loss noradrenalin. Norepinephrine is set by the nervous system to your fat cells.

This causes them to break down your body fat. It is turned into free fatty acids. These are then burned to produce energy. Many people believe that if you fast, your metabolism slows down. However, evidence shows that fasting in the short term may boost fat burning. There have been two studies that have shown fasting for 48 hours increases metabolism up to 14 percent, reduces insulin levels, and speeds fat burning. You probably already know about insulin because of its importance for diabetics. People who have diabetes have to take insulin to maintain normal function. However, many people are unsure of what insulin does in the body or even what it is.

Insulin is a hormone that is made by your pancreas. Its job is to convert sugar glucose in the blood into energy. The cells then use that energy as fuel. Insulin also has another role to play in the body. It drives the storage of fat. The level of insulin in your body will increase whenever you eat. It also decreases whenever you fast the lower level of insulin because when you fast can help to prevent excess storage of fat, it also helps the body to mobilize the fat that is already stored. As a result, it can boost your fat loss and help you lose weight more rapidly.

Is Intermittent Fasting Safe?

In this chapter we'll discuss whether intermittent fasting is safe. You may be keen to embark on an intermittent fasting lifestyle, but you might be concerned about safety. After all, not every diet is suitable for everyone. A key factor in safe and successful weight loss is getting sufficient nutrition. If you don't get enough minerals, vitamins and protein, you could become ill with too few calories and too restrictive an eating pattern. You may be unable to get enough nutrients. This may cause you to have medical issues. The good news is that intermittent fasting appears to be a safe way of eating for most people. However, there are a few cases in which intermittent fasting should be avoided.

Who should avoid intermittent fasting? There are a few groups of people who should take care when they do intermittent fasting. Although they may not need to avoid this lifestyle completely, they will need to show caution. The first is children. Children are growing and developing. They therefore need to eat enough calories every day. They also need to get enough nutrients in the form of minerals and vitamins. Without enough protein, they cannot grow properly. This could lead to a host of problems. Illnesses like scurvy can be caused due to lack of vitamins, although some experts suggest that children can fast safely. It's something that should be approached with caution.

Diabetics should also take care when they do intermittent fasting. It's true to say that if it has a number of potential benefits for diabetics, this is because of the effect on insulin and blood sugar levels. However, there are some possible dangers. If you fast and have diabetes, your blood sugar level could drop dangerously low. This is especially likely if you're taking medication to control the condition. When you don't eat, your blood sugar level will be lower. Your medication could then drop it even further, leading to hypoglycemia. This can make you pass out, feel shaky or go into a coma. Another problem is that your blood sugar level may get too high when you eat. This could happen if you consume too many carbohydrates.

If you're diabetic, always talk to a health professional before embarking on if you will also need to be more aware of the symptoms of low blood sugar. As long as you're cautious about what you eat and avoid heart exercise, you may be fine. The third and fourth groups who may wish to avoid IVF are pregnant and breastfeeding. Women doctors usually recommend that these groups don't try intermittent fasting. This is because nutrition is absolutely vital at these stages in a woman's life. Not only is she feeding herself, she's feeding her baby. Therefore, she needs to consume sufficient calories and nutrients to support two people. This can be difficult when fasting intermittently. It should therefore only be attempted under medical supervision.

Could intermittent fasting trigger an eating disorder? For most people, intermittent fasting is a successful way of eating that causes no problems. However, there are some people who won't thrive on this lifestyle. Some people have a natural tendency to develop disordered eating behaviors. These people may need to avoid intermittent fasting if it triggers an eating disorder. It's therefore vital to recognize if intermittent fasting has strayed into patterns of disordered eating. There are several symptoms to look for. You have anxiety about eating and food. You're feeling extremely fatigued. You're experiencing mood swings, menstrual changes and problems sleeping.

For those who have a genetic predisposition to disordered eating patterns, intermittent fasting can be dangerous. This is because there's a focus on not eating. Most diets focus on lowering your calorie intake by eating low calorie foods. IAFF minimizes your calorie intake by avoiding eating during certain periods. This can lead you to ignore the hunger signals of your body. Also, for someone with a tendency to develop eating disorders, you may become afraid of food due to. If this is because you may start to associate avoiding food with losing weight. Your brain may begin to reward you for not eating and develop a fear of mealtimes.

Some people find that dieting causes them to bingy. When they're in their eating window, they end up overindulging on high calorie foods. This mimics eating disorder behaviors. It's therefore important to be highly aware of any possible signs that your fasting is turning into an eating disorder. What are the side effects of intermittent fasting? Intermittent fasting offers many benefits, but it has side effects that may affect each individual differently. Some of the effects you might experience include feeling grumpy, irritable and grouchy due to hunger, experiencing brain fog or excessive fatigue, obsessing about how much you can eat or what you can eat.

Persistent dizziness, headaches or nausea due to low blood sugar, hair loss due to a lack of nutrients, menstrual cycle changes due to rapid weight loss, constipation due to a lack of fiber, protein, vitamins or fluid. The potential for developing an eating disorder, sleep disturbances. Most people won't experience these side effects to any serious extent. They will also usually disappear after a while. However, for some people, these problems are severe or long lasting. If so? You may want to stop intermittent fasting until you seek medical advice, can athletes try intermittent fasting? Some athletes swear by intermittent fasting as a way to improve their athletic performance. However, there's mixed research on the subject.

Some evidence suggests that if you don't consume enough carbohydrates, the duration and intensity of your training will suffer. Meanwhile, other research suggests that if it offers benefits for athletes, some of the potential benefits include growth hormone increases due to IAFF. This helps to boost muscle, cartilage and bone growth. It also improves your immune function, all good for athletes. It improves your metabolic flexibility so you can adapt more easily between energy sources. Your body will be better able to use carbs or fat as a source of fuel. It will also allow you to burn fat for much longer before your body switches to carbs.

As a result, your insulin will stay low and your post exercise recovery will improve. IAFF reduces inflammation. This aids your post exercise recovery. When you exercise, you incur a large amount of information that you must recover from. However, the faster that inflammation subsides, the better I can speed the process up. There are a few concerns, though. These include it could cause a testosterone drop that is problematic because it impacts on muscle protein synthesis. You may find it difficult to eat sufficient calories to allow you to gain muscle. Is it safe for women to fast? Many experts say that it's perfectly safe for women to fast. However, there is evidence that women have a greater sensitivity to starvation signals.

When the body senses starvation, it increases production of ghrelin and leptin. The hunger hormones. This causes a negative energy balance and often wild mood swings. As a result, women are also prone to other hormonal imbalances. If they do, if this can cause menstrual cycle difficulties, it may also interfere with the production of thyroid hormone. This could be problematic for anyone suffering from autoimmune conditions. That doesn't mean, though, that women can't try intermittent fasting. It only means that they need to take more care. It may be better for women to begin with a gentler form of IVF rather than a long fast. A 12 to 14 hour fast may be the best option. Some women thrive on intermittent fasting, while others find it doesn't suit them at all. It's worth experimenting to see if it works for you.

A Protocol For Intermittent Fasting

In this chapter, we'll talk about a protocol for six eight intermittent fasting. If you're keen to try intermittent fasting, you may want to start with six or eight fasting. This method involves fasting for 16 hours and then having an eating window of eight hours. It is one of the most popular forms of this way of eating if you're ready to get started. Here is the protocol for six eight if choosing an eating window when you're ready to begin six eight fasting. The first thing to do is to choose an eating window. This eight hour period can be at any time in the day. Therefore, you can choose the right time to suit your preferences and lifestyle.

When you have chosen your preferred eight hours, you must limit your consumption of food to those hours. How do you choose the right hours for you? Lots of people like an eating window from noon to 8:00 p.m. This is because they can fast overnight, skip breakfast and then enjoy lunch and dinner at the usual times. They can even add a couple of healthy snacks into their regime. For people who would prefer to have three meals a day, a nine a.m. to five p.m. eating window may be best. This allows for breakfast at nine a.m., lunch at noon, then an early dinner at four p.m. Others prefer to wait until early afternoon to break their fasts, then to have their last meal later before bed.

Whichever eating window you choose, make sure it's one that fits with your lifestyle patterns. If you choose wrongly, you won't be able to stick to your diet. Planning healthy foods to maximize the benefits of the 16 day diet, you should eat healthy foods as much as possible. If you fill up on foods that are rich in nutrients, you won't be hungry or crave unhealthy foods. This will help you to stick to your new way of eating in the long term. While you can enjoy some snacks and trees, you should balance every meal with a variety of whole foods. Some of the best include fruits like bananas, apples, oranges, pears, peaches and berries. Vegetables like tomatoes, leafy greens, cucumbers, cauliflower and broccoli.

Whole grains like oats, rice, quinoa, buckwheat and barley, healthy fats like coconut oil, avocados and olive oil. Lean protein like poultry, fish seeds, nuts, eggs and legumes. If you binge on junk food, you could end up negating the benefits of this diet. Therefore, you should still keep unhealthy choices to a minimum. Choosing calorie free beverages, you can drink any of your preferred beverages during your eating window, at least within reason. If you drink several family sized bottles of full fat soda, you probably won't lose weight in your fasting window. You need to only consume calorie free beverages.

If you consume any beverage containing calories, you are essentially breaking your fast. This boils your entire eating regime. Water, green tea, unsweetened coffee and tea without milk are all good choices. They will also help you to control your appetite and keep you hydrated until you break your fast. A weekly timetable, your weekly six eight eating timetable will vary depending on which eating window you choose. Here are three samples to suit different schedules.

Early eating meal plan A.T.M Breakfast Monday through Sunday, 10:00 a.m. snack Monday through Sunday, 12:00 noon. Lunch Monday through Sunday evening. Calorie free beverages Monday through Sunday.

Average eating meal plan at nine a.m. Calorie Free Beverage Monday through Sunday, 11:00 a.m. Breakfast Monday through Sunday, two p.m. lunch Monday through Sunday, four p.m. Snack Monday through Sunday, six p.m. dinner Monday through Sunday. Late Eating Meal Plan 11:00 a.m. Calorie Free Beverage Monday through Sunday, 1:00 p.m. Snack Monday through Sunday, four p.m. lunch Monday through Sunday, six p.m. Snack Monday through Sunday. Nine p.m. dinner Monday through Sunday.

Intermittent Fasting 24 Hour Protocol

In this chapter, we'll talk about a protocol for 24 hour intermittent fasting. If the six day diet isn't right for you, you may want to consider 24 hour fasting. This is known as the eat, stop eat method. It involves one or two non-consecutive days of fasting every week. Introduction to the Eat, Stop Eat method. This method was devised by Brad Palone, who wrote a book about this way of eating. His methodology was based on Canadian research into the effect of short term fasting on metabolic health. The idea behind Pillans method is to re-evaluate all you've learned about timing of meals and meal frequency. This diet is quite easy to implement.

You simply choose one day or two consecutive days of the week in which you won't eat for 24 hours. You can eat normally on the other five or six days. It's advisable, though, to eat healthily for the best results. Although it sounds counterintuitive, you'll still be eating on every calendar day with this fast. How does this work? Imagine you decide to fast from 9:00 a.m. on Monday until nine a.m. on Tuesday. You eat your last meal on Monday morning before nine a.m. You can then eat your next meal on Tuesday morning after nine a.m. during your fasting hours, you should stay well hydrated, drink lots of water and other beverages with no calories, like unsweetened milk free tea or coffee, choosing your fasting days.

If you want to try the stop eating method, you'll need to choose the right fasting days for you. This will be down to individual choice. First, you'll need to choose whether to fast for one day or two. You'll probably find it easier to start out with one fasting day per week. When you're used to it, you can increase it to two days weekly. Don't exceed that number of days, though. Some people find it easier to fast at the weekend because they don't have to focus on work. Others would prefer to fast on workdays so they have distractions to stop them from thinking about food, you will need to determine your own preferences. Remember, though, if you choose to do two days of fasting, they cannot be consecutive. This would be too long an extended period of fasting. You may wish to space your two fast days out fairly evenly.

Alternatively, you may wish to space them just a day apart, then enjoy eating the rest of the week. You may need to experiment to find the right pattern for you. A weekly timetable. These are some sample timetables to help you plan your 24 hour fast one day fast meal plan Tuesday at nine a.m. to Wednesday at 9am to day fast meal plan. Tuesday at 9am to Wednesday would be your fast and Thursday at 9am to Friday at 9am would be your other fast. You may prefer to begin your fast period at an earlier or later hour of the day. We have suggested nine AM to nine AM on the next day. However, you may prefer seven a.m. to seven a.m. or even 12:00 noon to 12:00 noon. You need to choose the right time for you as well as the right days.

Other Types Of Intermittent Fasting

In this chapter, we'll discover other types of intermittent fasting, although 24 hour and 16 eight intermittent fasting are the two most popular types, there are several others here. We'll take a closer look at five other kinds of fasting regimes that several people follow. 24 fasting 24. Fasting is sometimes called the warrior diet. It is one of the earliest diets to involve intermittent fasting made popular by Orrie Hoff Mackler, a fitness expert. This diet involves eating one large meal in the evening. This large meal takes place in a four hour eating window. During the other 20 hours of the day, only small amounts of raw vegetables and fruits can be eaten.

The food choices for this diet should be healthy, similar to those on the paleo diet. They should be unprocessed whole foods that contain no artificial ingredients. A timetable for this diet looks like this midnight to 4:00 p.m. small amounts of fruits and vegetables Monday through Sunday, four p.m. to eight p.m. large meal Monday through Sunday, 8pm to midnight fast Monday through Sunday five to fasting. This popular form of intermittent fasting involves eating normally for five days every week. There may be two days. Calories should be restricted to five to six hundred. Sometimes called the fast diet.

This way of eating was made popular by Michael Mosley, a journalist. Women are recommended to eat 500 calories on their fasting days. Men can have 600 calories on their fast days. You can choose which two days you prefer to fast. However, it's best if they aren't consecutive. On those days, you can choose to eat one meal or two small meals. Many people prefer to eat two meals of 250 to 300 calories each. This is a sample timetable for this way of eating. Tuesday and Friday eat 500 to 600 calories, 36 hour fasting. The 36 hour fast plan means you'll be fasting for a full day. Unlike the eat stop method, you won't be eating something every calendar day.

If, for example, you finish dinner at seven p.m. on day one, you skip all your meals. On day two, you won't eat your next meal until day three. It's seven a.m. This equals a thirty six hour fast. There is some evidence to suggest that this kind of fasting period can produce a quicker result. It may also be beneficial for diabetics. It may also be more problematic, though, since you'll be going for extended periods without food. A timetable for this eating plan looks like this Tuesday from midnight all the way to Wednesday, seven a.m. fast alternate day fasting. This way of fasting means that you fast for a full 24 hours every alternate day.

Some versions of this I-F diet allow you to eat up to 500 calories on your fast day. Others only allow you to have calorie free beverages. This isn't the best option for any newcomers to intermittent fasting. You go to bed feeling hungry several nights each week. This is hard to maintain in the long term. A timetable for this way of eating looks like this Tuesday, Thursday and Saturday, midnight to midnight, fast extended fast. Following the six eight or eat, stop eat method is quite simple. Some people, though, are keen to push the benefits of intermittent fasting to the limit. They prefer to do a forty two hour fast. This involves eating dinner on day one at six p.m.

all meals would be skipped on the next day. On day three, you would then eat your breakfast at noon. This would be a total fasting time of forty two hours. If you try this way of eating, you shouldn't restrict your calorie intake during your eating window. It's technically possible to extend fast for longer periods of time. In fact, the world record stands at 382 days. Of course, that isn't recommended. Some people do try seven to 14 day fasts due to the theoretical benefits they're said to provide. Some people say that a seven day fast can help prevent cancer. Others say that longer, fast promotes mental clarity. These benefits are unproven and are theoretical. It's probably best, therefore, to stick to one of the tried and tested. I have plans outlined earlier.

Maximize Your Intermittent Fasting Results

In this chapter, we'll talk about how to maximize your intermittent fasting results. Are you ready to try intermittent fasting? Whether you're doing it for weight loss or for the other benefits, you will probably want to maximize your results. Luckily, there are a few things you can do to get as much benefit as possible from your eating regime. Here we take a look at some things you can try to speed your weight loss, exercise and intermittent fasting. There is some research to show that if you exercise while fasting, there are additional benefits. There is an impact on your metabolism and muscle biochemistry. This is linked to your insulin sensitivity and blood sugar level.

If you exercise while fasting, your glycogen or stored carbs are depleted. This means you'll burn more fat to get the best result, and eat protein. Following your workout. This will build and maintain your muscles. It will also promote better recovery. You should also follow up strength training with carbs. Within a half hour of your workout, it's wise to eat food close to any modern or high intensity exercise chapter. You should also drink a lot more water to stay well hydrated. Keeping up your electrolyte level is important. Coconut water can be useful for this. You may feel a little lightheaded or dizzy if you workout while fasting. If you experience this, take a break.

It's important to listen to your body. If you're doing a longer fast, you may find gentle exercise like Pilates, yoga or walking or better. They will help to burn fat without making you feel unwell. Choosing the right regime for you to maximize the results of your intermittent fasting. You'll need to choose the right regime. As you've seen, there are several different types of intermittent fasting diets. Not all are suitable for everyone. You need to find one that works well for your lifestyle and that makes your life easier. When you choose the right regime, you'll stick to it in the long term. So here's some questions to ask yourself to help you choose wisely. Are you already eating healthily? Fasting is harder if you're currently eating a standard American diet.

This is because it is high in carbs, full of sugars and very addictive. If you jump straight into extreme fasting, you'll experience symptoms of withdrawal from sugar. This makes it hard to stick to your new diet. If you usually eat processed foods regularly, try beginning with a short fasting window. Meanwhile, detox from sugar and begin to eat more cleanly. Stop snacking and introduce Whole Foods into your diet. You can then increase the fasting window if necessary. On the other hand, if you already eat healthily, you can start with a longer, fast window. Can you manage to go for long periods without eating? Some people are able to manage fasting for a whole day.

Others can only manage a few hours. You may need to experiment, focus on the way fasting makes you feel. If you struggle too fast for long periods, choose a method like the five to or six eight. If you find it easy, you may be able to opt for a 36 hour fast straightaway. How does your schedule look? It's easier to fast if you're busy and distracted from thinking about food. If you fast at work or while you're working on something, you'll probably feel less hungry. If you work out, you may want to end your fasting window straight after exercising. If you answer these questions, you'll be best placed to choose the right regime to suit your life and preferences. This will give you the best chance of success.

Adding in Quito, some experts say that if you combine intermittent fasting with the keto diet, you'll lose more weight. So what does this involve? The ketogenic diet is a specific way of eating in which most calories come from healthy fats. The remaining calories are derived from protein. Very few, if any, carbohydrates are consumed on this diet. This low carb, high fat diet encourages your body to burn fat, not sugars to produce energy. If your body lacks sufficient carbs to carry out everyday activities, fat is broken down by the liver. It produces ketones and then they are used as fuel for energy.

The process is known as ketosis, hence the name Kaido. Like intermittent fasting, keto diets have a number of benefits. They can boost weight loss, reduce your blood sugar level and improve your brain function. Many people say it helps to reduce problems like diabetes and obesity. If you combine keto diet with half the amount of time you're in ketosis increases, this could make you feel more energetic, less hungry and speed your weight loss.

How To Get Started With Intermittent Fasting

In this chapter, we'll discover how to get started with intermittent fasting if you're convinced of the benefits of intermittent fasting. You'll need to know how to get started. After all, embarking on any new regime can be complicated. So how can you get yourself off to the best possible start? Here are some top tips. Starting with a less rigorous regime, it may be tempting to try to lose as much weight as possible by starting out with a long, fast. However, bear in mind this may not be the best approach. As we've already mentioned, it can't be difficult to fast for extended periods if you've never done it before. If you're used to a high carb, high sugar processed foods diet, you'll struggle to fast for 36 hours straight off.

If you find your first fast, impossibly hard, you'll probably put off the whole idea. Even if you are, the likelihood of sticking to it for any length of time is low. It's recommended to try any intermittent fasting plan for at least a month. This will give you enough time to see whether it's working for you or not. It will be very difficult for someone inexperienced to stick to an extended fast regime in the long term. It's therefore best to opt for one of the less rigorous regimes to start with. The five two diet allows you to eat some food every day. In fact, you can eat your regular meals on five days of the week. The other two, you still get 500 or 600 calories to play with.

This should give you plenty of options. As long as you make healthy choices, choose your meals wisely and you'll experience the benefits without ever feeling hungry. Alternatively, try the popular six eight method for a large proportion of your fasting time. You'll be asleep. You'll then be free to eat whatever you like within reason during your eight hour eating window. Many people like the freedom that this offers. When they get used to the 16 hour fast, they find this way of eating quite simple. If you want to work longer, faster. Once you're used to fasting, you can. However, many people continue to follow their initial plan in the long term and experience good results.

Staying hydrated. Whatever type of intermittent fasting plan you try, you need to stay well hydrated. Fasting is only referring to food and calorie containing beverages. It doesn't mean you can't have water and other calorie free drinks. In fact, you should drink more of them. Staying hydrated will ensure that toxins can be flushed effectively from your body. This will help to promote your weight loss and wellness goals. It will also help you to stay healthy in other ways. Your skin will be healthier, your bowel habits will be more regular. You'll also avoid headaches and other problems associated with dehydration.

Drinking calorie free beverages during your fasting window can also help to prevent you from feeling hungry. Often we think we're hungry, but we're actually thirsty instead. If you drink a glass of water when you're beginning to feel hungry, you'll continue fasting for longer. Try experimenting with different eating patterns. We have suggested some eating plan timetable earlier. However, that doesn't mean you need to stick to them. The days and times that we have suggested are just examples. They may not work for you. You need to choose the right days and eating patterns to fit your lifestyle, preferences and needs. Perhaps you prefer to begin eating as soon as you get up and then have your last meal early. Or maybe breaking your fast in the early afternoon and having a last meal just before bed is best.

You may prefer to fast at the weekend, so you don't need to worry about feeling tired at work or fasting on a weekday may be right for you. So you have distractions. There is no single perfect I-F plan for everyone. That means you may need to do a little experimentation. Weigh up the pros and cons of all the regimes that we've suggested. Think about which one you've been drawn to and give it a try. It's best to try to give it a month to see how well it works for you. If you're having problems, it's time to go back to the drawing board, try a different intermittent fasting regime to see if that better suits your lifestyle or move your eating windows around a little to see if it becomes more manageable. Don't be afraid to experiment. After all, experimentation could be the key to success.

Common Questions About Intermittent Fasting

In this chapter, we'll talk about addressing common questions when you're keen to start intermittent fasting, you want all the information you need at your fingertips. Although we've addressed all the key points in the first nine chapters, there are a few more questions to answer here. We address some of the most common questions about intermittent fasting. Hopefully the answers will help you to make a final decision about whether I could be right for you. It should help you to get started with your new lifestyle, exercise and fasting. Many people wonder whether they can carry on exercising if they're fasting. In most cases, intermittent fasting won't stop you from working out in the long run. It may take a little time, though, to adjust to your new regime.

Some people who follow this lifestyle even find they're more energetic while fasting. Some people worry that they'll lose muscle if they fast. This is something that is a danger with any diet. However, you can avoid this happening. If you eat plenty of protein in your eating window and do regular resistance training, you should be fine. It's advisable to exercise at the end of your fasting period. Usually you'll feel hungry around 30 minutes after finishing your workout. If you break your fast at that time, you'll feel satisfied. What should you eat during your eating window? When you fall and I have a lifestyle, there are no restrictions about what you can eat in your eating window. This is why it's so different from other ways of dieting.

You aren't restricted to amount's or specific food types. However, it's wise to remember that you should still make healthy choices. If you overindulge regularly, you won't see the benefits of AAF. The best solution is to eat a balanced diet in your eating window. This will help you to maintain your energy level while still losing weight. Foods that are dense in nutrients like seeds, beans, nuts, whole grains, vegetables and fruits are good choices. You should also consume plenty of lean protein. There are certain foods that are especially beneficial if you follow this way of eating avocados. Yes, they're high in calories.

However, they're packed with mono unsaturated fats. This makes them very satiating. If you add a half avocado to your meal, you'll feel much fuller fish. You should try to eat a minimum of eight ounces of fish every week. Fish is packed with protein, healthy fats and vitamin D. It's also good for your brain health. Cruciferous vegetables, foods such as cauliflower, brussel sprouts and broccoli are good choices. They're packed with fiber to help you avoid constipation and feel more for potatoes. Many people worry that potatoes are bad for you. However, they're very satisfying and we'll keep you full for longer legumes and beans.

Although these are carbs, they're low calorie, and give you lots of energy. They're also packed with protein and fiber. Probiotics eating foods rich in probiotics like sauerkraut, kefir and kombucha helps keep your gut happy. This will help you to avoid stomach issues when you're adjusting to this diet. Berries, strawberries, blueberries and others are packed with nutrients like vitamin C. They're also rich in flavonoids, something that is known to boost weight loss eggs. Every egg has a massive six grams of protein, simple and quick to cook. Eggs make you feel full nuts. Yes, nuts are high in calories. However, they're packed with polyunsaturated fat.

That helps you feel for whole grains. Yes, whole grains are also carbs. However, they're full of protein and fiber. You don't need too much to feel full for longer. A study has even shown that eating whole grains can boost your metabolism. What can you have in your fasting period? So you know what you can eat in your eating window? What can you have in your fasting period? The answer depends on which fast you're doing. If you're doing the five two diet, you can eat up to 500 or 600 calories on your fast days. Obviously, that's quite restrictive. So you can maximize the amount you can eat by including lots of low calorie, high nutrient foods. Vegetables and fruits are staples of your fast days.

If you're doing any of the other fasting methods, you can't eat any solid foods at all. You also can't have any drinks that contain calories. Luckily, though, there are lots of beverages you can have to stay hydrated. It's obvious that you should have lots of water and your fasting window sparkling and still water are both fine. If you wish, you can add a squeeze of lime or lemon for a little more flavor. You could also add more flavor with some orange or cucumber slices. You can't add any artificially sweetened enhancers, though. These could damage your fast. Another good beverage for your fast period is black coffee. It contains no calories and won't affect your insulin levels.

You can have decaffeinated or regular coffee, but don't add milk or sweeteners. If you want more flavor, try adding cinnamon or other spices. Some people say that black coffee could enhance I-F benefits. Caffeine may support the production of ketones. It can also help to support a healthy level of blood sugars in the long run. A note of. Warning, though, some people find that if they drink coffee during their fast, they get an upset stomach or racing heart, you may need to take care to monitor how you feel. If you drink black coffee, if you're fasting for 24 hours or longer, try a vegetable or bone broth.

Don't use bouillon cubes or can broth, though it's full of artificial preservatives and flavors that will damage your fast. Make it at home for the best results. T can also help you feel full. You can drink any type of tea in your fasting window. Oolong, black, green and herbal tea are all fine. Tea also helps to improve your fasting by supporting cellular and gut health as well as probiotic balance. Green tea is especially good for managing weight and helping you feel full. Apple cider vinegar offers many health benefits. You can add this to the list of things you can have during your fasting period. It will support your blood sugar level and digestion. It could even boost the results of your fasting.

There are, however, some drinks that you need to avoid while you're fasting. You may not realize that zero calorie sodas can break your fast. While diet sodas technically have no calories, they've been shown to inhibit fastenings' positive effects. This is because they get their sweet flavor from aspartame or other artificial sweeteners. These trigger your insulin response. You should therefore avoid drinking them in your fast window. Many people ask whether they can have coconut water or almond milk in their fast period. While both of these are healthy options and benefits for your wellness, they contain lots of sugar.

Since sugar is a carbohydrate, you'll no longer be fasting if you consume it. You shouldn't drink these beverages during your fasting period. One very common question is whether it's possible to drink alcohol. If you're doing and I diet, it's important to limit your consumption of alcohol to your eating window. This is because most alcoholic drinks contain a lot of calories and sugar. Therefore, drinking them will break your fast. Also, alcohol will have more effect on you if you have an empty stomach. Even a single glass of wine may make you feel unwell. Can children try intermittent fasting? There is no specific evidence to say whether it's safe for children to try intermittent fasting or not. Some experts say that it's perfectly fine, especially for those who are already overweight. Others say it's a bad idea.

Since children are going through a period of rapid growth, they need sufficient calories to support their development and growth. Children need to eat enough protein, vitamins and minerals. If they don't get enough, they could become ill. It's probably wise to speak to a doctor before putting a child on an IV diet. Is fasting unhealthy? It's only natural for people to ask whether fasting is unhealthy. Those who extol the virtues of more traditional diets say that fasting could slow your metabolism. This could cause you to put on weight, not lose it. Therefore, they say, fasting is unhealthy. However, this isn't the case at all.

People have been fasting for centuries with no ill effects. Studies carried out on people during Ramadan have shown that extended fasting caused no health issues for most people. There are few issues to bear in mind, though. Fasting isn't for everyone. Some people find it difficult to fit into their lives. They struggle to sustain this lifestyle for extended periods. They may find it difficult to fit in socializing, work and exercise around fasting windows. This can lead to an inconsistent eating schedule that may have unhealthy consequences. There are a few other issues to consider to some people who try to begin to lose touch with the signals that tell them that they're full and hungry.

This can make it hard to stick to IAFF in the long run without developing an eating disorder. Some people who are prone to eating disorders become obsessed with food and eating some beans during their eating window. Others push their fasting further and further and become fixated with not eating. It's therefore important to approach I-F with caution if you have a history of disordered eating. On the whole, though, IAFF isn't just not unhealthy. It can be positively good for you. It can help you to effectively manage your weight and avoid obesity. It can improve your metabolism and your insulin resistance. It can also decrease your inflammation and boost your cell repair, as well as support a healthier gastrointestinal tract.

Thoughts & Ideas

Now, you know, the benefits and possible problems associated with intermittent fasting, if you're ready to try it yourself. This chapter, Of course, should tell you everything you need to know to get started, identify why you want to try intermittent fasting. You may want to lose weight or improve your health. You may just want to see if it makes you feel more focused and energetic. If you know which benefits you'd like to see, you'll be in a better position for success. You'll also be able to prioritize the strategy and foods that will be best for your goals. As you've seen in this chapter, Of course, there are several different plans to choose from. You'll need to consider which one is right for you. You may prefer.

A daily approach was something like the six day diet. Alternatively, a weekly plan like alternate day fasting or five two may suit you best. You'll need to consider your schedule and your personal preferences. Think about the times you get up and go to bed. When do you tend to get hungry? How busy are you during your day? Do you work out? The answers to these questions will help you choose your eating window. If intermittent fasting is going to be successful for you, it needs to work effectively around your lifestyle. You need to be sure that you can keep your diet in the long term. You'll only be able to do that if it fits in with your needs.

Remember that intermittent fasting should make your life easier, not harder. If it's too difficult to follow, you'll give up too quickly. You should try to follow the diet for a minimum of a month to see if it's working for you. When you get intermittent fasting right, you should reap the benefits quickly. Not only should you lose weight, you should feel more energetic and healthy. You'll feel more focus and experience a wealth of health and wellness benefits from a reduced chance of developing diabetes to a potentially longer lifespan. The advantages are numerous. So what are you waiting for? It's time to give intermittent fasting a try for yourself. You're sure to experience the benefits.

Yoga Is Something Different

Yoga is something different to most people, it's quite diverse and practitioners have different expectations when they start. It's perfectly OK whether your goal is greater enlightenment, a more toned and muscular body or relief from disease. There's yoga for you. This chapter will serve as a guide. The philosophy of yoga has been around for 5000 years. That's staying power. And it's a philosophy, a way of thinking rather than a religion. In ancient India, the word yoga means union. It refers to a union of the entire self, mind, body and spirit. The union is achieved through physical poses, frequently called asanas.

Although Asana is not one of the many types of yoga, these poses are meant to heighten awareness of mind and body, which makes yoga a natural corollary to meditation. Today's researchers are discovering the many benefits of yoga. While it can increase spirituality, it also has the ability to heal many ailments and diseases, especially stress, immune system disorders and heart problems. It also provides increased flexibility, which can reverse the aging process. The more vigorous yoga practices are considered cardiovascular exercises. Along with a proper diet, you'll be able to lose weight. The gentler types of yoga do not have cardiovascular benefits.

So remember to do additional exercises. Why are people becoming interested in yoga? The most common reason is to improve flexibility and physical health. Besides the physical benefits, yoga also boosts mental power and paves the way to spiritual enlightenment. For most, it's the spiritual awakening that turns yoga into an important part of their lives. This is a gradual but wonderful development, an opportunity for personal growth. The essence of yoga is always to become a better version of oneself.

Science Of Yoga & Health Benefits

In this chapter, we'll talk about the science of yoga and its health benefits. People have been practicing yoga for thousands of years. While the original purpose was to elevate to a greater spiritual level, it became clear that yoga benefits the person as a whole. Modern scientific research has shown tremendous overall health benefits of a yoga lifestyle. Yes, yoga does improve the body, but surprising scientific research has shown that it changes the brain as well. It's about becoming a better version of yourself and getting in touch with the real authentic you.

As the brain becomes more uncluttered, it keeps us focused on the present. While yoga begins on the mat, it extends to our entire day as greater compassion and awareness becomes a part of our life. Yoga won't provide untold riches, although the physical benefits are remarkable, the world is already filled with abundance, much of which we ignore. The real beauty of yoga is that it grounds us to the present, connecting us to the abundance that is within our grasp. A better, more fulfilled life is within our reach when we let go and simply accept what is there. Each yoga pose, which usually involves stretches, has its own purpose and benefit. The practitioner becomes aware of tension and learns to release it.

Yoga poses are very specific and perfection comes with practice. But it is not the ultimate goal. Yoga involves a lot of stretching, but more importantly, it creates balance by increasing flexibility and strength. Whatever type of yoga you practice, your body and mind simply improve. Yoga is extremely diverse and individual, which makes it important to work at your own level of comfort. Please don't use the person next to you in class as a guide or even the teacher to work the poses in the best way for you. This isn't a speed contest and you have nothing to prove. Yoga is a lifetime commitment, not a competition. Even if you're not used to exercising, you can practice yoga.

You may not be as flexible as the next person, but you'll get there. Yoga is always a work in progress and never a competition. While it is a physical practice, yoga will inevitably touch on your spiritual side. It unifies mind and body to become one. Research conducted throughout the 20th century has found a myriad of physical benefits to practicing yoga relief from stress. Our lives are filled with daily stressors, and we know that stress can cause tremendous damage to the body and mind. The boss wants to talk. Your spouse is upset. The mortgage is overdoing the kids. They want the keys to the car.

Just another typical day. Holding yoga poses, stretching muscles, being focused on the present and breathing deeply and slowly helps us achieve a state of greater relaxation and harmony. We are able to consciously choose our response to stress instead of being at its mercy. Remaining calm under difficult circumstances is a choice, and yoga can provide the tools. Yoga and pain relief studies have proven that practicing yoga can provide tremendous relief for people suffering from multiple sclerosis, arthritis and other chronic conditions. We'll discuss its amazing effect on the autoimmune system and cardiac system at greater length and other chapters.

Yoga and breathing. Yoga combines physical movements with breathing slower, deeper breathing can alleviate stress, yoga and flexibility. Yoga involves a lot of stretching, which strengthens muscles. Since yoga impacts the entire body, flexibility and elasticity happens from head to toe. It also loosens tight tense muscles and helps us remain more relaxed. Yoga and weight management. Yoga does not burn up as many calories as some other exercise regimes. However, it does increase your body awareness. People who practice yoga become more aware of what they eat and the effect such food has upon their health. This usually leads to better, healthier eating habits and a natural loss of unwanted weight, yoga and circulation.

If your blood isn't supplying your body and brain properly with oxygen, your health will suffer. You need proper circulation for the brain to function. Energy and the growth of cells. Sluggish circulation can cause nerve and tissue damage, blood clots, dizziness, among other problems. The thorough stretching in most yoga poses will improve circulation. The Campo's described in this chapter is an excellent way to improve circulation. Yoga and cardio health for patients who have experienced heart surgery, depression and anxiety can be a natural result. Yoga can be helpful in managing this type of post-operative stress.

It can also lower blood pressure, serving as a preventive heart healthy measure. The specific heart benefits will be discussed later on. There's no hurry. Take your time. These benefits will take time to achieve. Yoga is not a two week miracle program. So as you begin with, your yoga chapters allow sufficient time for the results to manifest themselves. You should see a huge difference in approximately two months. Whatever your reason for practicing yoga, you should notice an improvement in all aspects of your being.

Yoga History

In this chapter, we'll learn about yoga history. Yoga has become quite trendy these days as practitioners in their yoga pants and mat head toward the popular yoga studios to attend their weekly yoga chapter. Well, many of these fashionable yogis probably are unaware of the long history of yoga dating back to ancient times in India and its spiritual roots? Most of what we think of as yoga only dates back 150 years, while people today practice yoga for their health. Its roots are entwined in rich spiritualism that took a lifetime to master. For ancient yogis, yoga was a way of life. Mention of yoga first appeared around 1500 B.C. in Hindu literature, the first writings in the traditional Sanskrit.

The term yoga, which means Yok frequently refers to a dying warrior rising to heaven and reaching a higher power. The original concept of yoga was clearly to elevate those who deserved it to a higher level, to connect the individual to the universe as a whole. For ancient Buddhists, yoga wasn't even a specific discipline. It grew out of the desire to attain spiritual goals and controlling both the mind and the body. To achieve this. These spiritual leaders recognize that man is fallible but always capable of improvement.

By changing dysfunctional thinking, they recognized the power of the mind to bring about inner peace and alleviate suffering by broadening individual consciousness and becoming open to new ideas. They already understood the basics of the mind body connection. Yoga, including meditation, was and still is a quest for knowledge. Ancient practitioners thought correctly. As it turns out, that knowledge would lead to a higher level of consciousness and existence. Old writings describe several levels of being with increasing knowledge, bringing the practitioner to a next higher level. It was viewed as a process for which many encompassed a lifetime of learning yoga.

The physical part of gaining enlightenment was to prepare the way to meditation, which was spiritual in nature. The physical side of yoga began to emerge around five hundred A.D. by the third century. Yoga was an accepted Buddhist practice involving a spiritual quest through meditation. This is the classical period where the writings of Viarsa introduced the all important yoga sutras, which lists yoga as a precondition for a higher existence. For several centuries, the practice of yoga became an accepted practice to attain important personal values, although it was still far from today's set of poses.

More meditative, it was intended to help transcend human suffering and rise above it. It was also used to broaden or deepen consciousness as a path to personal enlightenment. Yoga was seen as a means to overcome destiny and regain control of the self. The beginning of training and controlling the mind is clearly emerging up to the 15th century, while the West was in a state of constant strife and war, Eastern Buddhism focused on peace of mind. The difference between a Western and Eastern mind is becoming more noticeable. By this time. The emphasis of yoga shifts from transcending pain to reaching a higher plane of existence.

Man himself is to become a deity by the 8th century. Hatha Yoga, a mix of poses and meditation, came into practice. It's the beginning of modern yoga as we know it today. Modern yoga, the old spiritual quest of Buddhism, didn't reach the West until the 19th century, this coincided with an interest in Indian culture as a whole due to the burgeoning spice trade. Western culture became intrigued by the writings of Swami Vivekananda, a monk who traveled to Europe and introduced the intelligentsia to Buddhist spiritual writings, especially the fourth century yoga sutras, which involved clearing the mind of unwanted thoughts and learning to focus on one thing.

Yoga, as we know today, became popular in the U.S. in the 1940s, when young Americans began to take yoga classes. By the 1980s, the known health benefits of yoga increased its popularity. Although the practice was seen as more physical than spiritual by the majority of the practitioners by the 21st century, the devotees of American yoga have increased from four million at the turn of the century to 20 million by 2011. This increase in popularity is mainly due to the increased scientific studies of the numerous benefits of yoga, especially the alleviation of stress. Whether spiritual or not, people want to increase their health. Many people, however, still seek both mental and physical elevation.

Yoga offers both. While mastering the physical aspects of yoga is important, it's equally crucial not to lose sight of the spiritual benefits. Yoga is more than posting adorable selfies on Instagram. Thousands of years ago, yoga was a preparation for the spiritual enlightenment of meditation. It was intended to prepare and relax the body from meditative practice. It's important not to lose sight of that to achieve your spiritual side. Keep in mind the seven spiritual laws of yoga. One, you have unlimited potential. The purpose of yoga is to reach a high level of consciousness so the universe is filled with abundance to receive.

Learn to give three. Understand the universal law of cause and effect known as karma. Your actions, whether positive or negative, will be returned in equal measure so that you don't resist life's forces. Your desires will manifest themselves when you least resist. Five Be clear on what your desires and intentions are. Six Stop struggling and remain open to all opportunities that come your way. Seven Know what your true purpose in life is. Meditation, which will be discussed in the final chapter, will help you achieve the spiritual laws of yoga.

Emotions & Mind-Body Connection

In this chapter, we'll learn about emotions and the mind-body connection. The purpose of yoga has always been to connect the mind to the body that the Buddhists had in mind thousands of years ago. Even then, it was clear that when the mind and body work is one, the self becomes healthier, more aware and is able to function at a higher level. But how exactly are the mind and body connected? People who are aware of their thoughts and feelings are better able to cope with stress and life's adversities. They form better and healthier relationships. Ultimately, they believe in their ability to succeed.

We all face setbacks. It's how we handle them that makes the difference. Emotional wellbeing is rarely a constant. However, unexpected events can lead to depression, anxiety, stress and confusion. Losing a job, physical injury, the death or injury of someone we love or the end of a relationship can cause emotional upheaval. Even good events such as a new home, marriage or new job can cause anxiety as we face the unknown. When our mind experiences turmoil, the body immediately responds as if you needed a reminder. The body is there to tell you that all is not well. The body does that in a number of ways, such as developing high blood pressure and ulcer, insomnia, etc.. The symptoms are all physical manifestations of an anxious mind.

Whether we realize it or not, the mind and body work as a team. So where does yoga come into play? As yoga increases our mental awareness, we become more aware of our underlying emotions and thoughts that allows us to express and acknowledge them, rather than keeping them buried and allowing them to fester appropriately. Expressing negative emotions allows us to deal with them and put them behind us. When we deal effectively with negativity, we're able to acknowledge the more positive aspects of our lives. Sometimes we can become so overwhelmed we no longer see anything good or positive, even if it's all around us. Yoga provides that necessary balance. Yes, work can be stressful, but we see that there's more to our lives than that.

This is a healthy outlook that boosts the overall quality of life when we need it. A healthy mind-body connection provides us with the ability to cope with adversity as we become more resilient. Resilience is a skill that can be learned and developed. It prevents us from being victims of circumstances and gives us greater control over our lives. We can strengthen our resilience to relaxation and develop a calmer outlook. Both yoga and meditation are invaluable tools for taking greater control over our thoughts, feelings and our life in general. When we're in control, we sleep better, eat healthier and connect with others on a higher level. Our emotional health invariably affects our immune system.

As we will see in another chapter, a weakened immune system can leave the body vulnerable to colds, inflammations and infections. The myriad of ways that the mind impacts the body became clearer during the 20th century, when repeated studies reveal how stress and emotions can become inevitably linked and connected. Thankfully, modern physicians are taking a more integrated approach to their patients' health. More are recommending yoga and meditation not only for stress but for cardiovascular diseases as well. Discuss the overall benefits of yoga with your doctor. Whatever the state of your mental and physical health, it can always be enhanced.

Yoga Strength & Flexibility

In this chapter will discover yoga, strength and flexibility, strength training, usually in the form of lifting weights or Crossfade has been gaining popularity. Women especially are appreciating a more toned, muscled and strong body. Increasing bodily strength is important to prevent osteoporosis and the natural loss of muscles. As we age, strong muscles help keep joints healthy and prevent injuries while the benefits of strength training are clear. Some people question whether practicing yoga counts towards increasing strength and muscles. This may be especially the case for athletic males who view yoga as a girly activity. Bucking yoga really builds strength and muscles.

It depends on the type of yoga you practice. Certain types of yoga are deliberately gentle. Restorative yoga falls into that category. This doesn't make them any less effective. It merely means more people, especially older ones, can enjoy yoga as a benefit. As we discussed, yoga is for everyone. However, there are yoga exercises that are demanding and challenging and would be difficult even for a strong male. Poses such as Plank's and Warrior require support of the entire body and will certainly develop muscles and strength.

These poses strengthen the entire body, not just specific muscles that will get a workout during weight lifting. These poses can be done with small hand weights for maximum results. Thus, yoga can be better at building strength than some other forms of exercises. Ashtanga and Vinyasa yoga can increase strength through greater repetition of poses, especially in the upper body, region and legs. In addition, holding poses for a longer period of time, such as up to two minutes proposed is a terrific muscle enhancer. Just keep in mind it takes time to build that type of stamina. But building muscles is an individual goal.

How much muscle is enough for maximum muscle? Building weights can certainly help bring about quicker results. Many people use both yoga and weightlifting for some dramatic bulking up. Unlike weight training, yoga isn't specifically geared toward the physique. It's much more than exercise. With weightlifting, you could build muscles indefinitely by simply adding additional weights. If you wish, you can build isolated muscles such as your thighs into the size of a tree trunk. With yoga, you build strength in a more balanced way, as all muscles, big and small, are built up. The emphasis is on strength rather than bulk.

Your body becomes more resilient and allows you to use that strength in all physical activities, such as lifting, twisting and bending. Instead of a more muscular person, you become a stronger individual. You can incorporate other exercises into your yoga program. But yoga itself, when practiced regularly, will continue to improve your body and add strength and flexibility. Yoga stretches are widely known for improving flexibility. Flexibility and balance become especially important as we age and become vulnerable to injuries. Many people believe that you need to be flexible before starting yoga practice, but the opposite is true.

You can begin yoga in any physical condition and keep improving your flexibility. There are three specific areas of the body that are frequently tight: the hips, shoulders and the hamstrings. We spend a lot of our time inactive and sitting, and these muscles can become quite inflexible through non use. Daily yoga stretches will increase your flexibility tremendously as you provide these muscle groups with a real workout. As always, don't stretch your muscles to the point of pain stretched to the limit of your own comfort, and you will soon see the results. Now let's discuss another muscle that can be inflexible, namely the brain. Yes, the brain is indeed a muscle. If you have rigid attitudes such as that, things should be done only one way: you are limiting your mental power.

Perhaps your mind is frequently made up about certain issues and you see no reason to explore them further. The purpose of yoga is to unleash your mental powers. It involves change in all areas of your life. Yoga is a huge four letter word. The combination of yoga and meditation open up the mind to new ideas and ways of doing things. It encourages curiosity. Many people hold on to old traditional ideas because of fear. Yoga is meant to alleviate that fear and open up new life enhancing possibilities. When it comes to yoga, you will soon enjoy a more flexible body, as well as a mind that becomes open, flexible and curious.

Yoga Cardio & Weight Loss

In this chapter, we'll talk about yoga, cardio and weight loss. It's a well-known fact that exercise, especially aerobics, has a positive effect on heart health. Heart disease is a major killer as plaque in the arteries begins to block the natural flow of blood. More than 600,000 in the U.S. die of heart disease, yet it's totally preventable. The major causes are smoking, obesity, a poor diet and inactivity. A yoga lifestyle usually eliminates all four of these factors to ensure better cardio health. Many people avoid the word exercise, imagining pumping madly in an aerobics class or jogging endlessly around the track.

These exercises are certainly beneficial, but they aren't the only ones that can help us maintain a healthy heart and longer life. Yoga, with its gentle yet challenging poses, can bring about the benefits of aerobic exercise in an easier way. There have been numerous studies comparing yoga to no exercise at all and comparing yoga to regular aerobic exercises when compared to people who engaged in no physical exercise or exertion. Practitioners of yoga showed clear and tremendous improvements in heart health. They lost weight and achieved significantly lower blood pressure. Their cholesterol level also improved. These results were expected.

The surprise came when people practicing yoga were compared to the people who engaged in regular aerobics. There were no major differences between the two groups in weight loss, cholesterol level or blood pressure. The yoga group achieved the same level of benefits as the aerobics group. A group of independent researchers. The Cochrane Collaboration, confirmed the results, but indicated that how much and how long a person practices yoga did figure into the findings. People who attend a weekly yoga class will enjoy fewer benefits than those who practice yoga several times a week or on a daily basis. Many Americans suffer from atrial fibrillation, an irregular heart rhythm that can be caused by high blood pressure, stress and excess weight. Like regular heart disease.

Atrial fibrillation, too, can be prevented. A study at the University of Kansas used a group of 52 patients suffering from atrial fibrillation and had them engage in two weekly yoga chapters for several months. The results of the study found that the participants enjoyed an improved heart rhythm and a lessening of anxiety and blood pressure. Recent evidence suggests that yoga, when practiced regularly produces the same heart benefits as more traditional aerobic exercises. Transcendental meditation is a type of yoga meditation we will discuss later. A study of the American Heart Association found that transcendental meditation can lower the risk of cardiac death in almost half of the patients with heart problems.

Another study at the Medical College of Wisconsin assigned half a group of patients with high blood pressure to a transcendental meditation group and the other half taking blood pressure medication. The meditation group practices 20 minutes a day for up to five years. The study showed that almost half of the meditation group had a reduction in heart problems when compared to the group on medication. Further studies are being conducted, but there is clear evidence that yoga has a significant positive impact on heart health, yoga and weight management. While there are quicker ways to lose weight, yoga can help you shed a few pounds. Yoga doesn't burn the same number of calories as aerobic exercise.

You'll burn around one hundred and fifty calories an hour doing yoga, which you'll burn over 300, doing an hour of walking. But there's more to weight loss than burning calories. Even if yoga does provide a healthy workout, there is another subtle influence. However, yoga increases awareness of our bodies and the food we use to fuel it. If your diet consists of burgers and chips, the enhanced mind-body connection will reinforce the toxicity of certain foods and will make you reach for healthier, more life affirming choices. Toxic foods simply become less appealing. This means that most people will reach for a salad instead of a burger. If you want to lose weight on your yoga regime, opt for the more strenuous types of yoga, such as kundalini, yoga and yoga.

Types Of Yoga

In this chapter, we'll learn the types of yoga, there are so many different types of yoga disciplines, it can be confusing to pick one. Don't let the variety stop you from diving into the yoga pool. There are certain yoga types that are geared towards beginners, and these are your best options when learning about the movements. Also, keep in mind that the teacher can make or break the experience. If you don't feel comfortable in a particular class, it may be the instructor rather than the yoga explorer. Until you find your perfect yoga fit to begin yoga at home, you will need a mat, yoga blocks or towel for support when needed and the strap to use as a prop in certain bending poses. Hatha yoga.

Hatha yoga is the most general type of yoga and perhaps the most difficult to define. Depending on the teacher, classes can be slow and easy, but some may be more strenuous. To be sure, a particular Hatha class is suitable for you. Visit a class as a guest before signing up. Hatha yoga consists of gentle movements without a continuing flow between each pose. This makes it easy for beginners to learn the basics. It's extremely adaptable to individual needs and physical conditions and a great way to increase strength and flexibility while reducing the risk of injury. It is the best place to start and learn the basic poses before moving on to more arduous movements and positions.

The focus is on holding a pose and strengthening balance. Hatha yoga is slow moving, so if your goal is to move fast and sweat, it isn't the best option. The benefits of Hatha yoga is a decrease in stress and blood pressure as the body learns to relax vinyasa yoga. Vinyasa yoga has a quicker pace than Hathor and poses can rapidly flow into each other. Rather like dance steps. Each movement is linked to an inhale and exhale, thus linking movement with breathing. The mind remains focused and in the present there are no strict sequences. Deposits and teachers can mix and match to vary the routine. Therefore, if a particular Vinyasa class doesn't appeal to you, another might.

Yoga is less gentle than Haffa and pushes the boundaries of flexibility and strength. It provides a wonderful cardio workout as your body is continuously moving. Except when doing the restful downward dog, it is sure to work up a sweat. Relaxing music is frequently played in the background like Haffa. Vinyasa is an excellent starting point for beginning yoga students. Iyengar Yoga Iyengar. Yoga is an extension of Hatha yoga, specifically focused on bodily alignment and can be tremendously healing. It increases flexibility through slow stretching moves that are held for a period of time. These movements have meditative qualities. It tones the muscles and calms the mind. Better alignment can strengthen muscles, help with pain and improve posture.

Iyengar yoga involves the entire body and improves circulation and digestion with a better, healthier body. Better lifestyle choices usually follow. This form of yoga may use chairs, belts or other props to improve bodily alignment. Ashtanga yoga is perfectly appropriate for beginners. Ashtanga yoga is more structured than some of the other asanas. There are a series of movements, six in all, and each series must be mastered before moving on to the next Ashtanga. Yoga is not for beginners. It challenges strength, endurance and flexibility. Therefore, it's best to begin Ashtanga yoga. After some familiarity with the yoga disciplines, Ashtanga works the entire body, so results will come quickly.

It does require commitment and most practitioners of Ashtanga do the exercises every day. Each series can take years to master. People will love Ashtanga because it requires repetition of the same poses. There is no variation until you reach the next level. Bikram yoga. There are twenty six poses to be completed in a structured sequence for each Bikram chapter, which lasts for an hour and a half. The twist to Bikram is that it's practiced in one hundred and five degree heat. You will sweat and you will need to remain hydrated. The heat, Of course, adds an additional challenge. It also adds benefits such as ridding the body of toxins. Hot yoga, as the name implies.

Hot yoga is also performed in a room filled with high temperature. It differs from Bikram in that hot yoga is unstructured without the twenty six specific poses. This makes it suitable for beginners. But do consider the added challenge presented by the heat. Anderlini Yoga Kundalini uses meditation to energize the body, its effects on the mind are extremely powerful as it increases awareness and strengthens your inner self to allow for a more authentic you. This harks back to yoga's beginnings in its quest for spiritual elevation. Kundalini yoga blends movement with breathing and chants in yoga.

Yoga combines the physical with the mental and is specifically designed to provide energy and calm a busy mind. The benefits of regular practice are a sense of calm, reduction and stress, improved circulation and flexibility and greater joint mobility. The principle behind yin yoga is the yin and yang concept of Taoism, which seeks to balance all opposites in nature. The exercises are done on the floor and involve holding a pose for a long period of time. This affects the lower body parts. Specifically, the hips, thighs and spine poses may be held for five minutes or more. In a world that assaults us with stimuli on an ongoing basis, the mind easily becomes overloaded and overwhelmed. This is considered normal to such an extent.

People pride themselves on being Type A personalities. They are filled with a sense of urgency to always be on the move. The body is unable to relax and the mind cannot become quiet. Yin yoga brings balance back to the mind and body. The long poses stretch the tissues and strengthen the body while allowing awareness into the mind. Much energy is expended in suppressing unwanted thoughts and emotions in yoga releases that energy, restorative yoga, restorative yoga restores your mind and body. It is easy, slow moving with poses that are held long to provide a state of utter relaxation. Props such as Bloks may be used to help you hold on to your pose. Restorative yoga helps you slow down when everything around you becomes hectic. Think of it as an isle of tranquility in a crazy world.

Yoga Poses & Better Immunity

In this chapter, we'll talk about yoga poses and better immunity. A healthy immune system is the body's first defense against inflammation and diseases from cancer to the flu. To function properly, your immune system needs to be in balance. That means cells, organs and tissues function together as an army ready to defend the body against invaders such as germs and other impurities. The immune system produces antibodies to help heal infections and rid the body of toxins. Ever wonder why some people catch every bug that is making the rounds while others appear to be immune? Times of stress can render our immune system especially vulnerable.

That's why the healthier our immune system, the quicker we can overcome the effects of bacteria, germs and toxins. Healthy cells immediately come to our defense and attack those invaders. These helpful soldiers are the white blood cells. Yoga is a natural relax and stress reliever and an excellent way to keep our immune system at an optimal level. It provides that necessary boost during times of stress. Scientists have been studying the connection between yoga and the immune system. A study in the Journal of Behavioral Medicine indicates that yoga can be helpful in lessening inflammation in 15 separate trials.

Researchers tested whether the practice of yoga would affect inflammation. Most of the studies were done using easy Harth opposes. The results of these studies showed a pattern that yoga did decrease inflammation and had a positive effect on the body. The best yoga programs were those that lasted up to 12 weeks of hourly chapters. Consistent practice was the key to success besides inflammation. There are specific asanas that can help relieve the irritation of the common cold, such as the tortoise pose. Sit with your buttocks and legs pressed to the floor, stretch your legs open, inhale and lower your torso close to the floor. As you exhale, feel the stretch in your spine and inner thighs.

Keep the pose for ten breaths, place your hands beneath your knees and take a hold of each leg. Depending on how flexible you are, you can lean forward toward the floor as far as you are able, but don't force inhale to expand your chest and exhale as you fold your body downward for sinus congestion. The downward dog she poses can help alleviate congestion. This downward bending pose also helps with infections as it drains the lungs. Camel pose for bronchitis. If you suffer from bronchial congestion, the camel pose can open up the body to allow you to breathe easier. The camel pose will also help with neck and back pain. The camel pose can be strenuous on your back. So check with your doctor before getting started.

Start by stretching your spine by doing the Cobra pose. This is an excellent warm up and will prevent too much strain on the spine. The camel poses a difficult pose to master immediately. So take your time and work your way up to the full backward extension. Remember, no yoga poses are ever forced. Kneel on a mat with your hands on your hips, tuck in your chin and press your tailbone towards the floor.

Arch your pelvis forward if needed. Place your hands by your tailbone. This is an easy modified camel pose. Once you've mastered it, you can bring your arms back and grab your heels. Remain in the camel pose for sixty seconds until you begin to feel uncomfortable.

Whatever type of yoga you're currently practicing, it will help strengthen your immune system. The above forward and backward bends are simply extra helpful in giving your system a needed hand pose. There are approximately eighty four asanas and this chapter will introduce you to a few of the basic ones. A few dos and don'ts before you start your journey. Do wear comfortable shoes, do wear comfortable clothes, don't practice asanas on a full stomach, don't force any poses to the point of pain. Yoga is painless and should feel comfortable. Your flexibility and strength will improve with practice mountain pose. This is your starting point for all standing poses.

It may look easy as if you're simply standing there, but it is intended to make you feel grounded. Stand straight with your feet naturally apart, press all ten toes into the ground, raise your kneecaps and inner thighs for an upward lift. Tuck in your stomach and raise your chest. Keep your shoulders down. Hold the palm of your hands toward your body, inhale and feel your chest rise up further. Hold the pose for five seconds. Cat pose. This is. One of yoga's most popular poses, get down on your hands and knees, making sure your knees are aligned with your shoulders, keep your head neutral, exhale and raise your spine up and your head down.

Inhale and lower your spine and raise your head to the ceiling.

Do this several times. Downward dog, another favorite animal among yoga enthusiasts, this is a wonderful stretch. Go down on your hands and knees with your hands flat on the floor, inhale and raise your knees up. Your heels will lift your tailbone up toward the ceiling during the exhale, lower your heels to the floor and straighten the knees until your legs are straight. Keep your arms firm as you straighten them. Warrior one pose. Exhale and spread your feet about four feet apart, lift your arms until they are perpendicular to the floor, shift the left foot, 60 degrees to the right and the right foot, 90 degrees to the right, the heels should be aligned. Exhale and bend the right knee over the right ankle with practice at your right thigh will be parallel to the floor.

Raise the ribcage and press down on your left foot. You should feel the stretch up the back of your left leg to your belly. Bring the palms of your hands together. Remain in this pose for 30 seconds. Inhale, push the back, heel into the floor and reach up and straighten the right knee. Take a deep breath and reverse the legs and repeat the exercise. Extended puppy pose. This pose stretches the spine as it soothes the mind. Get on your hands and knees. Move your hands forward and curl toes under exhale and bring your buttocks back to your heels. Keep your arms stretched forward while keeping your elbows off the ground with your buttocks above your heels.

Lower your forehead to the floor, feel your spine stretch, breathe into your spine and hold the pose for thirty seconds. Triangle, the triangle stretches and tones the entire body, stand with your feet far apart, lift both arms to shoulder height, turn the right foot out by 90 degrees and the other foot in by 45 degrees. Lower your right hand to your knee or if you're able to touch your ankle. Raise your hand to the ceiling, hold the pose for eight breaths, then repeat the exercise with the other side, COBRA lay on the floor with your face down, your legs are stretched behind without touching. Rest your hands, palms down beneath your shoulder while your fingers are pointed forward. Inhale as you pull your chest and head upward. As your arms straighten and your hands keep pressing into the floor.

As you raise your chest, hold your shoulders back. Don't force any lift that doesn't come naturally. Hold the cobra pose for up to 30 seconds. Tree pose helps achieve and maintain balance while standing on one foot. This is a great asana for beginners. Start by standing with your feet together. Raise your right foot as high as you can to the upper left thigh. Lift your hands and press your palms together. Keep looking ahead while maintaining your balance. Plank pose moved to the plank pose from the downward dog, inhale and lift your torso forward until your elbows are on the floor, press lower arms into the floor and gaze at the floor, hold the plank, pose for 30 seconds and work up to one minute. This pose is designed to build strength. Keep breathing and make sure your shoulders are relaxed.

How To Get Started Doing Yoga

In this chapter, we'll learn how to get started doing yoga as you start your yoga journey. It's necessary to keep in mind how important your mental attitude is for success. Bodily agility and flexibility will come with practice, but to begin practicing, you need the correct mindset. For a beginner, it can be very confusing. Just picking out the right yoga outfit can be a headache. Then how do you decide which yoga practice is the best one for you? So start by relaxing and consider the following your roadmap to successful yoga practice.

Rid yourself of expectations if you viewed pictures of yoga poses and decided that you could never achieve that type of agility. Keep in mind that it undoubtedly took years, perhaps decades, for the model to get to that level. He or she was specifically chosen for his or her expertise. Yoga is not about achieving the perfect pose. It's about improved breathing and alignment one step at a time and the rest will follow. If you can't touch your toes, touch your knees instead toss and the expectations you may have and start with an open mind. Yoga is nonjudgmental. It is not a competition.

Although with practice you will naturally improve age and body, shape our mental limitations and have no effect on your ability to begin yoga practice if you are physically unable to do a particular pose. There are a dozen other poses you can master. Find the right teacher. As you probably figured out in high school and college, the right teacher can make a huge difference in any class if you don't feel motivated and inspired by your yoga class. Perhaps the teacher is wrong for you. This doesn't mean the teacher is bad in any way, but he or she is not helping you meet your goals. Consider whether the teacher is teaching things that you need to learn, regardless of how good the teacher is if he or she isn't helping you meet your needs.

Look for another one. Your best friend may rave about her hot yoga class, but if this isn't for you, you need to keep looking for another class. Perhaps you want something less physical, more spiritual. There are plenty of yoga teachers out there and one will be just right for you. Are you moving toward your goal? A good teacher will guide you step by step along the journey. If you feel at a standstill, perhaps the teacher is not for you. Can you ask questions? A good yoga teacher is available before and after class for his or her students and will listen and address individual concerns.

If your teacher is not approachable, find one who is. Don't hesitate to ask your teacher about his or her training or philosophy. The best type of teacher is someone who views yoga as a continuous work in progress and is still studying with his or her own teacher. It's yoga, not the outfit. You know, one of the major reasons people don't go or stop going to the gym, they feel self-conscious among a group of perfect bodies. Yoga has become so trendy, people are actually fretting about which designer outfit is best and what color mat they should buy.

Do you really need one hundred and twenty five dollars Dior pants to attain enlightenment, wear whatever feels comfortable and don't compare yourself to anyone else. Yoga is a personal journey, as mentioned in this chapter. Of course, before, it's not a competition. All you need for yoga is a simple pair of leggings, shorts, tank top or t-shirt. Seriously, you're not trying to make a fashion statement. The only thing you need to keep in mind is comfort. Special outfits are available for hot yoga. You'll want a yoga mat that lasts. So do choose a quality mat. It will be an excellent investment. Some yoga classes can cost up to twenty dollars. This can add up, but it shouldn't be a deterrent to get started.

There are ways to practice yoga on a budget. The local YMCA gyms and some community centers frequently offer yoga classes at low rates during warm weather. Yoga groups may meet at local parks when signing up for class buy in bulk. Signing up for 20 classes at a time instead of the individual classes may get you a discounted rate. Some yoga studios, rent mats and water bottles, may only charge a dollar. So the extra expense can add up. Bring your own mat and bottled water from home. Some yoga studios offer karma yoga classes. These classes are free in exchange for doing some work at the studio, such as manning the front desk and cleaning up after class. If cost is of concern, don't hesitate to ask about this option. Some studios will be happy to trade a class for a bit of service.

Rendered the best time to practice yoga. Handy excuse not to get started with yoga practice is time. The fact is we are all busy. We all have the same 24 hour day. We intend to accomplish something. We need to make time. Traditional yoga involves sunrise or sunset, but using any time for yoga is better than no yoga at all, although practicing yoga on a full stomach is not a good idea. Get up an hour earlier than usual and do your asanas before you do anything else. It energizes and activates your body and mind in the best possible way. The physical poses get your body going while the breathing clears the mind. Yoga intentions.

Some yoga teachers ask you to set your intentions at the start of the program. What exactly does that mean? Setting an intention is not needed for you to enjoy the benefits of your yoga chapters, but it can take them to a higher level setting. Your yoga intention brings yoga into your daily life. Yoga doesn't stop when the asanas are done. They're supposed to be at the beginning of your spiritual journey, not at the end. Yoga was originally developed as a spiritual quest. The rest simply followed intention's. Clarify your purpose in practicing yoga. It focuses on a personal quality that you wish to improve or enhance.

Perhaps you hope for greater patience, awareness or compassion toward others. Maybe you wish to let go of past hurts. Make that real in your mind. Your intentions are the bridge between your poses and the rest of your life. Yoga is not like walking out of the gym and forgetting about it until the next class. Mental practice should be part of your daily life. You will set your mind to make it real by keeping your intentions in focus. That is genuine spiritual elevation. Before you begin, talk to your doctor. It's true that anyone can practice yoga. However, you should discuss any possible limitations with your doctor before getting started.

This won't prevent you from doing yoga, but it might simply limit a few movements to prevent injury. Your doctor might also have some ideas about which type of yoga is best for you. Having a doctor who is knowledgeable and supportive of yoga is a tremendous asset. Slow and easy does it. If yoga is a new experience for you, it is natural to be excited and jump right in. But the goal of yoga is not who can do the most poses in the least amount of time. Yoga is a slow and deliberate process. Each chapter should be devoted to making poses easier work at your own level of comfort. It cannot be stressed enough that yoga is non-competitive.

If certain poses are more difficult than others simply practice, the more until they become easier. There's no time limit for mastering yoga poses. When poses become easier, go a bit beyond your comfort zone to reach the next level, but never to the point of physical discomfort. Begin at your own starting point. Joining a new yoga class where everyone else seems to know what they are doing can be intimidating. But that is the case. When you begin any new endeavor, regardless of anyone else, you are your own starting point. It is entirely irrelevant that everyone else is able to balance on one leg for sixty seconds while you keep tipping over instead of fretting. Enjoy the progress as you keep improving.

Savor who you are every step along the way. Self acceptance is the essence of enlightenment. The spiritual side of yoga encourages compassion. Start with yourself. 127. Transcript

In this chapter, we'll learn about preventing injuries, practicing yoga is as safe as walking. That being said, injuries are still possible and you should take care to avoid them. Start by following a few basic rules. Don't practice yoga on a full stomach and avoid alcohol. Remain hydrated at all times. Every yoga class should begin with warm up exercises. If yours does not look into another class. As we've discussed, the right teacher makes a tremendous difference and can reduce your chances of injury.

Certified teachers undergo up to 500 hours of training to qualify for certification. Make sure you are dealing with a qualified teacher. Don't try to do poses for which you aren't ready. This can cause severe muscle strain. Attempting poses for which you are unprepared is one of the leading causes of yoga injuries. Learn your body's limitations and respect them. You make the decision how far to stretch, not your teacher. You may be feeling more agile on certain days than others. If you are having a bad day, accept it and don't attempt difficult poses that may have been possible at other times. Listen to your body.

Certain areas of the body, such as neck, lower back knees and hamstrings are particularly vulnerable to injuries. Take care. With any poses involving those body parts, it is easy to become lightheaded when changing poses, so be sure to remain hydrated at all times. Most yoga poses can be modified by using blocks or towels. Don't hesitate to use these modifications until your body is able to create the poses more effortlessly. Don't begin yoga by jumping into risky poses such as a headstand. This can cause serious neck injury. Work your way up to the more difficult poses.

Yoga & Meditation

In this chapter, we'll learn about yoga and meditation, yoga is the bridge between meditation and spirituality. The original Buddhist used yoga as a means to prepare for meditation. Meditation, like yoga itself, is secular. It can be practiced by anyone. The purpose is to quiet, loud mental chatter and to calm the mind benefits of meditation. One meditation allows you to become more aware of your inner and outer life. You start to notice emotions and thoughts that you may have previously denied. It provides insight to improve your relationships.

Three: Being aware helps you act in the moment instead of acting out of habit. Negative emotions can have you act in ways that are harmful, even when you are unaware of the reason for your behavior. When you become aware of these feelings, you can deal with them in a positive way, for meditation allows you to be less critical of yourself and others. Five Meditation keeps you from acting on random emotions and lets you analyze facts before taking action. Six Meditation reduces stress and anxiety. Seven Meditation helps you adapt to changing circumstances.

How does meditation work? Much research has been done on meditation for the past decades. Physically, meditation lowers our blood pressure and calms our nervous system. When we meditate, our heart rate and breathing slow down through greater awareness, meditation allows us to change the way we think about past experiences. If you were continuously put down as a child, you begin to accept it as normal as an adult. Those same feelings are deep within you. You expect to be put down even if there's no reason for such expectation.

Regular meditation can change that negativity to allow you to accept more positive thoughts and emotions. Studies have revealed that meditation can actually change our brain structure. People who meditate have enhanced areas dedicated to awareness and focus. A study at Harvard University has shown that while age can diminish certain areas of the brain, regular meditators retain the brain capacity of someone decades younger. For anyone seeking a higher level of existence, meditation clearly has much to offer. Another Harvard study showed that with regular meditation, areas of the brain that deal with fear and anxiety were reduced, while areas involving empathy and compassion became enlarged. Changing how our brain reacts is the ultimate in taking control of our lives. How to start meditating like yoga.

Meditation requires commitment. It's an ongoing process. The more we meditate, the better we get. And there are no limits as to how well we are able to meditate. Ancient and current Buddhists spend a lifetime on meditation and self empowerment. Meditation requires a quieter place. Most people close their eyes and focus on their breathing, noticing every inhale and exhale. While other thoughts may intrude, they are simply acknowledged and set aside in a nonjudgmental way. Start with just a few minutes. It is surprisingly difficult to sit quietly for any length of time because we are used to being constantly active.

Work your way up to half an hour or 45 minutes, try to meditate at the same time every day so that it becomes a daily habit. Find a comfortable place where you won't be disturbed. Meditating after getting up in the morning can get your day started on a positive note, however, meditating before going to bed can help you sleep better. Of course, there's no reason you can't meditate during both times of the day. Finding time to meditate, claiming not to have enough time is simply an excuse not to get started. You don't own time. You make it by getting up half an hour earlier in the morning. If you have your own office, close the door during lunch time and use the hour or part of it for meditating.

Do you spend a lot of time on social media? Limit your time and you've bought yourself at least an hour to every day. Mindful meditation, one of the most useful types of meditations is mindful meditation. It brings greater awareness to our thoughts and emotions. Many people are chained to negative thoughts frequently about occurrences from years past. No matter how much time has passed, these emotions can still control our actions. Mindful meditation allows us to acknowledge those negative feelings, then put them aside so they no longer have the power to control us. Mindful meditation is based on one critical axiom that cannot be overcome.

Aided, you are not your thoughts. Some people feel controlled by their negative emotions, mindful meditation puts you in control like yoga. Meditation can change areas of the brain, increasing our ability for enjoyment and decreasing the areas responsible for depression and anxiety. Instead of having our mind jumbled with thoughts and feelings, mindfulness keeps us in the present to deal with what's happening now. This is a skill that can be learned from how to meditate mindfully. Mindful meditation couldn't be easier. If you can breathe, you can meditate. Simply follow a few simple steps to enjoy the relaxing benefits. Find a quiet place, preferably with natural light.

Ensure that you will not be disturbed if you can find a peaceful place outdoors, it would be ideal. A good amount of time to set aside for meditation is half an hour. But you can start with just five minutes and increase your time gradually. Like yoga. It should be easy and not painful or uncomfortable to wear comfortable clothing. You don't want anything tight disrupting your meditative flow. It is helpful to have a timer set to keep you from glancing at your watch. You can use a chair or sit on the floor using cushions. If you're on the floor, cross your legs in a comfortable lotus position, which is the traditional Buddhist meditating stance. If you're sitting on a chair, have your feet touched the floor or use blocks on which to rest your feet. Your torso should be straight but not stiff. Rest your hands on your thighs. You should feel comfortable at rest.

Most people prefer meditating with their eyes closed as it removes distractions. But if you prefer, you can leave them open next. Just relax and gradually begin to focus on your breathing as you inhale and exhale deeply. You notice how the air feels going in and going out. Feel the rise and fall in your chest. It is natural for your focus to wander as others enter your mind. There is no reason to get upset and pretend these thoughts aren't there. Acknowledge them and then return your focus to your breathing. If your mind wanders a great deal, simply observe what's happening in a non critical way. Don't force them away. Merely pay attention to what is happening.

One way to increase your focus is by counting. Inhale, count one exhale. Count to up to twenty, then count in reverse. Remain still for a few minutes after you have finished meditating. Notice how you feel. Your thoughts and emotions become an observer, not a critic. Meditation is as easy as this, yet it can bring about powerful changes when practiced. With yoga, you will notice your mind and body working in natural harmony.

Conclusion

People have been practicing yoga for thousands of years, and it is still attracting new advocates, especially those in the medical profession. There's no doubt that it has a lot to offer as we attempt to reach a higher level of existence. Yoga is not a religious practice. Nevertheless, it does put us in touch with our spiritual essence. The original Buddhist yogis practiced yoga to increase the Enlightenment and enhance their understanding of the world around them. Yoga was a preparation for meditation. The origin of yoga was far more spiritual than it is today, but it still enhances our spiritual self. Yoga improves our immune system, heart rate, cardio health, circulation and breathing. It reduces stress, anxiety and enhances flexibility and muscle tone.

The benefits of yoga can reduce the effects of aging both physically and mentally. There are many types of yoga, some easy, some gentle, while others are extremely demanding. They all provide benefits, but we should choose the yoga that is best for us. Nothing about yoga should be painful or forced. If you feel pain or discomfort during yoga practice, talk to your teacher. You are either doing the exercise incorrectly or you're in the wrong class. There are many classes from which to choose, so you never have to settle for one that makes you feel uncomfortable. Yoga poses affect our entire body as they stretch our muscles to the limit. Unlike other exercises, which may focus only on certain body parts, yoga poses involve the body as a whole.

That is why many consider yoga superior to aerobics or weightlifting. Of course, aerobics and weights can be practiced in conjunction with yoga for optimal physical benefits. Yoga connects the mind with the body to create one functioning unit. We are well aware of how the mind can affect the body and our overall health. Negative thoughts can cause serious diseases and inflammation, such as arthritis. The purpose of yoga is to clear the mind of negativity and bring optimal health back to the body. Never forget that the mind and body work together and use the following rules as the best way to approach your yoga chapters.

Everyone has his or her own starting point, so don't worry about weight, age or flexibility. Your poses will improve with practice, but it should never be a competition with the rest of the class. Finding the right teacher will make a big difference. A good teacher should answer questions and never force poses that are beyond the student's capability. If this is your experience, find another teacher. Many people begin yoga with certain expectations. However, everyone is different. You may never be able to do a headstand while the rest of the class appears to do so with ease. That's perfectly OK. The only rule in yoga is to work at your own level of comfort. Nothing should ever be forced. Start slowly.

People practice yoga for decades and are still striving for perfection. There is no perfect yoga pose. There is only you, your body and your mind reaching ever higher levels. Before you begin a yoga class, check with your doctor. Yoga movements are safe and injuries are rare. But you still want to ensure that there's nothing to prevent you from practicing yoga safely. As we have discussed, ancient yogis used yoga to prepare the body for their meditative practices to get the full physical, mental and spiritual benefits of yoga. Make meditation a part of your life. Yoga can add so much to your life and can help you become a better vision of yourself.

Don't miss out!

Visit the website below and you can sign up to receive emails whenever SHAKRUDDIN KHAN publishes a new book. There's no charge and no obligation.

https://books2read.com/r/B-A-DUGBB-VMWZC

BOOKS 2 READ

Connecting independent readers to independent writers.

Also by SHAKRUDDIN KHAN

The Smart Way To Personal Finance Success
Goal Setting 101 Achieve More Goals Than Ever! Faster!
Blockchain Masterclass for Businesses and Corporations
Master Your Mindset & Brain Framestorm Your Way To Success
Manipulation Techniques: How Can We Influence People's Thoughts And Behaviors
Leadership How To Influence, Inspire And Impact As A Leader
Learn How To Create A Safe Working Environment For Your Team
Productivity Hacks For Easily Distractible Entrepreneurs
IT / Non-IT Recruiter Training To Become A Recruiter (Junior)
Weight Lifting Pro Tips For Strength and Conditioning Weight Training & Muscle Building Tactics